Indefensible

INDEFENSIBLE

Adventures of a
Farm Animal Protection Lawyer

PETER BRANDT

Lantern Publishing & Media ● Brooklyn, New York

2020
Lantern Publishing & Media
128 Second Place
Brooklyn, NY 11231
www.lanternpm.org

Printed in the United States of America

Library of Congress Cataloging-in-Publication Data
Name: Brandt, Peter (Lawyer), author.
Title: Indefensible : adventures of a farm animal protection lawyer
  / Peter Brandt.
Description: Brooklyn, New York : Lantern Publishing & Media,
  2020 | Includes bibliographical references
Identifiers: LCCN 2020022486 (print) | LCCN 2020022487 (ebook) |
  ISBN 9781590566299 (paperback) | ISBN 9781590566305 (ebook)
Subjects: LCSH: Cause lawyers—United States—Biography. |
  Lawyers—United States—Biography. | Animal industry—Law
  and legislation—United States. | Animal welfare—Law and
  legislation—United States.
Classification: LCC KF373.B665 B75 2020 (print) | LCC KF373.B665
  (ebook) | DDC 340.092 [B]—dc23
LC record available at https://lccn.loc.gov/2020022486
LC ebook record available at https://lccn.loc.gov/2020022487

To my parents, sisters, and Valencia and Natalia

Author's Note

Some names in this book have been changed in order to protect the individuals' identities.

All of the author's royalties from sales of this book will be donated to non-profit 501(c)(3) organizations engaged in farm animal protection work.

All of the views and opinions expressed in this book are solely those of the author unless otherwise specifically attributed. None of the views and opinions expressed in this book are those of the Humane Society of the United States, its employees, directors, agents, contractors or affiliates (collectively "HSUS"). The author's characterizations and descriptions of the HSUS and any of its activities are attributable only to the author and not to the HSUS.

CONTENTS

Part III: In the End

About the Author
About the Publisher

PREFACE

As I finalized the book in the Spring of 2020, a pandemic born of humanity's exploitation of animals broke out, underscoring this book's primary point.

Though it appears to have begun in live animal markets in China, titans of the North American meat industry tripped over each other to do their part to help the novel coronavirus inflict maximum damage in the name of short term cash-grabbing. Many books will be written about this outbreak, and, strictly speaking, this isn't one of them. But indirectly it is, because it is about the self-destructive stupidity and willful ignorance that the virus relied upon as it burned through quiet counties in South Dakota and elsewhere, where the only job in town is cutting open the throats of pigs and other animals—animals bred, tormented, and killed for no decent reason.

In the spring of 2020, brilliant journalists explained how massive slaughter facilities helmed by multinational meat companies were ideally suited to spreading the virus among workers, their loved ones, and entire communities. As one worker put it, "If you're not in a casket, they want you there."[1]

As their employees died, executives resisted taking even the most minor of life-saving precautions, like slowing down the killing, spacing workers on the line six feet apart, and giving them effective protective gear. At one Canadian slaughterhouse "supervisors began trolling the plant in N95 masks and plastic face shields" weeks before workers got masks.[2] More than 900 of the facility's 2,200 workers contracted the virus, and as of this writing two of them died from it, as did the 71-year-old parent of another.[3]

The meat industry decision-makers that helped the virus flourish are as greedy as they are idiotic and, ultimately, self-destructive. So much carnage, all for forgettable products like the hot dog. Products that no one should be eating, let alone killing or dying for. As this unfolded, the League of United Latin American Voters asked its "community of 60 million members, and the entire country, to stand with essential workers and not purchase or consume any meat products once a week to highlight the need for protections for these workers."[4] This book provides many similar reasons why a further-reaching boycott would be in all of our best interests.

Peter Brandt
May 2020

INTRODUCTION

When I was five, a monkey called Cartoons reached his small black hand through his cage bars, grabbed a fistful of my yellow Seattle Supersonics t-shirt, and yanked it into his mouth. Cartoons only had the shirt for a few seconds, but it came back to me with a ragged, wet, silver dollar-sized hole. He could have been gnawing on my hand. That would've been bad for me, and it would've been bad for the pet store, since my parents would've responded by working to shut the place down—a rational response to a situation that endangered kids as it created a miserable life for the monkey.

The Mensa members who permanently cage a solitary monkey in a pet store are also the sort who don't bother to ensure that the monkey can't chew on passing kids. This self-destructive stupidity is a link connecting my earliest encounters with animal cruelty to what I often see in my work as a lawyer for The Humane Society of the United States (HSUS): taking everything from an animal, or billions of them, and threatening the well-being of humans in the process.

Recently, I started teaching law school students about my monkey run-ins (there have been more) and how these and other events from my life relate to legal issues involving farm animals. I teach using humor, partly because humor makes sense given the abundant absurdities in the world of farm animal law and policies. Also, I'm only sure people are listening when they're laughing at the right moments. I wish I could trust looks of despondency and stifled rage. Those are proper reactions given the grim material, but they are also just common responses to showing up to law school. Finally, I lean on humor and anecdotes because just about the only things that stuck with me from my days as a law student were the entertaining yarns—not sermons, rules, or statistics.

A good example of this is Katko v. Briney, the shotgun-trap in a farmhouse case universally taught to U.S. law school students.[1] The case is about a handsome bandit who serially burgled a couple in 1960s Iowa. Take a moment and do an image search for these three. If I could deduce who owns the rights to the 1971 pictures of them I'd be pasting them in here because they are worth far more than a thousand words apiece. Marvin Katko in 1971 is objectively handsome, like a George Clooney prototype. He's got a strong jaw and eyes that are somehow steely yet soft. It's as if Ed and Bertha Briney realized they couldn't compete with him in the looks arena so they said: *Fuck it, let's just lean into our homespun, "American Gothic" look.* They went so far as to don parkas that Shackleton might've worn in the Antarctic. And even though they knew full well their picture would be in the newspaper, they nevertheless pulled their hoods up and Bertha cinched hers dangerously tight around her face. They look like a pair of elderly eels pensively peering from caves on the dark Atlantic floor. To paraphrase my law school torts professor, given the aesthetic disparity between robber and the robbed, it's no wonder Katko won the jury over.

One night, frustrated with his inability to prevent repeated burgling, Ed Briney booby-trapped a door in an unoccupied house on his property. Later, Katko opened that door, causing a shotgun to fill his thighs with lead at point-blank range. As far as Ed and Bertha Briney were concerned, complete success! But the Clooney-esque Katko had the temerity to sue and he won a total of $30,000 in damages, which in 2019 would be equivalent to nearly $90,000. It's easy to see why that lesson stays with law students: no matter how pissed you are, you just can't rig up a shotgun trap in defense of your unoccupied little house on the prairie.

So, I teach farm animal law obliquely, using personal anecdotes as a way to get through complicated and sometimes horrific subject matter. It tends to keep students from buying shoes online while they're pretending to take notes. The content of those classes became the chapters of this book.

The same callous recklessness I first encountered as a child was also behind one of the most significant farm animal legal showdowns I've been involved in—and it is one of the more significant animal law showdowns in U.S. history. Only as an adult, and with an understanding that monkeys are wild animals who shouldn't be crammed into solitary confinement, did it dawn on me that I wasn't the idiot in the Cartoons story. When I was five, I blamed myself for losing clothing to a monkey. Like the pet store owner who caged Cartoons the monkey, those running a southern Californian slaughter facility made stupid, cruel, and self-destructive choices. In early 2008, *The Washington Post* reported on video footage taken during an HSUS undercover investigation at a Chino, California cattle-slaughter facility named Westland/Hallmark Meat Packing Company ("Hallmark"). The last chapter of this book describes in detail the lead up to that investigation and what happened in the wake of the HSUS's release of that footage. My colleagues and I watched hours of it in late 2007. More than a decade later, I still have a hard time watching the footage.

The cows documented in the investigation were mostly "spent" dairy cows. The dairy industry calls them that because they're too tired, old, or sick to produce enough milk to justify the expense of keeping them. The cows were already in terrible shape before dairy workers prodded them onto slaughter-bound semi-trucks. When the truck doors rolled open many hours later at Hallmark, some of the cows couldn't even walk.

The cows endured even more cruelty at the plant. The HSUS investigation documented workers ramming cows too sick or injured even to walk with a forklift. The cows were pushed and dragged along concrete toward the kill floor, a violation of federal regulations.[2]

In the end, the U.S. Department of Agriculture (USDA) made Hallmark recall 143 million pounds of ground beef because of the HSUS's investigation. A cow unable to walk is at a heightened risk of carrying bovine spongiform encephalopathy (BSE), more commonly known as mad cow disease.[3] Eating BSE-tainted beef leads to a fatal degeneration of the human brain, known as new variant Creutzfeldt-Jakob disease.[4] This abuse was all the more frivolous because it was in the service of producing dairy and beef, products that are not considered essential for a healthy diet under U.S. federal dietary guidelines.[5] This meat recall remains the largest in U.S. history.[6]

Hallmark endangered public health and put itself out of business. The company responsible didn't survive the investigation, recall, and related litigation.[7]

The following chapters argue that industrial animal agriculture's financial and hedonistic "benefits" are not worth their costs. Aside from cruelty, those costs come in the form of serious threats to nearby communities, wild animals and their habitats, clean water, and clean air. Animal agriculture is also a primary driver of climate change. Because its share of the blame is large and increasing, curbing animal agriculture is one of the few ways to make an immediate positive difference on that front.

The first part of the book focuses on the needlessness of industrialized agriculture and the life of farm animals from birth onward. The second part discusses the numerous ways that confining billions of farm animals threatens humanity, wildlife, and the environment. The final chapters cover the last days and hours of farm animals' lives, in semi-trucks and at slaughter facilities.

That dreamboat Marvin Katko charmed a $30,000 verdict out of an Iowa jury, but I bet he wouldn't have deliberately taken that shotgun blast to the thighs in the hopes of possibly winning a lawsuit later. The risk would be too great for far too little. Likewise, we should stop raising animals by the billions just to cut their throats or squeeze products from them that we do not need. It's not worth the pain.

PART I

BEGINNINGS

1

DIET AND THE UPPER AND THE LOWER PRIMATES
Vegan Is the 800-Pound Gorilla of Diets

"Sometimes before they fell asleep, Ivan would reach out and touch his human brother's face."—Sandi Doughton,[1] *The Seattle Times*, 2012

Remember the cronut: 2013's tasty new treat that no one needed? Millions love croissants and donuts, so it came as no surprise that their fusion became a favorite among aficionados of pastries and loose pants. They are a novelty. None of us grew up eating cronuts. There's no reason to think they're a necessity or a boon to anyone's health. They're just a treat, and I'm sure they're delicious.

Now, imagine it took 350 gallons of water to make each cronut and that every batch somehow made life-saving human antibiotics more likely to fail. Without antibiotics, the next time your cold turned into a respiratory infection, the tetracycline we all rely on would not be able to prevent your wet-hacking decline into life-threatening pneumonia. Now imagine—and this one is less of a stretch—that cronuts were linked to common, debilitating, and lethal chronic diseases. And what if pollution from cronut factories poisoned long stretches of Midwestern rivers and routinely killed every fish calling those waterways home? Suppose also that the process of making this flaky chimera required the killing of a mother gorilla sleeping in the deep shade of lemon-yellow flowering trees. Imagine that everyone buying a cronut was stopped at the register and made to watch a video of that mama gorilla's shooting.

IVAN'S EARLY DAYS

In 1964, in the forests of what is now the Democratic Republic of the Congo, during a vicious internecine war involving child soldiers and public executions, hunters shot infant Ivan's mom and put him, his baby sister, and four other western lowland gorillas on a plane bound for the United States. Ivan and his sister were purchased by a store in Washington State. Only little Ivan survived the trip.[2] In the following decades, Ivan became a celebrity.

I first saw Ivan through thick security glass in a South Tacoma shopping center in the early 1990s. At the time I was not yet an animal activist. I added this sad, tacky scene to my bulging mental accordion-file of reasons to be moderately ashamed of hailing from Tacoma. Many towns have a store like the B&I. It starts as a fruit stand or a hardware store in the 1940s and then, over decades, expands by accretion without any discernible plan, like a creeping mold, on the outskirts of town. Back when I went to the B&I in the 1990s, you could buy a rifle, groceries, lingerie, or a model airplane. Or you could play tic-tac-toe against a chicken who probably hated you almost as much as he hated tic-tac-toe. Or you could see Ivan.

For 27 years, Ivan paced a cold, concrete floor, imprisoned by three thick walls of glass and a fourth made of concrete and painted with a bland jungle scene. He was alone and on display for more than a quarter century, throwing bald car tires, pounding his glass walls, pacing, and watching television. When we were very young, Ivan and I both watched *JP Patches*, a moderately creepy local morning kids' clown show.[3]

In *The Urban Gorilla*, Allison Argo's 1992 short film, Ivan grabs a banana as an anthropologist named Bob Doherty lowers it from the ceiling on a thin fishing line.[4] Doherty volunteered at the store during

Ivan's final years there and would do things, like this levitating banana trick, to try to make Ivan's life less maddeningly dull and lonely. He showed Ivan how to finger paint and would generally just hang out with him, albeit with bars or thick glass separating gorilla and anthropologist. Doherty didn't kid himself about how far this went toward making Ivan's life what it should have been. He explained,

> If anything were possible for Ivan . . . I would like to see Ivan in an outdoor compound, I would like to see Ivan with true, real solid vegetation, I would like to see Ivan be able to feel and taste things that he's never been able to feel and taste before, and I would like to see Ivan, most importantly, with other gorillas.[5]

He wanted for Ivan what Ivan's life would have been—should have been—if men hadn't shot his mom and kidnapped him and his sister so they could titillate underwear shoppers halfway around the world.

A year after *The Urban Gorilla* came out, B&I's assets were divvied up among its creditors. My father had recently become a bankruptcy judge, and one of his first cases was the bankruptcy of "The World Famous B&I Circus Store." The chief headache in B&I's bankruptcy was Ivan.[6] A single store's bankruptcy usually doesn't even make the local papers, but because of Ivan, B&I's bankruptcy became national news.[7]

Google Ivan and you'll find a world of content, much of it focused on the cruelty of his confinement with scant mention of how and why he came to be confined. Yet, in analyzing what happened to Ivan, the logical place to start is by acknowledging that killing his mother and stealing him from the jungle was stupid and unjustifiable. It's likely that little attention is paid to Ivan's Act One—not because it's insignificant, but because by now it's assumed by most (with the exception of Ted Nugent and maybe a Trump son or two) that killing a mother gorilla and forcibly transplanting her son to Tacoma are terrible injustices.[8] And it is also widely assumed that the injustice is so obvious that it doesn't need to be re-stated. But to fully understand what went wrong in Ivan's life, it's important not to overlook the beginning: Although Ivan's confinement was horrible, it happened only because, in the span of a few minutes under a forest canopy, a passel of assholes shot his mom and stuffed him into a cage. But for those awful moments, Ivan's life could have been wildly better.

Also, focusing on those first few moments in the Congo reveals that although we now take for granted that what happened there was awful, that was not always the dominant view on shooting a mother gorilla and stealing her infants. As late as the mid-1960s when Ivan saw his mom shot, no U.S. federal law banned shooting a mother gorilla in Africa and absconding to Washington State with her babies. In 1970, six years after Ivan's abduction and at about the time Ted Nugent—by his own (later recanted) account—repeatedly shit himself to convince his local draft board not to send him to Vietnam,[9] the U.S. Fish and Wildlife Service classified gorillas as endangered under the Endangered Species Conservation Act of 1969.[10] That designation made abductions like the one Ivan suffered a federal crime.[11]

As with Ivan's life story, discussions of our appetite for meat, eggs, and dairy often skip the logical beginning. But the conversation should start with asking whether we need these products in the first place. That omission probably happens because it's generally assumed—and here the Motor City (alleged) Pants-Shitter would agree—that we consume meat, eggs, and dairy now and thus always will. Yet, if something we want to eat, like a cronut, had a massive human body count and if its production was burning through natural resources at high speeds as it polluted what remained of clean air and fresh water, then it might be impossible to justify that indulgence. As with Ivan's story, if you fail to focus on the logical beginning, you may overlook where things go irretrievably wrong.

IF I COULD TURN BACK TIME

Distracted and drunk driving kill far more people today than they would if we rolled back the clock to a time when cars moved at tortoise speeds or if we ditched cars altogether and went back to steamboats, bicycles, and horses. The problem of texting and driving wouldn't be a problem at all if we rolled back the clock even more modestly—just to the 1990s, when cellphones were only for talking. No one is clamoring for any of this because it is unrealistic. Yet, in the realm of meat, eggs, and dairy, otherwise serious-minded people float the idea of solving global public health and environmental crises by musing, as Cher famously crooned, "if I could turn back time." It hasn't worked and, as hundreds of experts on agriculture and public health recently noted, "[a] return to more traditional husbandry methods is unlikely to occur, as the prevalence of factory farming has been rapidly increasing in both the high- and low- and middle-income countries."[12]

Let's take a step back. What is factory farming and why does it spur some to channel Cher when trying to figure out how to end it? It is sometimes referred to as "intensified" animal agriculture, a practice of raising increasing numbers of farm animals at fewer locations. It took off during the middle of the twentieth century and really snowballed as we moved toward the twenty-first. The transformation of the cattle industry during this timeframe is a good example:

> In 1964, half of all beef cows in the United States were on lots of fewer than 50 animals. By 1996, nearly 90 percent of direct cattle feeding was occurring on lots of 1,000 head or more, with some 300 lots averaging 16,000–20,000 head and nearly 100 lots in excess of 30 thousand head. These feedlots represent waste management challenges equal to small cities.[13]

Paralleling the beef industry, the other animal-protein industries underwent similar consolidation and intensification.[14] Factory farming essentially involves warehousing animals. Most egg-laying hens in the United States experience this in its most extreme form: The birds are packed into cages so tightly they can barely move, let alone extend their wings, and those cages typically are stacked in rows up to eight tiers high.[15] And, for nearly all farm animals, rather than spending their time pecking, rooting, foraging, or grazing through pastures and woods as their ancestors did, they're confined in barren lots, sheds, or cages, and all the feed is brought to the factory farm.

There are many reasons why rolling back the clock won't work, but chief among them are the massively powerful multinational feed, meat, and pharmaceutical companies that rake in billions of dollars thanks to a multi-decade strategy of spreading this wasteful model to even the remotest nooks of every inhabited continent.[16] Nevertheless, journalists and authors continue to discuss factory farming using an approach that calls to mind a line from the British TV show *The Mighty Boosh*: "Elements of the past and the future combining to make something not quite as good as either."[17]

The treatment of factory farming, whether in a book, op-ed, or blog, usually follows this template: (1) We're obviously going to keep consuming meat, eggs, and dairy; (2) but let's masochistically discuss how horrible we are for supporting factory farming's abuses of animals and the environment; and (3) then let's harken back to how things used to be done better a half-century ago; before (4) we urge masses of unknown (and perhaps imaginary) people to somehow go back to the way folks did things back in the day.[18] The attraction of this approach is that it doesn't require the writer or the reader to do much of anything: We get to keep scarfing down our treats—now made more piquant, thanks to seasoning with a bit of guilt—and it's up to someone else to get animal production industries to go old school.[19]

Imagine that approach in other contexts: (1) "Well, of course we're going to keep drinking and driving; (2) but let's take a long, hard look at the highway carnage and fractured families that result from it. (3) You know, back when there were only a few thousand cars on the roads and they topped out at speeds of 65 miles per hour, the consequences of drunk driving were not nearly so devastating. (4) Oh well, hop in! We're going be late unless I floor it. (5) Hey, I'm a bit parched. Be a lamb and pass me that Super Big Gulp brimming with Red Bull and vodka." I got a little carried away at the end there, but you see the point.

Widely respected and popular writers who are otherwise thoughtful and persuasive seem to willfully avoid asking the fundamental questions about our meat, dairy, and egg consumption habits. In a 2009 *New Yorker* review of Jonathan Safran Foer's book *Eating Animals*, for example, Elizabeth Kolbert identifies the weaknesses in Safran Foer's take and Michael Pollan's, as presented in his book *The Omnivore's Dilemma*. Pollan opts for a lazy defeatism semi-rooted in the way humans behaved 10,000 years ago. We long ago domesticated and killed animals and used them for food, so, according to Pollan, since that train left the station many millennia before trains were invented, we might as well keep on doing things the way our loin-clothed, Mesolithic-era forebears did.[20] I solemnly promise to take this argument seriously just as soon as Michael Pollan spends a winter in Manhattan wearing outfits he fashioned himself using only leaves and bark.

In a 2013 argument before the Ninth Circuit Court of Appeals, a lawyer for Big Foie Gras took a similar approach while asking judges to strike down a California law that banned the sale of diseased fatty livers from force-fed ducks and geese.[21] For humane reasons, in 2004 California banned the force-feeding of ducks and geese for the purpose of fattening the birds' livers.[22] The state also banned all sales of those force-fed fattened livers.[23] The ban took effect in 2012, and right as it did, Big Foie Gras ran to federal court in Los Angeles arguing that the ban unconstitutionally interfered with commerce between the states and between Canada and the United States. The Big Foie Gras plaintiffs included one southern California restaurant group, Canadian foie gras producers, and one duck factory farm in upstate New York, which, like its Canadian counterparts, force-feeds and slaughters massive numbers of birds to sell their fattened livers at the price point of "Fuck You, Starving Children."

In court, Big Foie Gras's lawyer described the force-feeding method as one that has been around "for thousands of years" and explained, "there are Egyptian hieroglyphics on the sides of Egyptian tombs showing Jewish slaves, frankly, feeding geese to enlarge their livers."[24] If your defense of a practice is that it has such a long and distinguished pedigree that it once employed human slavery, your argument has problems. Big Foie Gras lost that fight.[25]

True, the force-feeding of birds is only about 5,000 years old, not the prestigious 10,000. This begs the obvious question: Why should anyone care if a practice is 10,000 years old, 5,000 years old, or 10 minutes old if it is *currently* harmful and without counterbalancing redeeming qualities? Around 10,000 years ago, we were beginning to enslave one another and we had long been bludgeoning strangers to death for no good reason.

Kolbert notes that Safran Foer faults Pollan for naively believing we will turn back the clock and raise chickens the way we used to—*i.e.*, by letting them feel the sun on their feathers daily instead of never. Then Kolbert rightly faults Safran Foer for peddling the same notion in *Eating Animals*, subbing in heritage turkeys for Pollan's organic chickens.[26]

It's no longer fair to paint Safran Foer as a champion of heritage turkeys' potential, because, in May of 2020, as slaughter facilities emerged as major COVID-19 hotspots, Foer penned a brilliant *New York Times* oped under the headline "The End of Meat." As the headline makes clear, it seems Safran Foer now places a lot less faith, if any, in the notion that a morally defensible meat industry is possible. This is a heartening development in a grim time.

Kolbert does not grapple with the central inquiry: Do we need to be eating any of this? Or, more accurately, do we need to be eating all of them? If we do not, that makes any negative consequences—and there are many—very difficult to defend rationally. As Tolstoy put it in his *Writings on Civil Disobedience and Non-Violence*, "A man can live and be healthy without killing animals for food; therefore, if he eats meat, he participates in taking animal life merely for the sake of his appetite. And to act so is immoral."[27]

Maybe the downsides of the bacon industrial complex can be argued away persuasively, but I have yet to see it done. Instead,

Kolbert asks, "But is even veganism really enough?"[28] Rather than try to answer the question, she simply says,

> The cost that consumer society imposes on the planet's fifteen or so million non-human species goes way beyond either meat or eggs. Bananas, bluejeans, soy lattes, the paper used to print this magazine, the computer screen you may be reading it on—death and destruction are embedded in them all.[29]

This sentiment will be familiar to anyone who's seen the closing moments of a 3:00 a.m. Vassar college dorm-room debate. Those tend to end with the spilling of a skull-shaped bong and with someone shouting through the dank haze: "Jesus! The world is already so fucked, why even try to do anything?!" This defeatism is something Kolbert faults in others in the context of climate change.[30]

You can argue against any attempt at improving yourself or society by pointing out that any given improvement on its own will not solve all of the world's ills. This is a good way to let people know you understand how harmful your behavior is and how bad you feel about it, while also letting them know that you're not going to do diddly-squat to mitigate that harm because improvement will not bring about perfection. I'm going to die someday, so I might as well eat that fourth donut and ratchet up my chances of dying under a defibrillator in a speeding ambulance at age 45.

Guidelines, Accommodation, and Burning Pintos

The key question is, Why do we assume that people should and will continue to eat meat, dairy, and eggs? To answer that we need to know whether they're essentials or if they're like the cronut, something we like but one we may not be able to justify given its costs. So, beginning at the obvious starting point: To stay alive, we need to consume calories. For many, that involves choosing among a range of foods. Millions do not enjoy those options, so what follows does not apply to them, but it is worth noting that part of the reason why millions go hungry and lack reliable access to healthy food has to do with the wasteful meat, egg, and dairy industries.[31]

Even by the conservative measures of the U.S. Department of Health and Human Services and the U.S. Department of Agriculture's jointly issued 2015–2020 Dietary Guidelines ("Guidelines"), consuming dairy, eggs, and meat products is not a requisite for a healthy diet.[32] The Guidelines self-identify as "food-based recommendations for people age 2 and older, including those at risk for chronic disease" and a "primary focus" of the guidelines is "promoting overall health and preventing—rather than treating—chronic disease in the U.S."[33] Yet, the Guidelines are too timid to recommend replacing foods known to be harmful with foods that have no negative health consequences. The Guidelines' lone categorical recommendation against eating a food pertains to raw sprouts, and that is based on concerns about food safety and sanitation.[34]

The absence of recommendations to avoid any other foods is remarkable, given that in 2015, based on a review of decades of research, the United Nations' World Health Organization (WHO) determined that red meat is "probably carcinogenic to humans" and hot dogs, bacon, and processed meats *are* "carcinogenic to humans."[35] To be fair, that WHO report came out a few months after the 2015 Guidelines, but the decades of science that informed WHO's meat and cancer conclusions had also been available to the people writing the Guidelines. Although the Guidelines don't identify any unavoidable health drawbacks of plant-centered diets (because there aren't any), they do point to devastating health consequences associated with animal-derived foods.

Yet, teasing those two key lessons out of the Guidelines is like looking for clues in a 144-page note from a hostage. The Guidelines explain that vegetarian and vegan diets are more than just acceptable. In many ways, they are far preferable for anyone hoping to avoid a protracted death induced by heart disease and cancer, respectively the first- and second-place killers of all U.S. adults. Pointing to a growing body of evidence, the Guidelines explain:

[H]igher intakes of vegetables and fruits consistently have been identified as characteristics of healthy eating patterns. . . . Strong evidence from mostly prospective cohort studies but also randomized controlled trials has shown that *eating patterns* that include lower intake of meats as well as processed meats and processed poultry are associated with reduced risk of [cardiovascular disease] in adults. Moderate evidence indicates that these *eating patterns* are associated with reduced risk of obesity, type 2 diabetes, and some types of cancer in adults.[36] (Emphasis in original)

The Guidelines never claim that consumption of eggs or meat (including poultry) helps to reduce *any* disease risk, not even something moderately annoying like athlete's foot. The farthest the Guidelines will go is to say:

[F]ood pattern modeling has demonstrated that lean meats and lean poultry can contribute important nutrients within limits for sodium, calories from saturated fats and added sugars, and total calories when consumed in recommended amounts in healthy eating patterns.[37]

That is a big mouthful of nothing. Note these carefully chosen words, "can contribute important nutrients." That's hardly a selling point as the Guidelines also link "meat" and "poultry" to the two chart-topping killers, heart disease and cancer. There's no claim that those deadly risks are counterbalanced by the unspecified "important nutrients" in animal products. And if those unidentified "important nutrients" were *only* available from meat, then the Guidelines could not conclude, as they do, that a vegan diet can be a healthy diet.

As noted earlier, the Guidelines make clear that avoiding plant-derived foods is not a healthy option for anyone. Every diet that the Guidelines identify as "healthy" mandates eating grains, fruits, vegetables, and legumes.[38] Indeed, the Guidelines go so far as to say that most Americans need to be eating more of these foods.

The 2015 Guidelines dropped a recommended limit on dietary cholesterol, which prior versions had included. Cholesterol is present only in animal-derived foods—*i.e.,* only in meat, dairy, and eggs, all of which also happen to be heavy with saturated fat. In the plant world, though, only tropical oils like palm and coconut oils contain a lot of saturated fat. So, all too often, if you're consuming cholesterol, you're getting a side of saturated fat. The Guidelines recognize Americans' penchant for saturated fat–heavy diets is connected to heart disease and other leading killers, but just because we may like to eat fatty foods doesn't mean we should or must.

What's more, the Guidelines acknowledge that no one needs to consume cholesterol and, as Dr. Kim Allan Williams, immediate past president of American College of Cardiology notes, we "should eat as little as possible."[39] So the upshot is pretty straightforward: There are strong advantages to plant-based eating and no inherent drawbacks, as compared to eating meat, eggs, and dairy, which confer no unique dietary benefits and are linked to the leading killers of all U.S. adults.

Despite all of this, the Guidelines set up a false equivalency in places. For example, on the very same page, it states both that "processed meats . . . can be accommodated" and that "[t]he inclusion of protein foods from plants allows vegetarian options to be accommodated."[40] The word "accommodate" does all the work in these claims, and it is used as a gauze, obscuring what should be illuminated. My need for a car "can be accommodated" by a vehicle that will *not* explode when bumped, as well as by my purchase of a vintage Ford Pinto that will become a rolling fireball with absolute certainty when hit from behind. You can "accommodate" innumerable idiotic, self-destructive choices in a lifetime, but that doesn't mean you *should.*

Sure, I might drive that Pinto for a decade without any problems, but the odds are good that a day may come when my morning commute is cut short by a fender bender that sends me scurrying from the car, my flailing arms ablaze and my corduroys fully Nugented. On the other hand, even if I chose the less combustible car, I might nevertheless get rear-ended, but the chances of my not-a-Pinto going up in flames are lower. Indeed, anyone with my best interests at heart would not recommend the Pinto to me if I could get a car that would be less likely to immolate me at a stoplight. And let's not forget that these guidelines are supposed to be *recommendations*. Lifestyle advice like those in the Guidelines, which does not say *any* choice—other than raw sprouts—is on balance a terrible option, is advice to be skeptical about.

RISKS AND STAKES

A closer look at the connection between meat consumption and cancer risk reveals why the Guidelines shouldn't whistle past the graveyard when talking about the two. As mentioned earlier, a 2015 WHO report connects processed meat and red meat to cancer. That report provoked an odd response from the American Cancer Society (ACS):

> They found that eating 50 grams of processed meat every day increased the risk of colorectal cancer by 18%. That's the equivalent of about 4 strips of bacon or 1 hot dog. For red meat, there was evidence of increased risk of colorectal, pancreatic, and prostate cancer.
>
> Overall, the lifetime risk of someone developing colon cancer is 5%. To put the numbers into perspective, the increased risk from eating the amount of processed meat in the study would raise average lifetime risk to almost 6%.[41]

But looking at an incremental increase in risk, without stressing what is at stake, provides a misleading "perspective." Obviously, the stakes make all the difference. Suppose there's a five percent chance that one route gets you to a movie five seconds late, whereas there's a six percent chance that a more scenic route gets you there equally late. You are not some crazed adrenaline junkie for taking the scenic route, because who cares? Worst-case scenario, you'll miss five seconds of previews.

On the other hand, imagine you must jump from a burning plane and you have two parachute choices: a red parachute, which has a five percent risk of malfunctioning and leaving you flattened on a canyon floor, or a blue parachute, which has a six percent risk of deadly malfunction. Besides the one percent difference in risk and color difference, the parachutes are otherwise identical. Given those stakes, a reasonable person would choose the safer parachute even though the other one is only a one percent riskier option.

The stakes are the same with hot dogs: life and death. So, a one percent increase in the risk of dying slowly from colon cancer should not be downplayed. In a sense, the colon cancer stakes are higher than the parachute hypothetical because death by parachute malfunction is quick for all but coyotes in classic cartoons. Colon cancer can torture a person for months or even years, and, in some cases, can financially ruin an entire family before death.[42]

Similarly, to look at incremental increases in risk as the ACS does in the statement above without asking the fundamental question of *why* anyone should even engage in the risky behavior is blinkered silliness. Going back to the ACS's response to WHO's meat and cancer report,

> We should be limiting red and processed meat to help reduce colon cancer risk, and possibly, the risk of other cancers. The occasional hot dog or hamburger is okay.[43]

Like the Guidelines, the ACS avoids the obvious and fundamental question: Even if the increase in risk is minute, why take the chance at all if you do not have to?

There's a chance that biting an apple will leave you dead from choking. There's also a chance that gargling a mouthful of small ball bearings may kill you. Now, we could just compare the risk levels between the two activities, but we'd be morons to do that without addressing the elephant in the room by asking: "Hey, Einstein, why are you gargling ball bearings?"

Eating an apple or anything else carries some choking risk, but not eating isn't an option. On the other hand, if no one is forcing you to gargle ball bearings and you do it just because you enjoy it, then it's optional and obviously best to just never do it. That's as true if even the "occasional" ball-bearing gargling session is less likely to kill you than doing it every day. Determining whether occasionally consuming carcinogenic treats is acceptable could not be farther from the key inquiry: Why the hell are you engaging in potentially lethal activities when you do not need to?

There is no credible study demonstrating that taking only a single puff on one cigarette in a lifetime is risky, but we now know tobacco is implicated in tens of millions of cancer-related deaths. Tobacco use is so monumentally damaging and expensive that the Centers for Disease Control and Prevention (CDC) categorically advises that no one should use the stuff *ever*.[44] So the equation is: risky activity + it's not required + there are healthier alternatives = don't do it. The CDC's reasonable approach to tobacco starkly contrasts with the Dietary Guidelines and the ACS's approach to meat carcinogens. For reasons they never make clear, both the Guidelines and the ACS solve that same equation by saying: How about you guys just limit how many bacon cheeseburgers you eat?

The CDC itself has yet to apply its no-nonsense approach to tobacco to foods like processed meats. In the words of Michael Greger, M.D., FACLM, best-selling author of *How Not to Die*:

Cigarette smoking in the U.S. peaked in 1964 and has been steadily declining ever since. What happened in 1964? The first Surgeon General's report on smoking was issued. The science on smoking and health hadn't changed suddenly in 1964. There was decades of science linking smoking with lung cancer. In fact, the report cited 7,000 studies. You'd think that maybe after 6,000 studies they could have given people a heads up? Tobacco was a powerful industry in 1964. But all it took to start a multi-decade decline in U.S. smoking was that public acknowledgement from the powers that be that smoking causes lung cancer. The CDC should say the same thing about processed meat.[45]

As a matter of common sense and consistent policy, federal agencies and the ACS should solve that carcinogenic + unnecessary equation consistently and not pull punches for childish reasons like "but a lot of us like hot dogs." Worldwide, you can find headstones bearing the names of millions of early arrivals who liked tobacco products. The CDC rightly thinks so little of the hedonistic "benefits" of tobacco that it never even mentions them when discussing tobacco's drawbacks. That is what we should expect from public health professionals, and, really, it's what we should expect from any grown up.

A Gorilla's Sunset

Ivan was moved to the Atlanta Zoo as the B&I dissolved in a bankruptcy over which my father presided. So, in the end, Ivan was with other gorillas, living in a small semblance of the forest taken from him. He hadn't been around another gorilla in nearly three decades. He found his place among them quickly though. In 2005, the associated Press reported that, at 41 years old, he might have found his first girlfriend. According to a zoo volunteer guide, "There have been certain looks between them over the moat."[46] During his last 18 years, he wrestled and played with gorillas, wore burlap sacks on his head to stay dry in the rain, and he never gave up painting.[47]

Even if cronuts were linked to the deaths of gorillas and/or humans, the end of working antibiotics, the wasting of oceanic amounts of fresh water, and the pollution of rivers, there would be some hard-nosed guys who would proudly eat them. I'm talking about the sort of uniquely American tough-as-nails contrarians who might waddle into their draft board interviews in pants brimming over with their own feces.

Some might enjoy a cronut even if it meant a gorilla died, so long as they didn't have to watch the video of that killing. For some, they might indulge if the only harm was to the gorilla and there was no harm to the environment, no waste of water, and no undermining of public health. For the rest of us—those who would sit out this pastry fad—our rationales would hew to a common theme: The treat's costs are simply not justifiable. As the following chapters argue in turn, we can't disaggregate the farm animal industrial complex's worst threats to animals' well-being from its gravest threats to human health and the environment.

To answer Kolbert's question above, "But is even veganism really enough?" It is certainly a good start. No one can ever do "enough" to fix everything. But doing nothing sure as hell won't fix anything. And it isn't a good look to do nothing when you easily could do something—like foregoing some treats—that can help make life less horrible for people and animals.

2

HAVING A LIFE SPAN IS NOT THE SAME AS HAVING A LIFE

Mistreatment of Young Farm Animals and Their Mothers

"When the children started their working season 'they were full of play and acted like real children' but as the days wore on they sat 'like little machines with their fingers tied up in rags.'"—J. P. Felt, *Hostages of Fortune: Child Labor Reform in New York State*[1]

Jane Addams endured a dark night of self-reproach in Madrid, decades before winning the Nobel Peace Prize for her work for the poor and for peace. In the spring of 1888, she went with friends to a bullfight. Only in the evening, hours after the event, did she realize in great "surprise and horror" that she had watched "with comparative indifference five bulls and many more horses killed."[2] She described feeling

> tried and condemned, not only by this disgusting experience but by the entire moral situation which it revealed. It was suddenly made quite clear to me that I was lulling my conscience by a dreamer's scheme, that a mere paper reform had become a defense for continued idleness. . . . Nothing

less than the moral reaction following the experience at a bullfight had been able to reveal to me that so far from following in the wake of a chariot of philanthropic fire, I had been tied to the tail of the veriest ox-cart of self-seeking.[3]

In the years that followed, Addams became a powerful leader in the fight to get children out of full-time labor.

There are strong parallels between the current systemic abuse of young farm animals and the historical exploitation of child workers in the United States. Long ago, animal activists picked up on the similarities between the way adults abuse children and animals. In 1874, the American Society for the Protection of Animals (ASPCA) brought New York State's first child abuse case, on behalf of Mary Ellen Wilson.[4] Mary Ellen's adoptive mother severely neglected her, cut her with scissors, and regularly employed a rawhide whip on the ten-year-old child.[5] Henry Bergh, the ASPCA's founder, used the courts to rescue the girl, placing her in an orphanage and ultimately with adoptive parents.[6] Her abusive adoptive mother was convicted on several counts of assault and battery.[7] The case led Bergh to co-found the New York Society for the Prevention of Cruelty to Children in 1874, which according to *The New York Times*, "was believed to be the first child protective agency in the world."[8]

Historian Diane Beers described the animal activism of the late nineteenth and early twentieth centuries as one that did not draw hard lines between victims. In the early part of the twentieth century, hundreds of animal protection groups were also outspoken champions of children.[9] As Beers describes it, between 1915 and 1945, the progressive activists, "particularly women, were attracted to animal advocacy and incorporated it into their own wide-ranging agenda."[10] Beers describes the progressive movement as comprised of those who

believed some societal ills begot other societal ills, which in turn weakened the entire moral fabric of society. Abuse was one of those ills and few progressives drew sharp distinctions between animal abuse, child abuse and domestic abuse believing instead that each fed on and perpetuated the other: they were elements of the same battle.[11]

Jane Addams was a leader among these progressive activists.

Read *Grapes of Wrath* or, if you're lazy like me, watch the film, and consider how astonishing it is that full-time child labor was outlawed in the age of the fictional—yet realistically rendered—Joad family of the 1930s. California orchard bosses exploited Tom Joad eight days a week even though he belonged to the most favored group on the continent: the white guys. So, how did five-year-olds gain legal protections in the Thirties? Operating at the peak of their powers, those kids could organize a stick ball game, not a union. Children depended entirely on decent adults to save them from callous adults.

In that sense, the relationship between children and adults is similar to that of farm animals to adults. This is not a comparison of farm animals to children; it's a comparison of how adults exploited children and how they continue to exploit farm animals. The active child exploiters took six-year-olds out of New York countryside summers and forced them into windowless buildings to can fruit for months on end. These adults succeeded thanks to the tacit support of the far more numerous passive adults who let it happen: the adults who bought the products shaped by sore young hands and who did nothing to help those kids.

That exploitative combination is at work today in the adults-versus-farm-animals context. True, there are similarities across victims: children, chickens, and calves cannot stick up for themselves (nor can they organize a union). But animals are far easier to exploit than children. Unlike children, farm animals can't organize a stick ball game, let alone a union. So the salient comparison is not between animals and children. It is between the way adults exploit both for no redeeming reason, converting millions of powerless lives from bright-eyed and joyful to abjectly miserable.

Exploitative child labor is far from a solved problem in the United States or elsewhere. Globally, slightly over 70 percent of today's 152 million child laborers work in agriculture.[12] Virtually none of the approximately 108 million children working in agriculture are paid.[13] Most work for and within their nuclear family,[14] and the work they take on is often dangerous.[15] Nearly half of all child workers are aged five to eleven, and about a third of them are twelve to fourteen years old.[16]

The focus here is on government-sanctioned full-time labor by minors, not on jobs like the paper route I had in the 1980s. I worked that route for an hour a day so I could buy cassettes at Tower Records. It's not always easy to draw the line between acceptable and relatively safe jobs like my paper route and field or factory work. One easy distinction, though, is that I didn't have to miss school to work forty or more hours a week on that paper route. I also didn't operate machines that can remove fingers. There are a lot of minors working in dangerous and exploitative situations like that today, but in the United States, in many cases, it is illegal.

Yet, child labor on U.S. farms remains far less regulated than in other contexts. In 2018, *The New York Times* reported that economically strapped farming families are putting very young kids in the driver's seat of tractors and other dangerous machines.[17] According to the CDC, agriculture is "an industry that consistently ranks among the most dangerous in the United States." Though firm numbers are hard to come by, at least a hundred children die every year working on their families' farms, and thousands more are injured.[18] And of course, many children work on farms that do not belong to their parents.[19] Federal law allows children as young as twelve to work as hired farm hands.[20] And state laws restricting children's work at others' farms vary and are often flouted.[21]

Look back a century or more and you will see children working long hours in dangerous jobs to enrich sociopaths who didn't have to worry about the law upending their taking-candy-from-babies schemes. In the United States during the late nineteenth and early twentieth centuries, kids worked in canneries, factories, mines, tenement homes, and a range of other settings. They operated machines with evocative names like the "mangler."[22] Workers fed cloth into the mangler's rollers and the machine ironed it. Sixteen-year-old Virginia

Adams operated a brand of mangler called the "Hazen annihilator," which she described as "hot enough to take the meat off my hand."[23] She spoke from experience. The annihilator caught hold of her and, as it burned the flesh on the back of her hand, it crushed the bones beneath it.[24]

CLUTCHING AT BROMIDES

Obviously, government-sanctioned full-time child labor didn't persist in the United States for as long as it did because most adults enjoyed destroying the hands of children. There were bromides and excuses that helped adults avoid understanding the causes and effects of putting kids to work full-time at twelve years old. In a 1903 essay, Jane Addams took apart one popular child labor fairy tale:

> It is said that the labor of these little children is needed for the support of widowed mothers. Some of us are sure that the widowed mother argument has been seriously overworked. In every community there can only be a certain number of widowed mothers, unless some plague has carried off the men in the prime of life. Out of that number of widows only another certain number will be absolutely impecunious, for if the community is prosperous some of the working men by benefit societies and insurances will have made some little provision for their families. Out of that certain number of impecunious widows only a few will have children between the ages of ten and fourteen, in which short space of time the temptation to the premature use of children's labor always lies.[25]

Obfuscations like the widowed mother myth endured partly because few people saw girls like Virginia—standing in worn-through shoes on cold laundry floors feeding endless reams of cloth into the annihilator long past sunset. As Upton Sinclair put it, "[i]t is difficult to get a man to understand something, when his salary depends upon his not understanding it!"[26] The line works just as well if you take out "salary" and swap in "meals," "shoes," and "smart phones."

As with child labor, many of us work hard at not understanding, not acknowledging, what is guaranteed to happen to millions of animals like the one-week-old black-and-white boy calf pulled from his mother's side at a massive dairy. It's hard to avoid the conclusion that he would be better off if he were quickly and humanely euthanized rather than what typically happens: the week-old calf will be put on a truck slick with the feces and urine of other terrified calves, driven to an auction, and, in a matter of days or months, someone will shoot a steel bolt through the top of his head and hang him upside down seconds before knifing open his throat.

ANGERING THE BULL

When I was seven, I went on a field trip to a dairy farm a few miles from my elementary school in Bellingham, Washington. I have no negative memories of the trip. It's possible we only saw a small, cleaned up portion of the dairy, far from where manure would have been stockpiled by the ton. It's also possible that I was distracted by the "open bar" of orange-and-vanilla swirled ice cream treats. We weren't told what happens to the male calves born to mothers who are repeatedly impregnated and struggle to find comfort on concrete floors.

My cousins lived in the country, a few miles from where Washington meets Canada and not far from that dairy I toured. I spent a lot of time at their house. My sisters and I ran around with our cousins, swimming in their pond and jumping into piles of hay in the barn. Looking back on those days, I realize it's almost too Norman Rockwell–ish to be believed. Dad and his brothers grew up nearby on the family potato farm and they were all driving a tractor years before they could legally drive a car. During my childhood, that area was largely a dairy farming community, as it had been for generations. Now the dairies are dwindling as residential developments creep north from Bellingham.

The black-and-white bull in the field by my cousins' place was likely an unwanted byproduct from a nearby dairy. With a few of my cousins I crouch-stepped through strands of barbed wire fence into wet clover and tall grass. I was following my six-year-old cousin as he closed in on that lone bull. He carried a stick about the size of a baseball bat. As we crossed into his field, the bull looked up, barely lifting his head from grazing.

Just as it was almost too late to do anything about it, I was suddenly one hundred percent certain that following my cousin to watch him "make the bull angry" was a terrible idea. I was about ten, so old enough to know that going out of my way to piss off a two-ton horned animal was not the stuff of brilliance. But because I was older, I didn't want to be the first to retreat. I kept walking toward the bull, trying to make each step shorter than the last. When my cousin was about thirty feet from the bull, he waved his stick over his head and yelled a stream of nonsense. That did the trick.

The bull lifted his white head from the clover, focusing on the foremost tiny idiot-ape. Across his black chest, the biggest muscles I had ever seen went taut as he started to charge. My cousins and I sprinted for the barbed wire fence. There was no chance of outrunning.

Thankfully, watching us scatter like roaches as a cupboard opens seemed to satisfy the bull. He stopped running. My idiot cousins and I escaped through the barbed wire.

This was a new flavor of terror. It was also the first time I realized that I was not the star of this picture but an eminently cut-able extra. I knew that the bull could ensure that the only way I might return to his pasture would be in a blow tube–controlled wheelchair. There's no way to be sure the bull was angered and then satisfied as he watched us scatter. This is where some might pipe up and whine about anthropomorphism: ascribing what some deem uniquely human characteristics to nonhumans. It's a simple concept packed into a fancy long word.

I've run into this often. I first heard it listening to talk radio in Los Angeles in the late 1990s. I was working for a statewide ballot-measure campaign to ban the use of leghold traps for wild animals. Those are the traps you see in cartoons. Hidden on a forest floor, they snap shut on any foot unlucky enough to step on the trigger. Animals thrash and injure themselves in the struggle to get free, sometimes chewing off their own foot to escape. A few women had called into the radio show to talk about how cruel the traps were, and then a man got on the air to admonish them for being emotional and told them not to guess at what those trapped animals might be feeling.

Much of the concern about how anthropomorphism supposedly leads us astray is based on the concern that animals cannot talk so we cannot really know what they think. This makes little sense. First, there are no truly universal human characteristics: Not everyone talks and not everyone has the same capacity for thinking abstractly, or even thinking at all.[27] Conversely, whereas attributes have been proposed as supposedly unique to humankind, not long after each is identified they have in turn been found in other species.[28]

Secondly, even among the adults that our legal system deems fully functioning and responsible for their own actions, verbal communication is rightly recognized as a means of deception. Accordingly, in many significant instances, our legal system has long refused to simply take us at our word. Imagine if it were otherwise: I could beat a felony theft charge merely by saying, "How dare you! I most certainly did not steal that truckload of vegan donuts"—even if my fingerprints were all over the steering wheel and I was caught on security cameras wearing a Halloween ninja costume breaking into the delivery truck's cab. Evidence of my actions is almost certainly going to win over the jury no matter how charming a tale I spin to the contrary. Likewise, you may wish to sue me, for instance, by alleging my factory is violating federal law by dumping bleach into a river. I can't get off the hook by arguing that the case is moot and offering nothing but predictable "protestations of repentance and reform."[29] In these and other instances, our legal system values behavioral evidence over mere words about what was or will be done.

Similarly, when animal behaviorists want to know what animals prefer, they look to how animals act, using something called preference or motivation testing.[30] An Iowa farmer once told me about the habits of his pigs. For years, they'd leave the barn every morning and spend much of their days outside. Then factory pig farms began popping up around his property, and it started to reek outside. It began smelling a whole lot worse outside his barn than inside it. His pigs were lucky to have had some say in the matter, and they voted with their hooves. They rarely ventured out. Similarly, if a hen has the option of not living packed with eight other birds in a cage the size of a file cabinet drawer, she will take that option. That tells us what she prefers in the same way as my scurrying out of a twentieth anniversary showing of *The Exorcist* at Mann's Chinese Theater tells you I can't handle scary movies, despite what I might say.

Matching the emotional and mental states in animals with subtle shades of (what we consider) the human color wheel of feelings and thoughts is usually a needless distraction. It's not possible to accurately do that even between so-called competent adult humans. It is capricious and unfair to insist on it between species as a precondition to considering how our actions harm animals.

The bull whose meal was interrupted by a pack of little pale idiot-apes was an upset bull judging from his reaction. What more do we need to know?

TREMBLING AND LYING ALONE

What more do we need to know in the context of a mother pig used for breeding who chews with a bloodied mouth on the rusted bars of a crate barely bigger than she is?[31] That is certainly not her way of voting for a life of immobilized confinement.[32] After a few litters, these mother pigs are cast off, like the male dairy calves and their mothers, the dairy cows who no longer produce enough milk to economically justify their existence. Temple Grandin, the farm animal behaviorist, described visiting "a stock dealer that specialized in cull pigs and sows. Many sows were lame, had prolapses or were skinny with ribs showing."[33] While still producing litter after litter, her piglets are taken from her within a few weeks of birth.[34]

During a piglet's first week of life, a hot iron or sharp clippers may be used to cut off her tail.[35] The goal of this is to prevent tail biting. Pigs with access to the outdoors, or even just fresh air, or with something to do other than just stand on barren ground indoors—like root around in straw—are less likely to bite each others' tails.[36]

Pigs' high intelligence is widely appreciated, but that intelligence comes with under-appreciated traits. They are curious, social, and playful animals. As my colleague, animal behaviorist Sara Shields, Ph.D., explains, "on pasture they spend more than half of their waking time rooting or foraging. They require meaningful occupation or they begin to explore the only available other options—the tails of their pen mates." So it's not surprising that tail biting is more common when pigs are overcrowded in barren confinement facilities with little of interest to occupy their attention.[37] Cauterizing off a piglet's tail causes "acute pain and trauma," as it happens, and can lead to lingering pain indefinitely.[38]

During the first week of life, male piglets are typically castrated.[39] Although the American Veterinary Medical Association (AVMA) recommends painkillers for the surgery, they often are not administered.[40] Painkillers cost money. In 2013, the AVMA explained that surgical castration "will be painful" unless anesthesia is used.[41] That suffering is seen in piglets' "elevated blood cortisol concentrations, high-pitched squealing, and pain-indicative behaviors, such as trembling and lying alone. Some behavioral indicators of pain may persist for up to five days."[42]

In 2011, an HSUS undercover investigator worked at a Seaboard pig breeding facility and video-recorded routinized cruelty and neglect.[43] The facility, in Goodwell, Oklahoma, held about 2,700 mother pigs night and day in gestation crates barely bigger than their own bodies.[44] During the thirty-day investigation, the investigator never saw a veterinarian at the facility, even though many of the sows desperately needed medical care.[45] The animals had large sores, lumps, scabs, open wounds.[46] Additionally, the investigator saw piglets having their tails docked and being castrated—all without a painkiller. Sometimes baby pigs were so mutilated by botched operations that they died.[47] Undaunted by any of this, Seaboard trumpeted on its website and in a sustainability report that it treated its pigs with "the most humane practices throughout the animal's life."[48] The HSUS disagreed and filed a complaint with the Federal Trade Commission (FTC), asking the agency to investigate this as false and misleading advertising.[49]

The selling of meat, eggs, and dairy products pays the mortgages of many a huckster, and some of the advertising claims would be amusing if they weren't used to prop up atrocious cruelty. The FTC evaluates advertisements by asking: What is the take-away message imparted to a reasonable consumer?[50] If the FTC starts asking your company questions about an ad for something you make, it would also expect you to substantiate statements about things that would matter to reasonable consumers.[51] So if a company claims to be "the most humane," the FTC may ask the company to substantiate that assertion. That's what the FTC did in response to the HSUS complaint. The inquiries from the FTC prompted Seaboard to back down from its ludicrous "most humane" treatment claim.[52]

Although it would be better to see a company improve its animal care practices rather than back away from ridiculous marketing claims, this sort of change is a victory nonetheless. Companies make humane marketing claims because they have good reason to think they will sway consumers and reap rewards in the marketplace. So, taking away a deceptive claim removes an ill-gotten gain: consumer dollars spent on a product that might not have been spent absent the lying.

Unlike newborn piglets, about half of the calves born to the serially impregnated dairy cows are considered unwanted byproducts. Newborn male calves are a problem for dairy farmers. They obviously can't produce milk,[53] so they are typically sold to be raised for veal or turned into ground beef.[54] Life as a veal calf used to mean a life of extreme confinement in a crate similar to those used for mother breeding pigs.[55] In recent years, the veal industry has begun moving away from this cruelty thanks to decades of public outrage, consumer boycotts, and six state laws banning the crates.[56] Some bull calves, about 15 percent of calves slaughtered, are killed at only a few days old, some with their umbilical cords still dangling from their bodies.[57] This is not an aberration; it's a norm across the dairy industry.[58]

A *Dairy Herd Management* article illustrates how the value and the fate of these unwanted infants fluctuate significantly. In 2014 in the Midwest, male dairy calves less than a week old sold for $400 to $600 each. Yet in recent years, dairies have at times struggled to cover the transport and other costs of getting calves sold. The animals could bring in as little as $5 apiece. In the lean times, "the not-so-funny joke that circulated in concentrated dairy regions was to be careful about leaving your pick-up truck parked unattended, lest you return to find bull calves in the back."[59] Hilarious. On my childhood field trip to a dairy, no one told me what happened to the boy calves. That's not surprising because no one tells children about the male calves' fate, and few adults seem to grasp it, though it's not a secret.

Like the boys, female dairy calves are routinely separated from their moms within hours of birth.[60] For weeks, these calves are typically tied to stakes with a tether only long enough to allow them to step inside a small hutch and step back out of it.[61] The industry's rationale for isolating and virtually immobilizing these baby animals is to protect them from picking up transmissible diseases.[62] Right. The dairy industry depends for its existence on separating the mother from her calf, and it isn't for the good of the calf; it's the basis of commercial milk production. Keeping calves away from their mothers allows milk to be diverted from her growing calves to more natural uses, like making cheese to stuff into pizza crusts.[63]

Upstate New York is home to many dairy farms, as well as the brilliant visual artist Sue Coe, who regularly hears the tethered calves crying for their mothers. The calves' mothers respond with their own cries. As Coe observed, "[S]ometimes lifespan and having a life are not the same."[64]

I HAD BIG DREAMS AND NONE OF THEM CAME TRUE

Those who care nothing about animals are also likely candidates for abusing and exploiting their employees. In 2015, an Ohio U.S. Attorney's office brought criminal human-trafficking charges against five men, accusing them of targeting people in Guatemala to bring them to Marion, Ohio, to live in squalid trailers and work at an egg factory farm. They "focused their recruitment efforts on individuals under the age of 18, believing it would be easier to bring them into the US, and that they would be easier to control, and that they'd be harder workers."[65] To entice them to take on the risk of illegally entering the country, the smugglers "falsely represent[ed] that they would be able to attend school once they arrived in the United States."[66]

In exchange for smuggling them into the country, the traffickers took deeds to the minors' families' homes in Guatemala and threatened to keep the properties if the debt for the smuggling was not repaid.[67] They required their victims to pay rent for the disgusting trailers in which they forced them to live.[68] The teenagers' paychecks went directly to the smugglers, who passed on only small amounts to their victims, pocketing the rest to cover "rent" and the smuggling debts.[69] According to the 2015 indictment, the smugglers "threatened the victims and their family members with physical harm, including death, if they did not continue to work and surrender their paychecks."[70]

The 2015 indictment tells the story of several victims. It alleged that the smugglers forced "Victim 1" to "work six or seven days a week, twelve hours per day, including times when Victim 1 was injured."[71] That work included cleaning the facility, loading and unloading crates of chickens, debeaking the birds, and vaccinating them.[72]

"Victim 2" was a minor lured into the scheme by the promise of education in the United States. Instead, according to the indictment, like Victim 1, Victim 2 was forced to work at the egg factory farm, doing "physically demanding work for six or seven days a week, twelve hours per day."[73] The smugglers refused his requests to receive more of his own paycheck.[74] "Victim 3" was also a minor lured in by the promise of a U.S. education.[75] When he complained about the working conditions at the egg facility, the lead smuggler, Castillo-Serrano, "degraded and demeaned Victim 3, calling him humiliating names and telling him that he was required to work for Castillo-Serrano."[76] Shortly after this conversation, Castillo-Serrano and an associate "moved Victim 3 to a trailer that was unsanitary and unsafe, with no bed, no heat, no hot water, no working toilets, and vermin."[77] They called Victim 3's father in Guatemala and told him they would shoot his son in the head "if Victim 3 did not continue to work. . . ."[78]

An Ohio Federal District Court has so far convicted four of the defendants, and lead smuggler Castillo-Serrano has been sentenced to just over fifteen and a half years in federal prison.[79] In announcing those three convictions, Ohio's Acting U.S. Attorney, Carole S. Rendon, explained that:

> [T]hese defendants preyed upon vulnerable children with false promises of a better life and instead forced them into manual labor in horrific conditions on an egg farm for little or no pay. We will continue to prosecute human traffickers, whether they force children into the commercial sex industry or enslave them in rural parts of our district.[80]

Note that Ohio's top federal prosecutor described working conditions at egg factory farms run by one of the state's largest egg companies as "horrific."[81] Obviously, no one deserves what these men put their victims through. However, "horrific" conditions for poorly paid workers shouldn't be tolerated, regardless of who the employees are.

Trillium Eggs, the company that owns the egg facility where these kids worked six or seven days a week, claimed ignorance about what happened there and has thus far escaped any legal consequences.[82] In 2014, federal agents subpoenaed Trillium's business records.[83] The company claimed to have been misled by the people indicted and convicted,[84] but didn't immediately sever ties with its labor contractor, even after it learned of the federal investigation. It's hard to see how Trillium missed the multiple teenagers working six or seven days a week at its facility.

At Castillo-Serrano's sentencing, a federal prosecutor read aloud a letter from one victim: "I did not do anything to deserve this. I just wanted to help my family. I had big dreams and none of them came true."[85]

TAKING BEAKS FROM BABIES

Part of the victims' work at Trillium included cutting off approximately one-third of the tips of hens' beaks with a hot blade or infra-red laser. As described by scientific experts, debeaking is "severely painful" and can lead to persistent chronic pain.[86] If you are wondering why one would separate a bird from her beak with a hot blade, it's because despite animal agriculture's decades of selective breeding, the hens stubbornly retain the instincts they have had for thousands of years,[87] including dust bathing to balance oil levels in their plumage, retreating to a nest to lay their eggs, and using their beak as the primary means for interacting with the animate and inanimate world.[88] As with tail biting among pigs, hens may peck each other's feathers when they lack anything else interesting to peck at. This can turn deadly when blood is drawn. And as with pigs, giving hens an outlet—an environment that is not barren but interesting, with things to explore—could mitigate or prevent this.[89] These birds, when they're given the space, have a shot at retreating from others that may be hassling them with pecking.[90] But there is no "away" to escape to in a cage.[91] Cage-free hens are also routinely debeaked. Despite having more room than those confined in cages, cage-free birds are typically housed in huge numbers within barren buildings.[92] Lacking enrichments to explore, these hens, like caged hens, will peck at each other.

The millions of male chicks generated by the egg industry are better off. Unlike their sisters, male chicks will not be kept alive in torturous cage confinement for more than a year before being yanked out and killed. These baby boys are typically killed upon hatching, often in grotesque ways like maceration—throwing fully conscious chicks into what is essentially a wood-chipper. Since they cannot lay eggs, these male chicks are unwanted byproducts, like dairy cows who no longer produce enough milk, male dairy calves, and breeding sows who can no longer generate litters of pigs to become bacon for ZZ Top–bearded hipster-bros and their female counterparts, Stevie Nicks impersonators.

CAR SEATS AND WIRE CAGES

In November 2008, in the wake of an HSUS-led campaign, a strong majority of California voters enacted a law prohibiting tight confinement of breeding sows, veal calves, and egg-laying hens. California, like many states, allows citizens to directly vote in changes to state laws, bypassing the state legislature altogether. This happens by collecting enough voter signatures on petitions to qualify for the ballot and then getting more "yes" votes on the initiative than "no" votes on Election Day.

At a 2008 San Luis Obispo public hearing on Proposition 2, the HSUS heard from activists, academics, agency employees, legislators, and people who ran large caged-hen egg facilities. The hearing happened a few months ahead of the November vote. Our measure had qualified to be on the November 2008 ballot, and once that had happened California law required legislators to hold a public hearing on the measure. Although it can't change the initiative's substance, the hearing is a big moment in a ballot initiative campaign. Supporters on both sides show up in force to speak on the record. I drove down from Sacramento to hear the opposition's far-fetched claims about the supposed benefits of confining millions of hens in tiny cages for life. In 2008, with many other HSUS attorneys, I investigated the opposition's campaign claims. We aggressively worked to undermine any of their claims that didn't hold water. And we succeeded.

Ryan Armstrong, owner of a San Diego County egg facility, was our opponents' primary spokesperson. His testimony put a positive spin on living inside a cramped cage. The cages he used, which our measure would ban, confined seven to nine birds in a space about the size of a file cabinet drawer.[93] The hens leave the cage only once, after a year or so, when their egg production drops and they're removed and killed.[94] Like their counterparts—worn out breeding sows and dairy cows—these hens are considered "spent" and marked for death when their upkeep no longer pencils out to profits.[95] By then, the hens are in terrible condition: skinny and missing feathers from molting and abrasion against their wire enclosures.[96] Many caged hens have bulging abscesses, prolapses, and other wounds. They're so small and in such bad shape that they're generally not deemed worth the trouble of slaughtering.[97] In fact, only a few slaughter facilities will even take spent laying hens. Undaunted by any of this, Armstrong said that confinement could be a good thing for the hens. After all, on his drive up from San Diego, he had confined his two-year-old son to a car seat. I concede that his analogy would sort of work were he to keep his son belted into that seat for a straight year.

Extreme inactivity and the calcium drain of laying an egg a day often leaves caged hens with osteoporosis.[98] Hens have been selectively bred to lay an egg every day; the hens of even a few decades ago were not so "productive." Their wild ancestor, the red Jungle Fowl, lays only ten to fifteen eggs per year,[99] far less than the roughly 365 that hens in the egg industry must produce. It's no surprise that far too many collapse in their cages, unable to stand and reach food and water as their tiny, brittle ribs break and press into their spinal cords.

At the San Luis Obispo hearing, the opposition campaign staff wore official "No on Prop. 2" t-shirts, with large lettering bearing their group's name: Californians for Safe Food. This alluded to their primary talking point: Eggs from caged hens are safe to eat, but cage-free eggs are a public health menace. At the hearing, they propped up a poster of a bar graph comparing *Salmonella* incidence in California (which was low) to other states' *Salmonella* incidence. Sounds reasonable. But their graph compared California's *Salmonella* rate to *all* the other 49 states' *combined Salmonella* outbreaks. A Beverly Hills mansion looks mighty affordable compared to the cost of a home in New York added to the cost of a home in every other state.

More importantly, the most comprehensive and recent science at the time showed that eggs from hens in cages were actually *more* of a food safety threat than eggs from cage-free hens. Some of my colleagues described the state of the science in 2008, noting: "The largest study ever conducted, an EU baseline survey of more than 5000 operations in two dozen countries, concluded that it was the large, cage facilities, and not the cage-free farms, which had higher salmonella risk."[100]

In the intervening years, the science has increasingly borne out this conclusion.[101] Visualize a single building that has cage space for 143,000 birds, each getting only about as much space as an iPad screen. Now imagine the birds have all been taken from their cages and gassed to death, and you have to clean the whole building, including each of its thousands of cages towering from the floor to the rafters. All those nooks and crannies on each of the thousands of cages make it impossible to clean that building in a way that will kill lurking *Salmonella*.[102] Before the hens are killed, their immobilization in cages is thought to make the facilities more attractive to rodents, who can transmit *Salmonella* from building to building.[103] Even after filling cage buildings with high-temperature chemical foam—the most effective way to disinfect—you will still find *Salmonella*,[104] and, in practice, that high-temperature foam is not what's used to clean these facilities. In fact, many of the buildings are probably never cleaned, as evidenced by animal groups' numerous undercover investigations and by the facilities at the center of a 2010 egg recall, the largest in U.S. history.

Serial Offender

According to the U.S. Food and Drug Administration and its Department of Justice attorneys, "During the spring and summer of 2010, an estimated 56,000 persons throughout the United States fell ill after eating eggs contaminated with *Salmonella Enteritidis*," and Food and Drug Administration (FDA) and state agencies traced the outbreak back to facilities in Iowa owned by Austin "Jack" DeCoster.[105] Those facilities caged about five million hens. The FDA visited DeCoster's "farms" in 2010 and determined that DeCoster's eggs were *Salmonella*-positive at a rate thirty-nine times higher than the national average at the time. Every one of DeCoster's dozens of caged-hen buildings was rife with *Salmonella*. FDA inspectors found "live and dead rodents and frogs in the laying areas, feed areas, conveyer belts, and outside the buildings" and "manure . . . piled to the rafters." Based on what it found, the FDA ordered a recall of about half a billion eggs laid in these disgusting buildings and others like them.

There's at least a tome's worth of material on the life of Jack DeCoster and his cronies. A complete discussion of the staggeringly villainous things he has been accused of doing, and in some cases proven to have done, across several states and many decades, is beyond the scope of this book. But let me whet your appetite with a few highlights that led up to the 2010 egg recall. In 1998, Mexico filed a federal class action lawsuit on behalf of about 1,500 Mexican nationals who, over many years, had worked at DeCoster facilities in Maine.[106] Mexico alleged that her citizens had to live in trailers without working plumbing—sometimes with up to sixteen roommates.[107] The suit also alleged these workers were promised raises they never got for working with chicken manure and that at least one Mexican worker was beaten by another DeCoster employee.[108] DeCoster paid $3.2 million to settle the lawsuit.[109]

A few years later, DeCoster settled a federal Equal Employment Opportunity Commission lawsuit based on the claims of eleven Hispanic women that the company's managers raped or sexually harassed them at DeCoster's Iowa egg facilities.[110] The lawsuit alleged that supervisors raped five of them and told each that they would be killed or fired if they resisted.[111]

Following a 2009 undercover investigation by Mercy for Animals at a DeCoster facility, the state of Maine brought his company up on ten counts of animal cruelty over its abject neglect of hens, charges DeCoster settled with a payment of $125,000.[112]

Iowa branded DeCoster the state's first "habitual violator" of its water pollution laws, and Occupational Safety and Health Administration (OSHA) likewise described him as a habitual violator of work place safety rules.[113] Because of his environmental habitual offender status in Iowa, Ohio prohibited him from owning or controlling CAFOs (or Concentrated Animal Feeding Operations, a.k.a. factory farms) in that state. Of course he did just that, though, investing more than $65 million in Ohio egg facilities and taking care to hide his involvement from regulators.[114]

By the time of the 2010 egg recall, DeCoster was one of Iowa's largest egg producers, as well as a major pork producer. Although the recall happened in 2010, DeCoster did not lose his egg facilities that year; he controlled them at least until his sentencing in 2015. DeCoster is largely who the Hawkeye state wasted its resources on when it sued the state of California in 2014 for banning the sale of eggs from Iowa's caged hens. Iowa, and the states that joined with it, lost their lawsuit.

The Ninth Circuit Court of Appeals upheld a lower court decision, finding that states cannot sue other states on behalf of only a segment of an industry, in this case the egg industry.[115] Undaunted, in 2017, Iowa and other states mounted once again basically the same lawsuit against California, this time filing it directly in the U.S. Supreme Court, arguing that jurisdiction in the highest court was required because no other court could resolve their claim.[116] Apparently they've forgotten that two lower courts had already done so. In early 2019, the Supreme Court declined to take the case.

Taking a wide view of how he fits in to the last several decades, what is striking is not so much what Jack DeCoster did, but that he remained a driving force in the industrial farm animal business decades after basically everyone should've deduced he was as ruthless as he was sloppy. It took an FDA criminal case over half a billion recalled eggs to finally derail Jack DeCoster.

At the 2015 DeCoster sentencing, the father of one young victim described how *Salmonella* poisoning nearly killed his son. *Salmonella* poisoning and the antibiotics required to treat it wrecked his son's young teeth. As his father put it, the boy now covers his mouth when he smiles: "I mean it breaks my heart to see that he is going to have metal teeth until he is old enough to get implants."[117]

In early 2018, DeCoster completed his three-month sentence in a pretty cushy cage, a minimum-security federal prison in Massachusetts.[118] As the early activists who shaped the child and animal protection movements recognized, the most abusive personalities don't discriminate when it comes to their victims. Encouraging the DeCosters of the world is disastrous for farm animals, children and their parents, workers, and the environment. The byproduct animals are the victims arguably hit hardest by the disaster of industrial animal agriculture. As mentioned earlier, these male chicks and dairy calves, and broken-down, "spent" dairy cows, hens, and breeding sows, have little, to negative, economic value, so the industry gets rid of them in the cheapest ways possible.

In some instances, there are low-ball markets where they can be sold for a few dollars on their way to ending up as veal (in the case of male calves) or low-grade meat. Some facilities specialize in slaughtering the most miserable and debilitated "spent" dairy cows and breeding sows, broken animals many plants refuse. Although so-called byproduct animals suffer greatly, nearly every member of the largest class of slaughtered animals, chickens used for their meat, is born into cruelty by virtue of selective breeding.

BERRY STAINED WHITE WINGS

I turned on my headlamp as I walked away from the SUV under a warm, cloudless Mississippi night sky. This was the second night my friends and I would spend catching broiler chickens—chickens bred specifically to be slaughtered for their meat. I walked across the gravel drive toward the end of the metal sheds where the birds lived their short few months between hatch and slaughter. Two of the five buildings that had been there a week before were destroyed by a tornado spun off of Hurricane Katrina. I didn't know that like remora on sharks, tornadoes travel with hurricanes.

If you're asking why the HSUS sent an out-of-shape lawyer to help animals in the wake of a hurricane, that is a fair question. It has a lot to do with my willingness to get a hepatitis shot and get on a plane to Louisiana with less than twelve hours' notice.

Ironically, we couldn't do anything for the white young chickens in the buildings that the tornado spared. We were there because the contract grower, a somewhat intimidating guy who raised birds for an international megacorp, was gentle-hearted enough to invite us—HSUS employees along with volunteers from two farm animal shelters—to help the other birds. We were only allowed to help the escapee birds who had fled the smashed buildings to surrounding fields and woods. The contract grower left us nearly a case of Bud Light cans floating in an old Styrofoam cooler.

We were in t-shirts as we worked through the warm September night under a sky lit by more stars than I had ever seen. For hours, we snuck up on sleeping chickens, roosting for the first time in their lives on low branches or nesting under leafy bushes or in the tall grasses. We gently caught them so they could be transported to sanctuaries.

The way to do this, as we learned, is to simultaneously close in on the sleeping birds from all sides and to hold their wings close to their bodies to keep them still as we lifted them.

Living in basically an overcrowded warehouse, the birds had never had the space to really separate themselves into subgroups. On those nights, we found them sleeping quietly in groups of twenty or thirty. To me, they looked indistinguishable from each other. My friend Miyun Park and I talked about how remarkable it was that under these circumstances any given group of twenty or thirty had collectively decided who was in and who was out of their club.

During the first night, we saw birds with purple stains on their glacier-white feathers. On night two, someone deduced that this came from berries in the woods that they'd been feasting on. Like egg-laying hens, these birds still knew how to forage like their ancestors, despite decades of selective breeding to make them meat-generating machines. They all knew how to make a go of it as birds, in trees and knee-high grass; they'd just never had the chance. Freed by the tornado, they found berries to eat and roosted in the trees as their kind have been doing for millennia.

A year or so after the rescue, I asked a friend who had been with me during this adventure how the birds were doing at the sanctuary she worked for. She didn't want to answer. I knew that broiler chickens often died young, but I had thought a lot of that could be chalked up to the terrible conditions they lived in: overcrowded and reeking strongly of ammonia from months, or years, of piled up manure upon which they walk, stand, and collapse.[119] But the insurmountable cruelty these birds endure is hard-wired into them.[120]

Of the more than nine billion U.S. chickens slaughtered every year, nearly all have been bred to gain weight far more rapidly than chickens did even a few decades ago.[121] They gain so much weight and at such an insane pace that their bodies will just give out underneath them.[122] By six weeks old, they spend up to 86 percent of their time lying down on the caked feces on which they live, too lethargic to walk more than a few steps to reach the feed, and this leads to lesions, like breast blistering.[123] Or their hearts just break under the unnatural, unrelenting strain of trying to keep a body alive that is about five sizes bigger than it was ever meant to be.[124]

The fate of the roughly 227,660,000 turkeys slaughtered annually in the United States is much the same.[125] They too have been bred to gain weight far too rapidly, and as with chickens, this causes them immense suffering. Thanks to selective breeding over many generations, turkeys raised for meat grow to twenty-five pounds in four months' time, whereas their wild counterparts only weigh about one quarter of that by the same age.[126]

While I was working on this book, my friend Miyun, who was our leader on that post-Katrina mission, sent me a photo of an incident I had forgotten. It was near the end of our time at the contract grower's Mississippi farm, probably an hour or so before dawn on the second night. We found an open pit, the size of a cheap motel's swimming pool, but much deeper. It was an open chicken grave. Coming within a few feet of its edge brought tears to our eyes. On account of my orangutan arms, I was drafted to put on a paper respiratory mask and lie down on the pit's edge. I used a long pole with a net on it to pull up living chickens who had fallen in. That mask didn't help.

THE CAUSE OF, AND SOLUTION TO, ALL OF LIFE'S PROBLEMS

During the late nineteenth and early twentieth centuries, advocates worked tirelessly to remove kids from the full-time labor pool. However, efforts focused only on children's interests may not have been the most significant factor in the passage of a federal law in the 1930s that outlawed the worst forms of child labor. That was likely the negative impact of a tot-based economy on adult wages and opportunities.[127] Sore child hands in New York tenements earned less than adult hands would have earned for the same work.

Huge populations of painfully impoverished adults threatened social stability and, ultimately, the bosses' bottom line. Eventually, those dual threats could not be counterbalanced by the marginal savings in wages flowing from exploiting child workers. So, in the early twentieth century, children increasingly swapped piecework and factory floors for homework and classrooms. No matter how bad schools can be, they are generally a better, safer place for seven-year-olds than canneries or industrial laundries. The rising tide of concern for impoverished adult workers raised all boats.

Homer Simpson once toasted "to alcohol—the cause of, and solution to, all of life's problems!"[128] The same can be said of adults without principle or the available bandwidth to focus on a given ethical problem. Adults, of course, were the source of the exploitative child labor problem, but they also solved a large part of the problem, by putting in place child protective laws.

Through her work, Jane Addams drove the movement that ended the legalized cruelty of putting kids to work full-time. Beyond the direct harm to the young, Addams also wrote forcefully about the wider negative repercussions of child labor, noting that, "such an industry is parasitic on the future of the community."[129] She went on to explain:

> [T]he factories say to the community; you have educated the children in the public schools, now please give them to me for my factory. I will use them until they begin to demand an adult's wages and then I will turn them out again. If I have broken them down, the community will take care of them in the poorhouse and hospitals. The community which allows this allows itself to be most unfairly treated. . . . By the time they are old enough to receive adult wages they are often sick of the whole business.[130]

Government-endorsed full-time child labor in the United States did not end for entirely noble reasons, but the important thing is that it ended.

Likewise, adults are responsible for routinized farm animal exploitation on a massive scale. Although concern for farm animals' wellbeing ought to be enough of a motivation, there is no shortage of terrifying, secondary factory farming threats to humanity to consider. These include heart disease, cancer, pandemic plagues, the loss of working antibiotics, and bursting lakes of urine and manure that kill fish as they displace all the oxygen from long stretches of rivers. The downside for humanity also includes all the modern-day Joad families who have no choice but to make a living cutting the throats of animals that the rest of us feed to our children, even as we hope those kids never see the disemboweling or, worse yet, someday make a living by killing while breathing air heavy with the copper smell of aerosolized blood.

Adults can see that this system ends both for the benefit of the victims and the victimizers. For no good reason, the system takes everything from those who never had anything to give. We may find the motivation to improve farm animals' lot partially just to save our own asses.

ONE LAST CAGED BIRD

A few years after I watched my six-year-old cousin anger a bull, I watched his mom disentangle a cormorant from thorny, bright-green blackberry vines. She wore gray work gloves, but as she pulled the bird from the thorns' grip, the cormorant's golden hooked beak tore into her forearms. She didn't flinch. I watched her work free one black wing and then the other. I knew I could never keep going as she did, ignoring the blood as it ran into her gloves.

She wrapped the bird in a Hawaiian-print beach towel and transferred her to a dog crate. My cousins and I piled into her baby blue Chevy van that always smelled of watermelon bubblegum. She drove the short few miles to Birch Bay. Through the carrier's bars I watched the black cormorant watching us with terrified blue-green eyes. The tide was out as we walked far out on the beach and let her go.

3

RICH, NOT FAMOUS, AND PUSHING DRUGS

Dangerous Drugs Sold by the Ton to Make Treats

"Rich and famous and doing good," mused Schlichtmann. "Rich isn't so difficult. Famous isn't so difficult. Rich and famous together aren't so difficult. Rich, famous, and doing good—now, that's very difficult."—Jonathan Harr, *A Civil Action* (New York: Vintage Books, 1996)

The stadium lights go dark as a photomontage of kids with outdated (but still totally rad) early eighties' haircuts begins on giant screens. In the darkness, a man's voice says: "Moments matter. Moments at FFA conventions *really* matter."[1] A spotlight illuminates a middle-aged rock star sitting next to his smiling assistants. The stands are filled with teenaged Future Farmers of America. "I was sitting right here in 1985 at my FFA convention. . . ."

His spiel increases in fervor as it progresses. He rises from his seat: "I'm gonna crank up some Eric Church 'Gimme Back My Hometown,' and I wanna hear that this 87th convention of FFA members will do more than any others before you. So I say you get on your feet and I wanna hear some noise as we start to crank up this music!"[2]

He makes his way toward the stage, initiating high-fives and taking selfies with the young audience. The kids generally look puzzled.

They're not asking for the selfies he mugs for with them. He takes those on *his* phone. The confused teens only start smiling when they realize they're about to be in a photograph. This is the modern equivalent of thrusting autographed photos of yourself at people who have no idea who you are. The millennials do an amazing job of concealing how star-struck they are by this Indiana-based, middle-aged white guy, who happens to be a very wealthy pharmaceutical company executive.

I've watched the entrance portion of this awkward video on YouTube at least six times. I have a hard time getting through the rest of it. The brown-belted office-park millionaire conveys his message well, but it's a facile one: There are many hungry people, the human population is growing, and it's up to you guys (the teenagers) to find a way to feed them all. He also is intent on convincing farm kids that Big Pharma is just out to feed the world (but of course never mentions all those billions they make along the way). How they would "feed the world" is something he never explains, as others have pointed out.[3] The video has been up since 2014 and as of this writing has had about 5,500 views, which is in the range of popularity of other FFA keynote speakers, but far below the highest numbers.

FAME'S OPPOSITE

"Okay, and did anyone help you today?"

I wanted to remind the woman ringing up the pants, which she and I both knew were a size too small, that a mere five minutes earlier she had helped me find them.

I'd make a great spy. Often, I run into people who've met me yet have no memory of me at all. To most, I am yet another white guy, and closer on the white guy spectrum to George Lucas than Brad Pitt. The opposite of fame isn't infamy—it's scenery.

My knack for approximating a wilting fern means fame is not in the cards for me, but I've nevertheless thought a lot about how to handle the fame that is never coming. The best part of my famous life will be getting more with less, coasting on past successes to get more of everything good with a lot less work. Fame is like a steroid: more muscle with less effort, with troubling side effects. My favorite run-in with a famous person happened in a coffee shop. In 2007, I would often walk with my wife to her office in downtown San Francisco and then make my way to a coffee shop at the center of the city where I'd work at a small table. A downtown San Francisco café is noisy as hell and might seem like a terrible place to hunker down and write a legal brief, but I was productive there. The dozens of voices just blended into white noise. Once in a while though, a voice would cut through the background din like a school bell at recess. One morning I was hammering away on my laptop and found myself thinking, "Jesus. I wish that dude would shut up." Then I thought, "Hey, his voice is really familiar." I looked up and saw comedian Dave Chappelle. Of all the famous people I could have run into in downtown San Francisco, he was the one person I would be happiest to see, and there he was joking with the barista, who happened to be a young stand-up comic.

I thought, "What the hell! I'll bother Dave Chappelle." My table was positioned like a sentry post by the door, so when he left he had to walk right by me. You can imagine how our conversation went: I gushed about what a fan I was and how *Chappelle's Show* got me through law school. He asked what I did, and I told him I was an animal lawyer and was working on a lawsuit against a pair of classy Floridians who called themselves "Wizard of Claws." The lawsuit alleged that they sold very sick puppy-mill dogs to people for upwards of $5,000 apiece. Their website touted celebrity customers. He seemed interested in the notion of an animal lawyer. I don't know why, but as we parted, I gave him my business card. He was in town doing sold-out shows for a week or so. He put my favorite barista on as an opener for one of those shows. I saw Dave again the next day. He didn't seem to recognize me, and I let him buy his coffee in peace.

WE DRUG THE WORLD

The drug company rock star's "we feed the world" line is a favorite talking point within the constellation of multibillion-dollar industries that revolve around mass-producing meat, eggs, dairy, and most of all, manure. It sounds lovely and communicates nothing. More importantly, the idea that multinational corporations will solve international food shortages is contradicted by their past and present failure to do anything of the sort.[4]

The "we feed the world" line is almost always coupled with predictions about the size of the human population in 2050. We will have an additional two billion people on the planet in 2050 and will need to generate more food with fewer resources. Proceeding from these solid premises, the argument falls off a cliff.

It's not controversial to use quantified birth rates and the current population to come up with a rough estimate of how many humans will be around in 2050. Where things go off the rails for the "we feed the world" set is their unstated, and unsupportable, assumptions about what will be on menus around the world in 2050. Like their business plans, their argument here depends entirely on the assumption that because many people like omelets, sausages, and hamburgers today, the unborn billions of 2050 will all share that proclivity for meat-, dairy-, and egg-focused diets.

Even now, around the world, the appetite for animal food products is not a constant. As income levels rise in some countries, that newfound financial surplus has tended to translate to more consumption of animal products. That trend is not universal, though, and even where it does happen, consumption tends to level off.[5] Yet in some countries, as incomes increase, there is much less of an increase in meat, dairy, and egg intake.[6]

One of the most damning aspects of this prediction about 2050 is that the people making it have a terrible track record when it comes to predicting events even a couple of years away. In 2011, the drug company rock star embraced some predictions about California's Proposition 2, the 2008 ballot measure that banned extreme confinement of egg-laying hens, veal calves, and pregnant sows. Those 2011 predictions were that:

Proposition 2 would increase egg production costs in California by 20 percent. This loss of competitiveness among California's egg producers could result in the complete elimination of that state's egg production industry by 2015, when the law takes effect.[7]

If you're wondering if you somehow missed the "complete elimination" of California's egg industry—the fifth largest in the United States—you did not.[8] It's hard to see the future when your crystal ball is coated in drug-laced manure. Since the folks are awful at it in the short term, it's unclear why anyone should trust them with prognostications about what people all around the world will be eating decades from now.

Predictions about technologies yet to be are often way off base. Come with me to 1973, and a camera-film manufacturer's boardroom fogged with cigar smoke. Silver platters piled with bear-claws and raspberry jelly donuts sit alongside ashtrays spilling onto an oak table big enough to have its own zip code. Since it is the early '70s, the executives are all, of course, older white dudes.

On the chalk board near the head of the table is a scrawled number in the billions. It's the predicted global population in the far-off future of 2020. As the sun sinks, eclipsed by the IBM building across the street, burnt coffee gives way to whiskey. The meeting stretches on past sunset, but the executives never mention Instagram or portable phones that take photos digitally without film. They don't see any of that coming. It wouldn't be fair to fault them for not foreseeing the iPhone at a time when, to paraphrase the band KARP, nylon was still a special treat.

Around the world, smartphone users barely noticed, if they noticed at all, as the once mighty Kodak went bankrupt in 2012. Obviously, people didn't stop taking photos when Kodak left the scene. The Brooklyn Bridge on a summer afternoon bristles with the selfie-sticks of half the population of Europe proving that they were there. We have supple, quick minds when it comes to abandoning practices or objects the moment we've found preferable replacements.

Trying to make predictions about dietary habits of people thirty years hence is confounded by huge variables and unknowns, including the sort of unforeseeable catalysts and unaccountable human fickleness that doomed Kodak. Many future-people are likely to adhere to a diet heavy in animal-derived protein, yet in the early 1970s, it also seemed reasonable to think people will always want to cart a heavy yet delicate camera with them to the Grand Canyon or Hawaii and that they'll perpetually be dropping off rolls of film at a little booth and returning a week later to find that half of their twenty-four prints are one hundred percent garbage.

Some might argue that our relationship to using animals for food is more profound and ancient than was our relationship to non-digital cameras. But it doesn't seem to matter to most of us how old a practice or object is once we see a better replacement in reach. As a species, we've been sleeping since night one, yet you won't find many clamoring for a return to the rustic pleasure of snuggling down to sleep on a pile of dry leaves amidst poisonous spiders a few feet from a fire smoldering on a cold cave floor. We will drop even ancient customs and long-beloved products and kill off entire industries in favor of something we tell ourselves, or are told by others, is better. "Better" is hard to universally define and even harder to foresee.

Big Ag has an arbitrary, tunnel-visioned fixation on the United Nations' prediction about the 2050 global population. The various bodies of the U.N. say a lot of things, and they're not all predictions about the population in 2050. For example, the U.N.'s World Health Organization is saying we need to stop dosing animals with antibiotics to make them grow more quickly because the practice is rendering important human antibiotics powerless. That's not an estimate about the future; it's a recommendation for dealing with a clear and present danger to human health. It's also not something Big Ag and Big Pharma want to hear, so you won't find them evangelizing about U.N. statements regarding the unjustifiable threat posed by stupidly juicing farm animals with antibiotics.

PRINTING A ONE HUNDRED TRILLION DOLLAR BILL
Our hankering for industrially produced animal foods plays a leading role in a crisis on par with Ebola and HIV/AIDS.[9] That's how U.N. Secretary-General Ban Ki-moon framed the issue of

antibiotic-resistant organisms. In 2016, he announced that the U.N. General Assembly was committing to action on this "fundamental, long-term threat to human health, sustainable food production and development."[10] This is only the fourth time since its 1945 inception that the General Assembly has taken such a stand on a health issue.

In the United States, about 80 percent of all antibiotics are consumed by farm animals, not humans, and there is no good reason for that.[11] There is a significant overlap between powerful antibiotics used to save the life of sick children and those given to farm animals simply to "promote growth" or to prop up the immune systems of animals kept in dismal conditions.[12] According to WHO, the science shows that "using antimicrobials in food-producing animals selects for antimicrobial resistance in bacteria isolated from food-producing animals, which then spread among food-producing animals, into their environment, and to humans."[13] Dosing farm animals with antibiotics, particularly with low level doses for extended periods of time, gives microorganisms millions of host animals within which they can evolve and develop resistance to the drugs.[14] As described by Johns Hopkins' Center for a Livable Future:

> Antibiotics in livestock feed are not administered at sufficient doses to eliminate disease. Rather, the continual "nontherapeutic" low-doses are only capable of eliminating the more susceptible bacteria; in a contest of "survival of the fittest," this inadvertently promotes the reproduction of antibiotic-resistant strains.[15]

The resistant microorganisms move from animals to humans through many avenues, including contact between workers and farm animals and by eating meat from infected animals.[16] By undermining antibiotics, we are in the process of turning back the clock to Victorian times, when you'd cough once while emptying your chamber pot and a fortnight later your family would be tossing dirt onto your coffin.

The link between sub-therapeutic use of antibiotics in farm animals and multi-drug-resistant *Staphylococcus aureus* (MRSA) is well established.[17] MRSA is one of the most common antibiotic-resistant infections, killing upwards of 11,000 people every year in the United States.[18] Victims of this infection can endure painful, pus-filled abscesses and rashes, which can result in permanent disfigurement.[19] There are two big categories of MRSA patients: those who acquire it in a hospital or medical setting, and victims of "community-acquired" MRSA—that is, people who pick it up elsewhere. Over the last decade, hospital-acquired MRSA cases have declined significantly while community-acquired infections have increased.[20] A 2013 study of thousands of Pennsylvania residents shows that those closer to pig manure and fields coated or injected with it are at a higher risk of picking up MRSA.[21] Proximity can increase your chances of MRSA infection by up to 30 percent.[22] The study showed that the nearer one is to these fields, the greater the risk.[23]

There is no upside to our creation of microorganisms resistant to antibiotics. The worst-case scenario—the one experts agree we are already living in—is that dosing farm animals creates a strong risk that, in about a decade or two, you may die from something that is currently treatable, like a respiratory infection or an infected cesarean section incision. Dumping antibiotics into farm animals to promote profits is not the only cause of antibiotic resistance, but it is a big part of the problem, and there is simply no rational justification for it.

Currently, around the world, about 700,000 people die every year due to infections that our antibiotics used to reliably trounce. Among these victims, about 200,000 are newborn children with infections that are now untreatable. The body count is expected to grow, and possibly spike, as more antibiotics become toothless.[24] In a 2017 World Health Organization–funded meta-analysis of all the research on the connection between the use of antibiotics in agriculture and its impact on antibiotic-resistance in humans, researchers observed that "[b]y 2050, an estimated 10 million deaths per year globally will be attributable to antimicrobial resistance, with a cumulative economic cost of US $100 trillion."[25]

In its recommendation for a complete ban on growth-promoting uses of antibiotics in farm animals, WHO noted that the evidentiary support for the ban was "low," but nevertheless concluded that evidence justified the ban.[26] It did this by looking at what was at stake, the potential loss of working human antibiotics, and weighing that against any "undesirable consequences" of such a ban.[27] The stakes make all the difference. In the context of stopping growth promoting uses of antibiotics, WHO concluded that:

> Potential undesirable consequences associated with complete restriction of growth promotion use of antimicrobials in food-producing animals (e.g. increased use of veterinary antimicrobials, adverse effects on animal health, animal welfare, food safety, the environment and animal production, increased costs of animal production, and economic impacts) appear to be relatively small or non-existent.[28]

In recent years in the United States, the subtherapeutic use of antibiotics in farm animals had been dramatically increasing. Between 2009 and 2013, the sale of antibiotics important to human medicine for use in farm animals increased by 20 percent.[29] In 2017, the FDA, working with Big Pharma, changed the farm animal antibiotic rules to require a veterinarian's prescription or plan for the use of medically important antibiotics.[30] So the new rules mandate a more compelling rationale—on paper if not in fact—for using antibiotics en masse in farm animals. The 2017 rule change may lead to dressing up the same old malarkey in a better-looking rationale: Farm animals still get drugged at the same rate, but now with a better cover story.[31]

There's good reason to think that this is what is happening. An extensive 2017 report from a panel of distinguished medical experts identified the flaws in the FDA's approach. They noted that no one can track prescriptions to look for "patterns among veterinarians, or even to identify high prescribers as the first step in helping them modify their use of antibiotics."[32] That's a big problem for a couple of reasons. First, there's the shopping around concern, *i.e.*, if one veterinarian won't prescribe the antibiotics, you call another and so on until you find one who will take your money and give you the drugs.[33] The panel also pointed to a 2011 Government Accountability Office (GAO) report that identified a significant potential for conflicts of interest between veterinarians and the behemoth meat companies that employ them.[34]

In the spring of 2017, the GAO took another look at antibiotic-resistance issues and the work of the FDA and USDA. The GAO concluded that there is no way to know if federal efforts to reduce the subtherapeutic use of medically important antibiotics in farm animals are working or failing miserably.[35] The GAO noted that it's impossible to gauge the effect of the 2017 mandatory changes to labels because there is no "use-by" date on the drugs sold before 2016. Thus, unknown amounts of the drugs may still be in use for years, consistent with pre-2017 labels that allow for "growth promoting" use.[36] More fundamentally, the GAO pointed out that neither the FDA nor USDA's Animal and Plant Health Inspection Service (APHIS) "have metrics to assess the impact of actions they have taken. . . . Without metrics, FDA and APHIS cannot assess the effects of actions taken to manage the use of antibiotics."[37]

Indeed, looking back, since the rule change, that seems to be exactly what happened. As *The New York Times* reported in 2018, cattle feedlot operations and Big Pharma alike agreed that the rule change really didn't change things on the ground, because the same old drugging can continue under the better looking guise of preventative medicine. According to the *Times* piece, "Zoetis, a major livestock drugmaker, said on its website that farmers 'will see little difference' in its tetracycline feed additives, beyond needing the appropriate paperwork from veterinarians."[38]

You may think it's not fair to only look at the side of the scale sagging under the weight of nearly three quarters of a million dead people a year without looking at the other side of the scale. It is certainly true that it has never been easier to find a ninety-nine-cent hamburger in every corner of the world. Our drugging of billions of animals for no good reason is something only people under the sway of self-destructive dumb-dumbs would put up with.

Garlic Won't Save You from Anything but Kisses

In the fall of 2017, I developed a respiratory infection, which I tried to knock out using the hippy go-to remedies: vats of ginger tea, round-the-clock moping on the couch, and eating more garlic than a seventeenth-century Czech peasant. Near the end of week two, with no real improvement, I knew I had to check in with Western medicine. I was prescribed erythromycin, a powerful macrolide antibiotic. The name was familiar to me because I learned about it as I studied its close relative: tylosin, a macrolide antibiotic given to tens of millions of U.S. farm animals.[39] The drugs are functionally one and the same, as an organism resistant to tylosin is also resistant to erythromycin. According to WHO, tylosin belongs to the class of drugs of the highest importance to human medicine.[40] During my coughing hippy-fest fortnight, my respiratory infection had begun to turn into pneumonia, but the macrolide knocked it out in just a few days. If I were in the same condition a century earlier, I easily could have died from pneumonia—and a few years from now, I may be right back in that situation.[41]

Beyond helping stay-at-home litigators beat pneumonia, "macrolides are one of few available therapies for serious *Campylobacter* infections, particularly in children."[42] *Campylobacter* is extremely common, and WHO noted that "the absolute number of serious cases is substantial."[43] As with so many of animal agriculture's downsides, the real kick of *Campylobacter* is felt by those who least deserve it and who are least able to survive it. It is one of only four main causes of diarrheal diseases, which afflict more than half a billion people annually, including two hundred million kids under five years old.[44] Those in developing countries are hit especially hard, per WHO: "*Campylobacter* infections in children under the age of 2 years are especially frequent, sometimes resulting in death."[45]

Historically, about 71 percent of U.S. cattle have been dosed with tylosin, and it has been the second most widely used antibiotic in pigs.[46] Like many pharmaceuticals, the drug remains active in manure to a large extent and can persist a long time in both water and soil.[47] U.S. Geological Survey experts conducted a survey of "a network of 139 streams across 30 states during 1999 and 2000," in which they found active tylosin in 13.5 percent of them.[48] According to a 2006 study, high levels of tylosin-resistant organisms persist in soil "for years after usage ceased."[49]

Of the many compelling reasons to shun animal food products, none is more compelling than the use of antibiotics in raising billions of farm animals. This may be the dumbest and most apocalyptically self-destructive thing we do with farm animals.

ADVERSE EVENTS

Right now, without a prescription, you could buy a bag of ractopamine. If you opened that bag and touched the powdery white drug, and then touched your nose, you'd better hope that someone is ready to rush you to the nearest hospital. That powder on your nose could be your ticket to a multi-day stay in an intensive care unit. While there, doctors may struggle to understand why your heart is close to exploding. The label on that bag not only would have told you never to touch the drug, it would have told you to basically wear a HAZMAT suit when you're handling the stuff. There is nothing like the wholesome pleasures of fresh air and doing chores around the farm while wearing "protective clothing, impervious gloves, protective eye wear, and a NIOSH-approved dust mask."[50]

Nevertheless, in a (now removed) online ad shot at an Iowa pig factory farm, you can see the unsheathed arm of a person dumping the drug into pig feed without the prescribed space-suit.[51] Wearing the recommended full-body protective wear in the ad would signal how frightening the stuff is and undercut the ad's faux-folksy tone. Nothing says simple, homespun goodness like a guy dressed as a crime scene coroner dumping a bag of powdery white drugs into farm animal feed with the accompaniment of an insipid acoustic guitar soundtrack.

Given the need for such serious protective gear, it is surprising that the drug is administered to 60 to 80 percent of all pigs slaughtered in the United States.[52] It belongs to a class of drugs called beta agonists.[53] The only other beta agonist that the FDA has approved for use in farm animals is zilpaterol. Although zilpaterol remains FDA-approved, its producer yanked it off the market in 2014 after meat industry titan Tyson Foods publicly said that it would not accept any cattle who had been given it. Tyson made that decision on the heels of something that happened at its Wallula, Washington, slaughter plant. Fifteen zilpaterol-drugged cattle had arrived at that facility barely able to move because they were missing hooves.[54]

Beta agonists are used only to increase profits. They have no therapeutic value. They increase profit margins by causing animals to convert more of the calories they consume to muscle, so, basically, they work like steroids. An animal is put on the stuff for the last few weeks of life and puts on a lot of muscle without necessitating a corresponding increase in feed or exercise. But like steroid use, the beta agonists have side effects.

When a drug maker learns that one of its drugs was involved in some adverse human health situation, for example when someone feels ill or goes to the hospital or dies, the company is supposed to report the incident to the FDA. The same goes for adverse events involving animals. The reports are brief and often terrifying, and they withhold from the public identifying details like victims' names. So, for example, all you can see are descriptions like the one about *this* poor guy. In July 2003 in rural Illinois, a man in good health fed his animals "Ractopamine for the first time . . . between 7 to 11am" and,

> shortly after, he was admitted to the ER with a high heart rate. Spent the whole day on a cardiac monitor. At time of the call to [Rocky Mountain Poison and Drug Center] the man was home with a slightly elevated [heart rate]. Mixing the Ractopamine was the only thing different he had done that day. He had used protective gear but unsure if he showered after exposure.[55]

A year later, in Indiana, a 48-year-old "[w]oman touched unopened bags of ractopamine to smell the product then touched her nose with her hands. Within one day the area around her nose broke out in pimples. Her nose remained sore for 10 days."[56] There are many other weird and frightening reports of adverse events in humans who touched the powder or otherwise handled it without wearing the body condom mandated by its warning labels. The reports do not represent the FDA's conclusions that ractopamine definitely caused each adverse event. Nevertheless, this is a drug that the government insists be labeled with a warning that anyone handling it should be sealed up in a protective suit with goggles and a respirator.[57]

Although the FDA allows the use of ractopamine in farm animals, more than sixty countries ban it, including Russia, China, and every member of the European Union.[58] The European Food Safety Agency (EFSA), the official food safety agency of the European Union, is unconvinced that human consumption of any amount of ractopamine residues in food is safe. EFSA noted that the FDA had approved the drug for use in farm animals based on scant human testing data. The only human safety test involved a mere six individuals, all healthy young men, and one guy dropped out when his heart began pounding uncontrollably. [59] According to EFSA, the small and uniformly male and healthy sample size did not account for vulnerable populations like the elderly, children, and people with heart disease.[60] In short, EFSA didn't buy the claim that this tiny, limited, human safety test could support setting any threshold of safe levels of ractopamine residues in human food.[61]

The FDA has approved ractopamine for use in pigs, cattle, and turkeys. It is a serious, multi-pronged threat to pigs' welfare and health. Death and lameness, a painful physical disability often resulting in an abnormal gait or inability to walk, are the largest categories of adverse events in pigs. The drug increases their heart rate, makes them hyperactive, and triggers a stress response.[62] Stress suppresses pigs' immune systems and also makes the animals aggressive and more difficult to move.[63] A pig who is difficult to guide from a pen to the semi-truck that will take her to slaughter is a pig who is more likely to be hit or shocked with an electric prod.[64] Aggressive pigs are also more likely to bite or otherwise injure the people who try to handle them.[65] Those bites can cause infections, including infections resistant to antibiotic treatments.[66]

The FDA has more adverse event reports for ractopamine used with pigs than it has for any other animal–drug combination,[67] and they commonly include trembling, lameness, recumbency, reluctance to move, stiffness, hyperactivity, hoof disorder, dyspnea (difficulty in breathing), collapse, and death.[68] One Iowa pork producer gave his pigs the recommended dosage during the last three weeks before sending them to slaughter. He reported the pigs developed "blotchy whitish/reddish spots over their bodies" and were "so stressed while being moved or sorted that the pigs would lie down and die."[69] This happened consistently over a two-year period until he stopped using the drug.[70] (Why it took him two years is another story. . . .)

After the FDA approved the drug in 1999, the agency was surprised by the frequency of negative side effects. In 2002, the FDA took the unusual step of mandating the use of this warning label on all ractopamine products for pigs: "CAUTION: ractopamine may increase the number of injured and/or fatigued pigs during marketing."[71] "Marketing" is an FDA euphemism for forcing pigs onto semi-trucks and then dumping them in pens where they wait their turn to be stunned, stabbed in the neck, and bled to death.

A collapsed pig at a slaughter facility is a magnet for *Salmonella*, and a *Salmonella*-carrying pig can pass that on to those who eat his or her butchered flesh.[72] *Salmonella* is a leading cause of food poisoning, annually killing about 450 Americans and sickening well over a million.[73] In addition to causing pigs to collapse on semi-trucks or in pens, ractopamine also has been shown to significantly increase the growth rate of *Salmonella*.[74] It's the gift that keeps on giving.

HERE'S HOPING THAT NO ONE CARES

The website of the National Pork Board, an industry trade association, is home to a thirty-three-slide 2013 PowerPoint presentation rife with advice on how to spin the story of animal cruelty, antibiotics, and ractopamine built into Big Pork's business model.[75] The PowerPoint is the creation of the public relations firm Maslansky and Partners. In it, the firm gives an overview of its views on how the public feels about drugs and cruelty in the pork industry. Based on its own ill-described one-time survey of consumers, Maslansky argues that consumers basically don't care about cruelty, ractopamine, or antibiotics. Instead, apparently, we care only about ourselves and our own safety. The message that consumers are nothing but self-centered sociopaths has got to be welcome news for an industry that depends heavily on using a drug like ractopamine and castrating week-old piglets without painkillers.

However excited the pork industry may be about that message, it cannot be reconciled with a variety of robust surveys finding the exact opposite. A growing number of people care quite a bit about the suffering of farm animals. In a survey commissioned by the American Farm Bureau, "95% of people said it was important to them how farm animals are cared for" and 76 percent said they valued animal welfare over cheap prices.[76] Of course, there will be a gap between what people say and how they act on any given day, but that's hardly unique to animal issues. Survey people about how they feel about five-year-olds working long shifts in sweatshops and the results are going to be consistently negative, even if those answers are contradicted by some of the respondents' clothing purchases. But failing to uniformly live up to a consistent ethic is categorically different from Maslansky's pork-baron-pleasing line about people just not caring about the welfare of animals.

State election returns also show that people care about more than just themselves when it comes to torturing farm animals. In recent years, voters in Florida, Arizona, California, and Massachusetts chose to ban gestation crate confinement for pregnant pigs and make it punishable with fines and, in some cases, jail time.[77] (Though incarcerated, pig producers would still have more space in their cells than gestation-crated sows.) All of the roughly 78 percent of voters who made that a legal reality in Massachusetts in 2016 must have been on Maslansky's "do not call" list.[78]

The business-casual pharmaceutical rock star likely means well. We like to see ourselves as the hero rather than the villain or an extra in the film of life. He may really believe the line he's feeding us about Big Pharma feeding the world, but there's no good reason for us to buy it. The company he heads up sells tylosin and developed and was the first to sell ractopamine.[79]

The faces of the kids in that arena bear expressions that seem to ask, *Who is this guy and why is he the star?* They're not dumb. They know he has drugs to push and that his message about feeding the world conveniently fits into that sales pitch. It's comforting that the number of views for his speech on YouTube is a fraction of the number of views for the speeches of America's actual future farmers. Those kids, the FFA organizational officers, tell stories about their lives and on occasion play the banjo and deliver Christian-focused comedy. They don't have products to sell—just the tepid stories and aphorisms that seventeen-year-olds gravitate toward when they know adults are listening.

The Big Pharma executive will remain wealthy, and he'll keep believing and saying the things that make the multinational multimillionaires who pay his salary happy. But the distant look in the eyes of the future farmers in that stadium is the best he can hope for among audiences. Those kids won't make him famous. They don't relate to him, despite his obsequious effort to shoehorn a Snapchat reference into his talk.

And he will have a very hard time connecting with a wider audience, as evidenced by his decision to share an anecdote about his interaction with a pair of chickens. Annoyed by his mother-in-law's preference for free-range chickens, he took her to a chicken farm, where, with his bare hands, he ripped off the heads of two chickens and then disemboweled them to show her the birds' intestines. One was a free-range bird and the other wasn't. His aim was to show her how much better looking the insides of a confined chicken were than the one allowed to move around more.[80] At best, this anecdote *might* go over well with a narrow segment of the Norwegian death metal scene.

Let us put aside for a moment that this gentleman thought it was okay to rip apart conscious chickens with his bare hands to make a point to his mother-in-law (and the true point of that display may be other than as described). That is the sort of incident tailor-made for deep shame and regret. Barring shame and regret, or better yet prosecution, even if he believed what he did was somehow acceptable, he should have been saying to himself: *I definitely should not tell that anecdote to a reporter for the* International Business Journal, *because even if my buddy Øystein "Lord of All Stabbings" Borknågårson and I think what I did was cool, I bet it's going to go over exceedingly poorly with everyone else.*

Fame and mainstream acceptance will elude those who fail to notice that most people don't accept that animals are here to be ripped apart for the most trivial of human whims. Likewise, as the public learns more, they will not tolerate animal drugs that harm animals and massively endanger people while serving no worthwhile purpose.

Lovely Scenery

A few years after Dave Chappelle had the honor of meeting me, I saw his former writing partner and *Chappelle's Show* co-creator, Neal Brennan, in a Santa Monica restaurant. Neal was alone and probably about to leave, so I went over to bother him. A couple weeks earlier, I had seen him do stand up in Portland, so we talked about that. Then I started to tell him the story about how I met Dave at that San Francisco coffee shop.

Right as I got to the part where I said, "I wish this guy would shut up," Neal stopped me and said, "It was Dave Chappelle." Then for some reason I deadpanned this semi-joke: "You know, I gave Dave my card but he never calls me." Because of my delivery, or because it's not really a proper joke, Neal thought I was being serious. I guess he thought I had really spent evenings sitting by the phone expecting that call from Dave to chat about what had happened in that Florida "Wizard of Claws" case (they went bankrupt). I tried to make clear that I wasn't that delusional and then I said goodbye, thinking that that had gone about as well as I had expected.

As I mentioned, often, even people who have met me before fail to recognize me. After I said goodbye to Neal and rejoined my parents' table, I sat down just as my mother was telling our waiter who I was and what my conversation with the guy across the room was all about. According to Mom I am a well-known animal lawyer who is often recognized by fans like that guy sitting over there. I have checked "get famous" off the to-do list.

PART *II*

A WIDENING AMBIT
OF DAMAGE

4

In the End the Coyote Wins

In Pursuit of the Uncatchable

"And then, in the instant that a wild new hope is lighting up his face, the coyote turns and smiles blandly upon him once more, and with a something about it which seems to say: 'Well, I shall have to tear myself away from you, bub—business is business, and it will not do for me to be fooling along this way all day'— and forthwith there is a rushing sound, and the sudden splitting of a long crack through the atmosphere, and behold that dog is solitary and alone in the midst of a vast solitude!"—Mark Twain, *Roughing It*, 1886[1]

One hot California afternoon, by a six-foot-high embankment at the end of a dirt road, I found a small black-and-white cat lying on her side in tall grass. She was barely breathing. That embankment held back millions of gallons of putrefying chicken manure, in a golf course–sized manmade lake. The ammonia from the shit lake hit me like a rock between the eyes. On the left side of the road, a dozen goats bleated at me from a fenced yard that they had nibbled bare. A few hundred feet from the goats, in a field behind a house, I found the little cat with her bald, sunburned ear.

Olive, as she came to be known, was starving to death by a massive egg farm near Stockton. Her eyes weren't just shut—they were crusted shut. She was a kitten who had only ever known toxic, stinging air. She clawed at the tan dry grass as I lifted her. I thought I would be taking her straight to a veterinarian to be euthanized. But in my car a few miles north on I-5, away from the poisonous lake, Olive came to life, running under the passenger seat and climbing into my lap.

Eight years later, one morning in the spring of 2016, before coffee or feeding the cats, I opened the curtains and saw a skinny German Shepherd loping down the street. I looked out into the darkness for a self-satisfied hippy, the type who usually accompanies "friendly" off-leash dogs. This dog's gait was inexplicably different, undoglike. I realized the dog was a coyote.

I skipped feeding the cats and stepped outside to make sure that Walter, the cat my neighbor refused to bring inside, was safe. Walter is not native to this continent.[2] So he stood no chance against a coyote, whose ancestors traversed these streets a million years before there were streets.[3] Cats first came on the scene in 1620, riding over on Pilgrim ships.[4] Coyotes have also been here longer than we have. Estimates vary, but they place the first human arrivals in North America about 975,000 years after coyotes.[5] I walked a few houses down and saw Walter's black ears lifting up over the soft rim of his porch bed as the coyote ambled down the middle of the street and hung a left at the bottom of the hill.

I knew I couldn't stand guard all morning. My neighbor already hated me because I had called animal control about Walter's awful living arrangement. I waited a minute to see if the coyote would come back before I headed home. That was when I heard yelling. Now the coyote came trotting back toward Walter and me.

"Get out of here, asshole! You killed my cat, you coyote asshole! Stay out of this neighborhood, motherfucker!"

Walter flattened himself on the porch, black ears disappearing below the rim of his bed.

On the far side of the street, the coyote passed me at barely a trot. Even so, she was increasing the distance between her and the bundled-up, fiftyish guy who was huffing and puffing up the hill after her, screaming. As she passed under the halogen streetlight's white glow, she didn't seem worried; she seemed embarrassed on her pursuer's behalf.

As the man came close, I wasn't sure what I should do. He saw me staring at him in the dark. I thought it would be weirder if I said nothing. As he jogged by, I asked, "She got your cat?"

"Yeah. Maybe it wasn't this coyote, but I saw one carry her away in his jaws and then my neighbor found her head." He continued shouting and running up the hill. "Stay out of our neighborhood, asshole!"

At the top of the hill, the coyote broke left. From there, it was an easy shot through a yard and over a tall chain-link fence into a graveyard.

The Embarrassing in Pursuit of the Inedible

The federal government has spent decades and millions of dollars paying assholes to shoot coyotes from planes.[6] Many more coyotes perish in far worse ways: thrashing for hours or days in steel-jaw leghold traps scattered in wild grasses and across forest floors, or choking on yellow poison that bursts from puncture collars on the necks of innumerable sheep.[7] The collars, misleadingly called "Livestock Protection Collars," don't kill coyotes fast enough to actually protect the sheep wearing the collar.[8] The collar's poison slowly rips up the coyote from the inside. Death takes up to seven hours.[9] It is so highly toxic that it lingers in the food chain, killing animals, like bald eagles, who eat dead coyotes.[10] Litters of infant coyotes are also "fumigated"—killed by poisonous gas canisters tossed into their dens.[11] Employees of a federal agency, euphemistically called Wildlife Services, killed 68,292 coyotes in 2018.[12] That's a bit more than one coyote killed every eight minutes. The government doesn't do this for me or for Walter the porch cat. They kill coyotes primarily for sheep ranchers.[13]

Ranchers also kill coyotes; some hang their corpses on fences.[14] The artist Sue Coe documented one such vicious display outside Chico, California. In her illustration, a coyote hangs crucified on a barbed wire fence wearing glasses, a woman's wig, and a handwritten sign around her neck that reads: "Will Work for Food."[15]

Despite the bullets, traps, and poisons, the coyote's territory has continuously expanded across North America for decades.[16] Increasingly, studies have dispelled the notion that lethal predator control works. Indeed, rather than limiting the number of farm animals that coyotes and other wild animals kill, such control mechanisms may actually increase the number of dead farm animals.[17] As one group of experts who reviewed predator control studies explained:

> Although it seems obvious that killing a carnivore about to take a lamb should ensure the latter's short-term survival, most lethal methods are applied indirectly in wholly different situations. Lethal intervention is usually implemented after carnivores are observed near livestock or days after a predation event has occurred, sometimes far from where the attack occurred.[18]

Unsurprisingly, this often means that the "culprit" animal is not the one killed.[19] Taking out one predator opens up a vacancy that can "be filled by more numerous, smaller species of predators that in turn might prey on livestock."[20] It's also now well established that when we kill coyotes, the remaining coyotes birth larger litters, "resulting in higher population growth rates and population densities during subsequent years."[21] On the other hand, non-lethal methods, such as using guard dogs or ribbon-like flags on fencing, seem to be more effective.[22] Unlike the widespread killing of predators, non-lethal methods have not been connected to an increase in farm animal predation.[23] Lethally punishing wolves and coyotes for eating sheep is as sensible as shooting a dog for eating a steak set down before him.

As others have pointed out, if you can't make your business work without a federally funded militia, poisons, traps, and airborne snipers, then the problem is your business model.[24] By comparison, the technology and entertainment industries are exponentially more important to the U.S. and California economies than the state's sheep ranchers ever will be.[25] Yet, there are no federally backed private mercenaries ensuring the success of a new sitcom or app.

A TINY HEART

Olive became the most playful and affectionate of our cats. She also had a sense of humor. She loved to start in the basement and sprint up the carpeted stairs into our kitchen, round the corner into the living room, and then pounce onto a soft catnip toy. The best part of this sequence was when she turned from the kitchen into the living room. Like a little Evel Knievel banking his motorcycle, she would tilt nearly to the ground as she took this 90-degree turn at top speed, her little back legs pedaling as she nearly spun out on the linoleum.

Every few months, she had a seizure. The episodes and their frequency might have been related to her exposure to hydrogen sulfide by the egg factory farm where I found her. The seizures terrified her. She would run and try to crawl underneath something when they came on. We had to grab Olive and hold her so she wouldn't hurt herself.

Eventually, eight years after I picked her up from the dry grass by the manure lake, we discovered a tumor had destroyed her right inner ear and was growing through her skull and into her jaw. In the end, when she tried to yawn, the tumor would stop her as she opened her little mouth.

The vet came to our house to administer the injections that would end her life as humanely as possible. We wanted to keep her calm, so we held her. The first injection anesthetized her, and the second, a bright blue liquid, killed her. For a tiny heart like Olive's, this happens quickly. Only when her little lungs stopped rising, did we cry.

At the risk of giving too much away, death is coming for you and everyone in your care. There are choices that, up to a point, might forestall or soften the inevitable. With Olive, we softened her ending. We cut short the tumor's slow erasure of a loved one. Letting a cat roam under blackberry bushes and across lawns, as my neighbor did, was a choice he may now regret, though it was made with benign intentions. His cat, who didn't understand coyotes, pined to go outside and he acquiesced. The rancher who serially kills coyotes understands those predators, but he won't abide their refusal to respect his plans. So, he keeps putting steak after steak under the muzzle of hungry mother coyotes who have babies to feed. If he cares about his sheep, and I believe some do, then the cycle of bait, kill, and repeat is all the more mystifying.

5

REAPING DROUGHT BY DESIGN

Water, Food, and Productive Land Converted to Oceans of Manure and Urine

"I wish there were no machines, and everyone led a pastoral existence. Trees and flowers don't deliberately cool you out and go beep in your ear."—Neil Pye, *The Young Ones*, "Bambi"[1]

In *A Small Star in the East*, Charles Dickens' 1868 essay about an afternoon tour of impoverished London's East End, he comes off as a bit of a prick, albeit of the most compassionate, well-intended kind.[2] Dickens invites himself into a home where he meets a woman dying of lead poisoning and another hoping to get hired at the lead mill:

> She knew all about the sufferings of the unfortunate invalid, and all about the lead-poisoning, and how the symptoms came on, and how they grew: having often seen them. The very smell when you stood inside the door of the works was enough to knock you down, she said, yet she was going back again to get "took on." What could she do? Better be ulcerated and paralysed for eighteenpence a day, while it lasted, than see the children starve.[3]

For many years, as you entered my hometown Tacoma on Interstate 5, you'd see a sign boasting that it is an "All-American City." Behind it, in every shade of matte gray, behemoth cranes move cargo between boxcars and ship hulls where the silty Puyallup River meets Commencement Bay. The thrice-received "All-American" awards are probably owed in part to the city's once-thriving lead and copper smelter, built into a valley along the bay. The smelter employed thousands for almost a century as it breathed carcinogens into us.

The plant began smelting lead in the late nineteenth century and did so until the 1920s, when it changed owners and metals—going from lead to copper as part of the American Smelting and Refining Company (ASARCO). ASARCO was affiliated with the Guggenheims, the titans of the twentieth-century steel industry.[4] Ringed by its workers' small houses with lawns of perennially dead grass, ASARCO smelted until 1985, when a weak copper market, government investigations, and lawsuits shuttered the operation.[5]

The smelter wasn't actually in Tacoma, it was in the tiny town of Ruston. In late-nineteenth-century photos, Ruston looks like a mining town high in the Sierras. Its small, unpainted buildings, partially on stilts, lean into the piney hillsides of the valley that empties to deep Commencement Bay.[6] Tacoma grew up on all sides of little Ruston, and to the casual visitor, Ruston seems like one of Tacoma's neighborhoods.

Eventually, people realized the smelter was, by degrees, poisoning everyone and the ground we walked on. In the mid-1990s, ASARCO sent my parents a settlement check of a few thousand dollars.[7] Years of class-action litigation crystallized into a final formula allotting cash based on a combination of proximity to, and duration of residence near, the 562-foot-tall smoke stack. We lived a mile or so from the recently shutdown smelter. In my neighborhood, I competed with the rodent community for the dusty, iodine-colored grapes growing in my neighbor's yard. It wasn't until years later that I was told not to eat anything that grew in the neighborhood because the soil was laced with arsenic, the favorite poison of would-be killers of czars and bed-and-breakfast guests.[8]

Arsenic is the assassin's go-to for a reason: It's really bad for you, especially when it's spewed out by smelters.[9] It is also a "known carcinogen," and as demonstrated by a recent study, arsenic exposure is linked to "cancers of the lung, skin, kidney, bladder, colon, uterus, prostate, stomach, and liver."[10] In addition to cancer, arsenic exposure is linked to cardiovascular disease, as well as "skin diseases such as hyperpigmentation and keratoses, peripheral neuropathy, and adverse reproductive effects."[11]

ENTER THE SALON

At 17, I tore up North Tacoma's poisoned ground at the wheel of a burgundy 1973 Oldsmobile Cutlass Salon, perfecting what my pal Mike called the "Salawn job." The '73 Salon topped the list of cars my parents never should have let me drive. It weighed in at about four thousand pounds and was roughly the size of a small farm.

Decades later, it's easy to second-guess their decision to let me drive it. It's even easier to shake our heads about the early-1970s thinking that brought the Salon into being in the first place. Why did Oldsmobile think the world needed a family sedan the size of an aircraft carrier? Meanwhile, Honda was making the Civic, which was about one fourth the size of the Salon and far more fuel-efficient. That last part came to matter a great deal during the oil crisis of 1973. Nevertheless, in the early '70s, the heyday of waterbeds, fondue, and deep orange shag carpets, the Salon was exceedingly popular.

My parents handed me the Salon's key thinking it would be hard for me to hurt myself in anything so gigantic. Their concern for my well-being was inversely proportional to the threat that I, a teenage idiot, posed to anyone unlucky enough to be in front of the Salon while not inside a sturdy, multi-story building. I shudder still at the choices I made behind the wheel of that burgundy lead sled. Because I didn't drink or do any drugs as a teenager, I had to work harder than the average dummy to jeopardize my friends' lives and futures. This is what I was up to on my last day of high school as I piloted the Salon into a large vacant lot. My girlfriend and two of her friends were with me as the sun set through fir trees on a ridge high above us. There were the beginnings of a few dirt roads dividing the forest here and there.

A week before, I'd scouted out this lot with my pal Randy. He and I had driven the Salon slowly up a steep dirt road. The road ended at the top of the hill, but I kept driving. It felt like we were in a *Monty Python* Terry Gilliam cartoon: a huge burgundy tank of a sedan rolling through dark forest shadows, not following even a deer trail. Somehow, I navigated the car through, and, as was my wont at the time, I gunned it. The Salon roared out of the woods to the alarm of rush-hour commuters.

So, on the evening of our last day of high school, I was back on familiar ground, but this time with a car full of ladies to impress. They were going to love this. I pointed the Salon's bow up that same steep dirt road and floored it, prompting immediate concern from my girlfriend and her friends. I affected my wry, "James Bond" smile. They didn't know that I knew this would work. All three said things like: *Slow down!* and *You're not going to fit through those trees!* and *Fuck!* I grinned as the Salon accelerated, kicking up an arsenic dust cloud in slanted sunset light. We were nearing the tree line at the top of the ridge. It did look like it would be a tight fit through the fast approaching pair of giant Douglas fir trees framing the dirt road, but I had just done this the week before.

Hitherto, I'd never heard a sound like bark crumpling metal as it scrapes off paint, and I haven't heard it since that evening. The Salon went from about twenty miles per hour to zero as I wedged it deep between those two trees. Turns out, I was on a different dirt road than I'd been on the week before. If you think it was easy to pry that car free of those trees, then in the words of Judas Priest, "You've got another thing coming." My companions' hooting laughter didn't help.

Then began weeks of cover-up. Near my house, I'd park with the Salon's passenger side covered by a juniper hedge, leaving the less-damaged driver's side exposed—even though that side was barely less jacked up than the other. Both sides were crumpled with bark smashed into what was left of the burgundy paint. The car looked as if a fir tree had used it as toilet paper. I gave up on hoping to fix it.

When the jig was finally up, I told my parents some malarkey about trying to do a U-turn on a heavily wooded median. This lie was an odd choice, as it made me seem no less a dummy than the truth would have. To my surprise, they were bemused, not alarmed. They'd let me drive the Salon partly because they knew it was worth as much as a weekend stay in a Des Moines Holiday Inn. They weren't insisting that I fix it at my expense. However, a few months later, in the middle of the night, someone smashed in the Salon's back window. That was the end of the line. It was also the end of the car that had rolled off the line in Lansing, Michigan, the year I was born and carried me and my older sister through high school. With its flanks stripped of paint by a pair of trees and a missing back window, it just wasn't worth fixing up.

I had taken the car for granted, never thinking critically about hanging onto a rolling two-ton leaded-gas smokestack. Like the smelter, the mighty Salon no longer made economic or environmental sense. The smelter had been one of Pierce County's largest employers.[12] Thanks to cars like the Salon and places like the smelter, "lead has become the most widely scattered toxic metal in the world."[13] The Salon got about twelve miles to the gallon, which was normal in a 1973 family car. But two decades later, leaded gas, like cheese fondue at a hot tub party, was correctly seen as 1970s silliness that we were better off without.

In the late 70s, studies of the communities around an ASARCO smelter smokestack in El Paso, Texas, led to the ban on the leaded gasoline the Salon chugged.[14] One confounding and tragic aspect of lead exposure that these studies revealed is that it can impede a child's neurological development while the child displays no symptoms. In 1989, a leading medical expert on the dangers of lead explained the risks:

These data draw a convincing picture of lead's broad impact on children's intelligence, growth, ability to hear and perceive language, and to focus, maintain, and shift attention. They certify, to the satisfaction of all but representatives of the lead industry, that lead is a potent, versatile, and widely distributed toxicant.[15]

By the summer of 1992, the Salon was out of our lives, replaced by a car that ran more efficiently on unleaded gasoline. And a few months after the Salon left us, so did the neighborhood smokestack. In January of 1993, what had been the tallest smokestack on the planet in 1917 imploded before a cheering crowd. In Tacoma, the self-styled "City of Destiny," something like this explosive ending had been foreseeable for decades.

The smelter began operating in 1888, when Tacoma was in its infancy. In the 1880s, Tacoma was a boomtown, thanks to its selection by the Northern Pacific Railroad as the Western terminus for its rail-line from Minnesota.[16] But Tacoma's growing population, around 36,000 by 1890,[17] was a fraction of what it would become in the next century.

As Dickens' article demonstrates, industrial lead work was common in the mid- to late-nineteenth century in places far more densely populated than Ruston and Tacoma. As with London's lead mill, wealthy Tacomans kept their distance from the smelter. Tacoma's fancier homes, including the house where I berthed the burgundy Salon, were at least a mile or more away from the small, whitewashed houses surrounding ASARCO.[18] The point here is that it likely did not seem unreasonable to Tacoma's city fathers to encourage smelting lead in a growing city.

On the other hand, long before the first lead smelting in Tacoma or London's East End, at least some people knew lead was dangerous. The first law we know of banning the use of lead due to its toxicity dates back to seventeenth-century Germany.[19] Based on a physician's discovery that leaded wine was causing colic, Duke Eberhard Ludwig of Württemberg banned leading wine in 1695.[20] Centuries before the Duke's law, however, many had deduced that the highly malleable and useful metal was bad news for human health.[21]

By 1888, in Tacoma, there were sound reasons upon which the gray-sideburned city fathers could have relied in concluding that a lead smelter would be bad for emerging neighborhoods or the people who handled the smelting. But, of course, the lead smelter—and the copper smelter it would become—were great for those who pocketed the cash and tax revenue from it. And what a coincidence that they lived far enough away that their lawns weren't permanently dead![22]

By the time the smokestack was shut down, the whole operation was in the midst of an EPA-mandated cleanup. By then, the stack was surrounded by nearly two hundred thousand people in one of the state's largest cities.[23] After the stack was rubble, anything not removed was sealed in plastic, and a layer of soil sprinkled with grass seed blanketed the site.

The copper ASARCO made was useful in medical devices and hospitals, among other unique and important applications.[24] Yet, copper mining and copper smelting have significant environmental and public health consequences—like the faintly bitter-almond-flavored grapes I ate from my neighbor's vine. Assuming that some copper smelting may be justified, it still made no sense to keep on smelting it in the middle of what became Washington's third-largest city. In El Paso, a city with an even larger ASARCO smelter smokestack, the mayor opposed the company's 2009 efforts to re-start its smelting. The mayor stated, "Maybe stick them out in the middle of nowhere, but to be right in the heart of a city is not a good thing." That smokestack, even taller than Ruston's, remains dormant.[25]

An Overdue Reconsideration

A moment of reckoning, one along the lines of reevaluating the Salon and smelter, is overdue for the meat, egg, and dairy industries. There's probably a good chance that those products were always with you, like the Salon was always with me and the Smelter with Tacoma. Assuming that the lead-then-copper smelter and the Salon made sense when conceived, each came to the end of the line as its cost eclipsed any benefits. The smelter helped Tacoma grow and to enjoy thrice "All-American" status, but evolving understandings of its impact on public health and the environment caught up with it.

In the twentieth century, as we came to realize their social, environmental, and public health costs, we sited smokestacks and similar polluters far from densely populated areas. Of course, it's easier to carry on with dirty and dangerous work if it's hidden from the increasingly urban consumers and voters who benefit from it. Many such operations, especially those related to industrialized animal agriculture, are now continents and oceans away from the populations that support them. Not only are we so much further removed from farming in the United States than our parents and their parents were, as practices intensified and animals were consolidated en masse often inside windowless sheds, but production also has been increasingly outsourced to other, lesser developed (according to some) countries.

Like the Salon I wrecked, the animal protein industries are inherently inefficient, wasting huge heaps of grain.[26] For every 230 calories of feed eaten by beef cattle, roughly 10 calories are passed on to those who eat the animal.[27] It takes between 70 to 110 calories of feed to make 10 calories of dairy, eggs, chicken, and pork products.[28] All those lost calories are burned up by the animals' metabolism or become manure and urine. No reasonable person would invest in a proposition knowing that the return will be $10 for every $230 invested—with piles of steaming feces as a bonus. That's a 4.3 percent rate of return on investment. The asininity of that inefficiency alone should be enough cause to shift away from the industrial farm animal complex. Yet it hasn't. And there's more.

In the process of burning up the majority of calories invested, the whole endeavor does enormous collateral damage. We could try to tinker with the basics and maybe bump up that return by a few percentage points just as my parents could have spent time and money designing a spoiler that might've made the leaded-gas-powered Salon a bit more aerodynamic, taking it from twelve miles per gallon to thirteen. That would make sense only if there were not already less costly, more efficient, and readily available alternatives.

The academic literature and reports from intergovernmental bodies, like the United Nations, support what has long seemed obvious: Those of us who can eat less, or zero, animal product should do so. In a 2017 report, the United Nations described agriculture as "the single biggest land use covering more than one-third of the world's land surface, not including Greenland and Antarctica."[29] The vast majority of that farmed land is devoted to producing animal products such as meat, dairy, and eggs. As a 2018 meta-analysis of studies including data from 38,700 farms in more than a hundred nations pointed out, "the impacts of animal products can markedly exceed those of vegetable substitutes . . . to such a degree that meat, aquaculture, eggs, and dairy use ~83% of the world's farmland and contribute 56 to 58% of food's different emissions, despite providing only 37% of our protein and 18% of our calories."[30]

The industrialized model rapidly spreading worldwide doesn't allow for animals to graze on verdant pastures. Rather, farm animals are confined in what experts refer to as "landless" facilities, where feed is brought in—sometimes from a nearby source but often from another region or even another continent.[31] When it comes to chicken, pigs, and egg production, the industrialized method long ago eclipsed the traditional farm, and it's projected to continue to grow in popularity.[32] At this point, globally, farm animals consume almost twice as many calories from feed as they directly nibble from pastures.[33] The inherent wastefulness of this approach is propped up by those of us who continue to vote for such unsustainable practices with our wallets. Not everyone can boycott products that demand and waste so much in the way of resources, but there are plenty of us who can and should.

Wasting Calories

Extreme poverty and hunger persist around the globe and not because we aren't cranking out enough bacon and Denver omelets. About fifteen years ago, the FAO reported that "[a]lthough enough food is being produced to feed the world's population, there are still some 840 million undernourished people in the world, 799 million of whom live in developing countries."[34] In 2013, with 30 million more undernourished people since 2002, the U.N.'s Human Rights Council

(UNHRC) pointed out that "the planet could produce enough food to feed twelve billion people." The UNHRC explained that it "[c]onsiders it intolerable that, according to an estimation by the United Nations Children's Fund, more than one third of the children who die every year before the age of 5 years do so from hunger-related illness."[35]

By 2017, the FAO reported that about "795 million people still suffer from hunger," and that "global food security could be in jeopardy, due to mounting pressures on natural resources and to climate change, both of which threaten the sustainability of food systems at large."[36] We already produce enough food to feed the human population, and if we made better choices—including not wasting land, water, and calories by diverting each to fatten warehoused farm animals—we could feed up to 12 billion people instead of choosing to let children starve to death in many parts of Africa and South Asia.[37] Moving away from industrialized animal protein won't, on its own, solve the problems of inequality and hunger worldwide, but it is undeniably a smart step in the right direction at a time when standing still or continuing to silly-walk toward mid-century will have severe consequences.

Although shifting to plant-based agriculture makes sense in terms of feeding the hungry, sparing the environment, and protecting human and animal wellbeing, we continue to convert wild lands to grow farm animal feed. This feed is put on slow boats headed to the European Union, the United States, China, and elsewhere to be fed to farm animals who convert nearly all of it to feces.[38] If we weren't so removed from the process, and so inured to it, this whole setup would appear as it is: callous, unfeeling, and stupid. It's as if we've retrofitted millions of 1970s Oldsmobiles to run on breadcrumbs snatched from starving children. Simply improving yield or producing farm animal feed with less plant-food input will not be enough to feed a human population expected to grow by two billion people by 2050.

Currently, millions starve, and they are located disproportionally in impoverished countries. These are the places that animal-agribusiness executives may visit for photo ops but wouldn't raise their children in. Those executives peddle the spurious talking point that we need to globally expand the factory farming machinery that makes them millions—not for profit, but to feed a growing global population. Yet they never explain why upping farm animal yields will help feed our growing population when we already have the capacity to feed everyone (but fail to do so). As experts pointed out in the *American Journal of Public Health*, "Evidence that transnational industry initiatives are overall improving food supplies in any setting, let alone improving public health, does not exist." Instead, what big agricultural interests are renowned for doing is forestalling, fighting, and diluting any sort of restrictions on their ability to do whatever they want to. That is a problem:

> [s]ignificant protection or improvement of public health has always involved legislation, the best of which carefully enables and encourages the equitable enjoyment of life. Examples include the protection of wildernesses, control of immigration, closed sewers, speed limits, pedestrian precincts, prohibition of smoking in public places, and indeed restriction of baby formula and weaning food advertising.[39]

Instead, millions of people currently die of hunger and millions more live with permanent mental, physical, and emotional damage that could be prevented if agriculture was organized more intelligently and humanely. Part of that re-organization would involve ensuring that the productive outputs of farmland can be consumed or sold locally by those farming it, rather than being packed up and flung across an ocean to distant factory farms.

It's a classic tree-barked-Salon problem: Why spend limited funds and rapidly dwindling time trying to fix an inherently inefficient crap-mobile? That makes no sense when less costly, more efficient substitutes are readily available now. Despite all the time, energy, and money thrown at the problem—or tree-stained sedan—it's likely it won't improve, and even if it does marginally improve, it won't be enough to justify the time and effort, and the result won't be better than available alternatives.

WASTING WATER

It shouldn't come as a surprise that farm animal agriculture, the largest human use of land, also sucks down a huge amount of ever-diminishing fresh water. The farming of animals, just one sliver of the agricultural pie, pulls in almost half of all the water used by the global agricultural endeavor.[40] Raising animals for human food uses about 15 percent of the entire planet's drinkable water.[41]

Projections for 2050 indicate that producing enough farm animal–derived food products at a business-as-usual rate for a population expected to reach about nine billion people by mid-century will almost certainly dry up regional surface and groundwater supplies. Industrial animal agriculture is expected to expand in the U.S. Midwest, central China, and South America, particularly eastern Paraguay, northern Argentina, and southern Brazil, which means that feed-crop production will take over more land in these areas. But all of this may ultimately be stopped or limited when the wells run dry. The water will run short as industrialized feed cropping replaces pastures and mows down forests in South America and especially Sub-Saharan Africa and South Asia.[42]

In 2014, those mewling hippies over at the U.S. Department of Defense (DOD) who produce the Quadrennial Defense Review Report pointed out that "[c]limate change may exacerbate water scarcity and lead to sharp increases in food costs."[43] Animal agriculture is a major driver of climate change. According to the DOD:

[T]he pressures caused by climate change will influence resource competition while placing additional burdens on economies, societies, and governance institutions around the world. These effects are threat multipliers that will aggravate stressors abroad such as poverty, environmental degradation, political instability, and social tensions—conditions that can enable terrorist activity and other forms of violence.[44]

Beginning in the winter of 2006 through 2010, Syria endured the worst drought in its recorded history. Experts link the severity of that drought to climate change.[45] Thousands of Syrian farmers were forced to abandon their dying crops and move to cities. The drought contributed to the mass bloodletting. This is the sort of threat multiplication described in the 2014 report of the hacky-sacking longhairs over at the DOD. In 2019, DOD reiterated that climate change impacts, such as droughts and desertification, are "drivers of instability and factional conflict" in Africa, as are flooding and tsunamis in Indonesia.[46]

The sharp end of these multiplying threats will be pressed most often into those least able to protect themselves: the poor.[47]

Even model projections that postulate a shift to near-vegetarianism still show that agricultural demand for water will outstrip supply in some regions.[48] This may prompt the response: If both the bacon-and-cheese diet and vegetarianism will contribute to the wells running dry by 2050, why not eat the bacon and cheese? Dietary changes alone will not be enough in some regions to solve the dry-wells problem. Given South Asia's large and growing human population, even a complete shift to veganism will cause an 80 percent increase in irrigation water demand.[49] But that is far better than the business-as-usual alternative, which will cause a 200 percent increase in the demand for water to irrigate the area—water to cycle through billions of farm animals, producing mostly urine.[50]

In rainy areas like the western side of Washington State where I grew up, "the increasing appropriation of arable land" to feed farm animals "may, more indirectly, lead to depletion of available water because it reduces the water available for other uses, particularly [human] food crops."[51]

WASTING LAND

According to one popular canard, much of the land used for farm animal grazing could not be used to grow anything else edible. There is some land like that, of course, but it's not a big piece of the global grazing pie. Around the world, only about 14 percent of grazing is happening on ground that is suitable *only* for grazing.[52] So, about 86 percent of grazing is happening on ground that could support

89

growing fruits, vegetables, legumes, or grains. More problematically, this canard suggests that grazing is predominantly how we fatten farm animals. In the United States and many other parts of the world often referred to as "developed" (e.g., China and the European Union), that hasn't been the case for years.

Using land for farm animal fodder removes the potential of growing something edible for direct human consumption or leaving it as a much-needed refuge for flora and fauna. For example, consider the sexy lentil and other hot-to-trot legumes that grow well in a huge variety of settings. That versatility explains why "[i]n developing countries, pulses," a legume subcategory that includes lentils, chickpeas, and other beans, make up "75 percent of the average diet."[53] Some varieties can grow in arid conditions and poor soils where no other crop will.[54]

Unlike the farm animal feed crops planted for the animal-protein industries in Europe, the United States, and elsewhere, lentils can be eaten locally or sold. This provides a healthier, more sustainable nutritional and economic safety net than growing feed destined for the beaks of laying hens or castrated piglets on another continent.[55] It shouldn't be up to urbanites in places like Berlin and Los Angeles to decide whether farmers in Tanzania plant lentils for local consumption or corn for cattle on another continent, but it's not some cabal of flannel-shirted activists in a corner booth at the vegan Chicago Diner who are meddling in that crop-choice decision in Tanzania.

If you have fifteen acres of waterfront real estate on Puget Sound, you could put a smelter there. However, the cost of doing so goes beyond the foreseeable harms smelting will cause. You also need to factor in the benefits you could reap if you used that land for something else. In Washington State, for example, alfalfa and other farm animal hay and feed crops displace wiser uses of productive land.

Washington has some of the world's best farmland, and most of it is east of the Cascade Mountains. West of the Cascades, where I grew up, life happens under a near-constant drizzle nine months of the year, but the land east of the mountains is much more arid.

Washington is the nation's top grower of apples, sweet cherries, and blueberries. The state also produces huge amounts of exciting foods like wheat, barley, wrinkled seed peas (top U.S. producer), lentils (third largest U.S. producer), and just regular peas (same, bronze medal).[56] Together, mice and I consumed much of Tacoma's annual grape yield during the 1980s. But now, a booming wine industry ensures that most Eastern Washington grapes avoid mice maws. Washington is second only to California in the premium wine market.[57]

All told, there are only about 14.6 million acres of farmland in Washington State.[58] Nearly 3.2 million acres of that land is devoted to growing feed for farm animals.[59] So, over one-fifth of the state's available farmland is devoted to producing fodder that will mostly become manure. Except of course that this fodder, and the wasted space and fresh water it represents, does not just vanish. It turns into a serious public health and environmental liability as it putrefies in manure cesspools.

NEIL, ARE THESE SOUTH AFRICAN LENTILS?

After threatening life and limb driving myself home from school, I often watched the British show *The Young Ones*. Neil, the show's hippy roommate/indentured-lentil-cook, ruined lentils for me for about two decades. The final parting of company between lentils and me came when I watched sallow, slouched, long-haired Neil, dressed in impossibly drab burlap hues, salvage a meal by scraping concrete gray lentil paste off a dirty wall. I got over it and have come to love the lentil, as we all should.

Growing legumes, like the lentil, is a far more efficient use of land and water resources than anything having to do with animal agriculture. Lentils have a dramatically smaller water and carbon footprint as compared to meat and other protein sources,[60] and they are a low-fat, protein-packed superfood, supplying B vitamins and minerals. According to the FAO, they "also contain bioactive compounds that show some evidence of helping to combat cancer, diabetes and heart disease."[61] Unlike cheddar cheese and sausages, which have been linked to increases in obesity, "some research indicates that eating pulses regularly can help control and combat obesity as well."[62] Lentils and the "wrinkled seed pea" may not seem sexy, but then neither is envisioning your great grandkids on desert sands battling to the death over a dusty, thirty-year-old bottle of Fuji water.

We can do better with those roughly 3.2 million acres that Washington's farmers devote to alfalfa and other farm animal feeds. Instead, we can and should use the land to grow apples, lentils, peas, wheat, cherries, and strawberries.[63] Calories from those foods are nearly a hundred percent available for human consumption, compared to the 4.3 percent return on the calories we cycle through cattle raised for beef, for example.[64]

In Washington, we pack about one-fifth of the alfalfa produced in Washington and six other Western states onto container ships in West Coast ports and take it across the Pacific, largely to be eaten by cows at factory farms in China and elsewhere.[65] Indeed, in the very productive land around Washington's Columbia River Gorge such exports claim the majority of alfalfa produced.[66] The U.S. dairy industry wastefully cycles most of the remainder through cows here, primarily confined at factory farms that look indistinguishable from their Chinese counterparts.

Like the smelter and the Salon, even if these arrangements might have made sense when they were first developed, they need to be re-evaluated now. In many parts of the world, it's difficult to discern agriculture's best path forward and the choices individuals ought to make. That said, we shouldn't leave the patently stupid options on the table. Cutting down Brazilian or Sub-Saharan African forests or plowing grasslands to grow soy and corn to feed to confined pigs and chickens in Germany or Indiana makes sense only for those who profit from it. Taking these options off the table helps clarify what is admittedly a complicated question: How will we feed developing parts of the world where populations are expected to grow massively in coming years? For millions of us in the United States, the European Union, and other so-called developed regions, our options are better. Not everyone has the privilege to have a wide range of options. That doesn't excuse those of us who do. We should not be supporting engines of starvation that turn the potential of land, water, and calories into oceans of manure.

FROM MOLTEN SLAG TO LUXURY

In the 1980s and early-1990s, the ASARCO plant looked as permanent to me as nearby Mount Rainier. Now, where the smokestack stood, you can buy a high-priced home with a panoramic view of Commencement Bay. Down the hill, where the valley meets the bay, there's a city park where copper by the ton was loaded onto freighters for generations. All eleven acres of that park are layered on top of a "capped"— *i.e.*, hopefully sealed—slag peninsula. It is 125 feet deep, built up by years of toxic waste dumping.[67] Although that might have seemed a sensible use of the bay decades ago, try it today and you are likely to find yourself bankrupted by fines and lying awake at night on a cot in a federal prison cell.[68]

Next to the park, there's a multiplex movie theater and a few shops at the base of several eight-story condominium buildings.[69] The change from active smelter to condos is an improvement. For those of us who remember the smelter, it's eerie to see it papered over. But regardless of how you feel about the condos, they're not belching arsenic and other carcinogens all over South Puget Sound, so far as we know.

Historically, as middle classes grow in developing countries, they largely follow in the footsteps of developed countries, replacing plant foods with more meat, dairy, and eggs. Cities in China and India have had, or currently have, their versions of the East London smelter-adjacent home Dickens visited in the 1860s. Similarly developing countries are in the midst of, or will likely have, decades like the 1960s to the 1990s in the United States and the European Union. Back then, animal agriculture's industrialization was at its moral, public health, and environmental nadir. Largely unchecked, its expansion polluted land, water, and air. If the demand for industrialized farm animal products holds in those places, it, combined with huge population growth in the developing world, will push us into a *Mad Max/Bladerunner* reality by 2050.

But there are reasons to be hopeful that the trend will not hold, at least not everywhere. For one, as it's playing out in developed countries, the switch from plants to more meat and dairy tends to level off. According to the FAO, "Meat consumption boomed between 1981 and 2007, but in most parts of the world growth in demand is slowing."[70] There are only so many sausages a nation can choke down before wising up.[71] Indeed, for reasons that are not well understood, in the developing world, as middle-class populations increase, they have not uniformly followed the trend of swapping out veggie portions for large amounts of meat.[72] Incomes in Vietnam are roughly equivalent to incomes in India.[73] In recent years, the Vietnamese have increased their meat intake at a rate that has outpaced increases in incomes.[74] In India, on the other hand, individual meat consumption is more than ten times lower than it is in Vietnam, and has not increased much even as income levels creep up.[75] Some of these variations across nations have to do with religion, but that does not fully explain what's going on.[76] In India, for example, millions avoid beef for religious reasons, but they are not swapping in other meats in place of beef.[77] Obviously, India dwarfs Vietnam's population. If meat consumption can be held down or decreased in India, that portends better than if India increases its meat consumption.[78]

ASARCO's 562-foot-tall smokestack was built on a public-health-protective theory: Let's pipe that smoke up as high as possible so less of it will settle on us. All they succeeded in doing was creating a toxic smoke plume that overshadowed not one county but four, dropping arsenic over several hundred square miles.[79] We learned over time that the "taller-is-safer" theory was dead wrong. Accordingly, we made several dramatic changes that left us with condos in the place of a smokestack and its glowing molten slag hardening in the bay below Ruston. Every day of hesitation before making those changes made things a bit worse and more difficult to remedy. More than three decades after the smelter shut down, and millions of dollars later, the state and federal cleanup crews are nowhere close to done cleaning up the smelter's multi-county, multi-generation poisoning.[80]

The Michiganders who brought us cars like the Salon were also doing their best to make a car that might safely cart around '70s babies like my sister and me. Yet, lead from our use of smelters and leaded gasoline has never completely left the environment, and it remains pernicious.[81]

THE LIGHT AT THE END OF THE TUNNEL

You can walk the railroad tracks from the ASARCO site to Tacoma's Union Station, which opened in 1911. Rich railroad barons hired renowned New York architects to design the redbrick structure, which boasts a 90-foot-high baroque-domed central hall.[82] The barons who built Union Station saw nothing but growth ahead in the passenger train industry. They were wrong. Ridership peaked in the 1930s. By the early 1980s, right around the time ASARCO shut down the smelter, the station shut down, too. It didn't make economic sense as a train station. Amtrak made its new, and current, Tacoma home a bit farther down the tracks in the grimmest little one-story building I've ever seen.

In 1992, the old Union Station came back to life as a federal court-house. When he became a bankruptcy judge, around the time ASARCO cut our family a settlement check, my father went to work there.

Once restored, Union Station served as a magnet, attracting and supporting other businesses. Today, the stretch of Pacific Avenue the station sits on is nothing like the stretch of abandoned buildings and strip clubs that it was in the '80s and '90s. Many of Pacific Avenue's old buildings remain; they've just been adapted. Thus, what was once a newspaper building is now a University of Washington satellite campus.

Moving on from endeavors that don't make sense anymore does not always require flipping a switch and detonating strategically placed explosives, as we did with ASARCO's smokestack. Burning up copper ore in the middle of a growing city, building leaded-gas cars the size of barges, or maintaining a Cathedral-sized passenger train station in Tacoma all became unrealistic in the late twentieth century. The trick is spotting the best moment to make changes before that moment passes. But even after the best moment passes, change is usually possible, and it usually makes more sense than hugging tighter to a sinking chunk of glacier-shattered ship hull. As I learned in the City of Destiny, hiding from the facts will not forestall the foreordained and foreseeable.

6

IF YOU MOSTLY MAKE CRAP, EVERYWHERE LOOKS LIKE YOUR TOILET

Animal Agriculture Is a Major Air and Water Polluter

"A New York congressman has asked the Federal Communications Commission to prevent any telecasting of daredevil Evel Knievel's jump over the Snake River Canyon gorge in Idaho. . . . 'I have received newspaper reports and photos from concerned parents in Idaho which already show youngsters on bicycles and jerrybuilt ramps trying to perform Evel's stunts over local streams. . . .'"[1]

When I was a five-year-old risk-taker, my mother bought me an Evel Knievel action figure. He came with a motorcycle that our dachshund Joe Cool slinked off with. In the privacy of his office (under the dining room table), Joe chewed that motorcycle into a perfect mound of white and black bits. This left Evel overdressed for the stunts he now had to perform on foot. Just like the man himself, my plastic Evel had a white jump suit with blue-and-red trim, stars across his chest, and a white cape.

In 1974, using his rocket-powered motorcycle, the Skycycle X-2, Evel attempted to jump the Snake River gorge near Twin Falls, Idaho. The Skycycle X-2 looks less like a motorcycle, and more like a twenty-foot-long jet-propelled schlong. The drive from Portland, Oregon, to Twin Falls takes you over the canyon near his jump site. Crossing that bridge drives home what a stupid idea his stunt was. It feels like a ten-minute drive over a ribbon of concrete 500 feet over a white-capped river. But, watching the jump footage on YouTube, as Evel saunters into frame in his white, star-spangled jumpsuit, I still think he looks like the baddest dude ever invented.

Despite efforts to ban the live broadcast, it went forward. Around the country, paying customers gathered in theaters to see the jump broadcast. Seconds after launch, something went wrong. The Skycycle prematurely ejaculated its parachute. According to the Wikipedia account, Evel reached the other side of the canyon, but instead of landing there, he and his Skycycle with its opened chute drifted back and slammed down on the launch side of the canyon. Somehow all Evel broke was his regal, manly nose.

Sitting on the floor of my grandmother's Torrance, California, living room, I watched Evel attempt some other idiotic stunt a few years after his Snake River boner. This was my first time seeing Evel, and I was beyond smitten—so much so that my grandmother and my mother decided not to tell me that Evel was our distant relative. "Knievel," which sounds as fake as "Evel," is a real name. Years later, my grandmother would mention the Knievels when telling old family stories.

Mom knew what would happen if she told the five-year-old me that any amount of Knievel blood flowed in my veins. She could see me in a succession of hospital rooms, spending all of my childhood in traction. She waited to tell me until I simmered down, sometime in my thirties.

A Snake Runs Through It
"And what's your name?" I asked.

"I'm not telling you."

"Can a city employee have a secret identity?"

"I don't have to tell you my name."

98

I was sitting in my dark basement office in the summer of 2002. That summer I was an intern at the Idaho Conservation League, helping to fight factory farm pollution in Idaho. I was talking to an employee who maintains blueprints for buildings in the tiny town of Weiser, Idaho. There were probably no more than ten Weiser city employees. So, if I ever need to pin a name on this guy, it wouldn't be hard.

Weiser City Hall's Captain Anonymous had just finished telling me about a light industrial area on the town's outskirts when he refused to give me his name. The area was a cluster of about five warehouses next to a beef cattle feedlot. That feedlot was ringed by residential neighbors who were angry about the feedlot's smells, flies, and dust, and about what it might be doing to their drinking water. I had called Captain Anonymous hoping he would explain the blueprints that his office had given me in response to a public records request.

"That's just an old industrial drain," he told me.

"So, it's a drain from the warehouses to the Snake River?" I asked.

"Yeah," he said. "A long time ago it was a drain, but it hasn't been used in years."

I had just watched a video made by a neighbor of the feedlot, a mom of two boys. She was furious at the place. She had a view of it from her living room and had watched its steer population go up dramatically. The place had a hotel-swimming-pool-sized, concrete, open-air manure structure directly across the street from the warehouses, but its size didn't make sense. It was way too small to hold the waste from so many animals. Given the herd size, you'd need a lake-sized cesspool, sometimes referred to as a "lagoon." So, what was the point of the Motel-6-style toilet-pool?

The neighbor shot her video at night, during a monsoon. She held the camera and a light as her husband held aside a heavy manhole cover on the edge of the road, just across the street from the manure pool. She narrated the video, saying something like, "As you can see, it's raining hard, and down there a whole lot of brown water is flowing from the feedlot. It smells horrible." Her video showed that a small, brown river flowed from the feedlot toward the industrial area across the street. I needed to figure out where it went after the industrial park.

I called Weiser City Hall because I suspected that the pipe I saw on the industrial area's blueprints was almost certainly going to drain to the river that was only about one mile away. The feedlot's mini-lagoon didn't have to be bigger because, in the middle of the night, they would flush a whole lot of bullshit directly into the mighty Snake River, the very river my Knievel kinsman had tried to jump. Not on my watch.

SEE NO EVEL

Although it considers them a leading source of water and air pollution, the EPA doesn't even know how many CAFOs are out there or where they all are.[2] CAFOs are the largest of the factory farms. The EPA has a hunch that there are around 18,000. A 2008 Governmental Accounting Office report stated that no one has a handle on where, or how numerous, these polluters are, as the state and federal accounts are incomplete and inaccurate.[3] The report reached the obvious conclusion that the EPA needed this basic information to effectively mitigate or prevent CAFO water pollution.[4] More than a decade later, the EPA still lacks that data. Recently, with the aid of satellite imagery, an Iowa state environmental agency discovered more CAFOs than they expected.[5] About five thousand more.[6] This underscores why, in the straight-shooting words of the *Des Moines Register*, "our streams often smell like toilets."[7]

The toilet smell is not the most worrisome aspect of the problem. Huge amounts of manure find their way to groundwater, rivers, and streams by way of leaking cesspools, and from the fields manure is liberally sprayed on or injected into. That waste brings dozens of dangerous pathogens—like *Salmonella*, tuberculosis, and trichinosis—into our drinking water, and also contaminates water supplies with active residues of powerful antibiotics and other pharmaceuticals.[8] The nitrogen in manure can squeeze the life out of streams and rivers, and it contributes to the ever-growing New Jersey–sized dead zone in the Gulf of Mexico near the mouth of the Mississippi River.[9]

Even though the Weiser feedlot was piping manure directly to the Snake River, it also managed to contaminate the aquifer beneath it, threatening all of its neighbors.[10] The environmental attorneys I interned with in Boise sent the feedlot a letter threatening a federal Clean Water Act lawsuit over their drainpipe shenanigans. In 2003, the Idaho Conservation League filed that lawsuit, which quickly led to the place shutting down.[11]

Oddly, along with the feedlot operator, a group of Catholic Benedictine monks retained an ownership interest in the real estate and became its sole owners in 2006.[12] The monks wisely and humanely refused to sell the property to anyone planning to use it as a feedlot,.[13] But by then, state authorities had taken a hard look at the aquifer under it and found a lot to be frightened of.[14]

They discovered that the groundwater under the feedlot was contaminated with "nitrates, ammonia, *E. coli*, the hormone estradiol and cattle antibiotics, such as sulfamethizine."[15] Nitrates in drinking water are deadly, especially for infants. Drinking nitrate-contaminated water can lead to Blue Baby Syndrome, which turns infants a bluish gray.[16] If it is not treated promptly, it can quickly lead to coma or death.[17] The place is anomalous in that it's a CAFO that government agencies have actually taken a hard look at. There are thousands more that the EPA cannot take even a soft look at if it wanted to because the agency has no clue how to find them.

Is it Too Late to Change Your Mind?

Grandma was born into a farming family in 1914. She grew up on the Nebraska prairie, attended a one-room schoolhouse, and later taught in one. Her husband, my grandfather, grew up on a Nebraska farm that his family had homesteaded since about 1878. The state gave his family's farm a "Nebraska Pioneer Farm Award." Many of my relatives still farm that patch of southwestern Nebraska. So, in 2012 I was amused, as was Grandma, when Nebraska's governor said of my employer, "We will kick their butt out of Nebraska. HSUS is anti-agriculture. We don't want them in Nebraska."[18]

After Nebraska, Grandma moved to California, living in San Francisco and various spots around Los Angeles County. In 1930s San Francisco, she walked down the hill from her home and paid a nickel to see the Marx Brothers. She told me they were even better live than in their movies. In the 1980s, she retired with my grandpa to Lompoc, one of California's best impressions of a small Nebraska town.

Between 2007 and 2010, I lived a few hours north of Lompoc in Sacramento. For work, I periodically traveled to California's Central Valley and would sometimes drive the extra few hours to stay with Grandma in Lompoc. In 2009, when she was in her mid-90s, I told her about an environmental case I was working on against an egg factory farm owned by a company called Olivera Egg Ranch, located just south of Stockton. Like many people, she'd never heard of the standard practice of caging egg-laying hens.

Although she lived through it, the industrial chicken revolution of the mid-twentieth century happened unbeknownst to her. When she left her parents' farm for California, chickens roamed free and roosted in the barn at night. During my mother's early childhood in Compton, they got their eggs from a guy creepily known as "the bachelor," who had hens down the street from them. Grandma hadn't noticed that, starting in the middle of the century, egg-laying hens were increasingly imprisoned in wire cages.

I don't remember Grandma having much of a reaction as I told her about the welfare impacts of caging hens. But Grandma was a German/Irish Catholic Nebraskan, and they are often impossible to read. As a people, we have what's known as "resting coffin-face." When amused, Grandma had a beautiful soft laugh and a twinkling eye, but I couldn't detect most of her other emotions as they came and went. My father's side of the family is German and Slavic. With that genetic combo, no matter how I feel, I usually look like I'm asleep with my eyes open.

I visited Grandma a while after telling her about the egg factory farm case and caged hens. After greeting me, she immediately had me follow her at her top-speed shuffle over to her olive-green refrigerator where she proudly showed me a dozen free-range eggs. She explained that they were the only kind of eggs she would buy now. Months later, after I told her about how breeding sows were imprisoned in crates, she foreswore all pork products. She made that change at close to age one hundred.

A Failed Cesspool Jump

The Olivera egg farm case that converted my grandmother to free-range eggs is bookended for me by black-and-white homeless cats. Little Olive is the beginning bookend cat. The case formally began in the fall of 2008, just after I found Olive with her pink, sun-scarred ear near the facility's four-city-block-sized cesspool of bubbling chicken manure.

Months before I met Olive in 2008, I was in that same spot, in a car with my boss at the end of a dirt road.

"It doesn't smell that bad," my boss said.

"Roll down the window," I replied.

"Oh my God!"

The sun was setting as we got out of the car. The road ended at a bare-dirt embankment about six feet high. We walked up it and looked across a purplish-brown lake of chicken shit. On the opposite shore stood several metal buildings that together confined about 700,000 caged hens. On our side of Lake Feces, the back end of a huge sedan jutted out of the cesspool. God knows how it came to have its grille embedded in the soft earth nine feet below the surface. If it had been occupied on entry, the occupants likely would have died from hydrogen sulfide asphyxiation.

Some people wonder why the HSUS gets involved in environmental lawsuits against slaughterhouses and factory farms. What do environmental disputes have to do with improving animals' lives? But the two are certainly not mutually exclusive. To put it another way, packing huge numbers of birds into buildings ten times as large as traditional barns is horrible for the hens, and that high population also means a huge amount of manure and urine produced in a concentrated area. Those massive stockpiles of waste amp up the air and water pollution threats as well as threats to the quality of life of the communities near these facilities. Just ask the neighbors of the Weiser feedlot Superfund site.

Leaving Gilroy

The Olivera company first came to my attention in 2005 when California animal activists sent the HSUS a video of hens in manure-caked cages that looked about thirty years old. The property owner had called animal groups hoping to get help for the birds when his tenant simply abandoned tens of thousands of hens in wire cages inside long metal sheds on a field near Gilroy. Apparently, the landlord and his tenant, Olivera, had been fighting over the property and this led to Olivera just splitting, leaving all those hens behind to die, still locked in cages. Several rescue groups saved as many hens as they could. My friend and colleague Jennifer Fearing helped in that effort. She described the smell as "overwhelming" and saw dead birds "scattered in the aisles," while "others were rotting in their cages."[19] In addition to Olivera's spats with his landlord, local government inspectors had cited the company for running a substandard, stench- and fly-generating egg operation.

Wealthy people typically will find a way to promptly shut down the source of swarms of biting flies or the smell of a million urinals wafting in through their open windows. The well-to-do are good at removing those situations—or preventing them in the first place—thanks to their influence and wealth. They command the attention of local politicians and regulatory agencies in a way that less privileged people usually do not. I have seen state and local governments take a blame-the-victim approach to low-income communities dealing with CAFOs springing up around their homes. In Idaho, just outside Twin Falls, people living near CAFOs told me that state government agents referred to them as "odor eaters." From a CAFO owner's perspective, low-income communities are the best neighbors because they may lack the connections and resources required to shut down nuisances.

Between 2008 and 2011, along with many talented lawyers, I represented several neighbors in a lawsuit alleging that Olivera's facility near Stockton was a nuisance and that it violated federal laws requiring air-pollution reporting. The neighbors suing the operation alleged the manure lagoon from the roughly three-quarters of a million hens made their homes unlivable. The piercing sinus pains and headaches from ammonia and the clouds of flies made spending time outdoors unbearable. But many had no choice but to be outdoors much of the time because they farmed vegetables on their property. These neighbors had lived in their homes for years, if not decades, before the property at the end of their road became a massive egg factory farm.

NEW PIONEERS

"The smell is so terrible . . . it's like a dead body"

"Well how would you know what that smells like?"

"I saw dead people in the camp."

This line of questioning about a nine-acre lake of liquefied manure in the deposition of an Olivera neighbor was not one that Olivera's lawyers would be repeating during the trial in front of a jury. This is why they tell you in law school to never ask a question that you don't already have a very good idea of the answer to.

More than three decades earlier, after many months in a Thai refugee camp, Dara came to the U.S. A few times a week, she drove a truck for hours to Bay Area farmers markets where she sold the bok choy and other vegetables she grew near the Olivera facility. While I was working on the Olivera case, I bought vegetables from Dara one bright Wednesday afternoon near San Francisco City Hall, just blocks from where my Grandma would have seen the Marx Brothers perform.

Dara worked the land the way my grandparents did in their Nebraska childhoods. Unlike my grandpa's family, Dara had to buy her land at market rate. Another key difference between Dara's farm and my grandparents' was that after hours under a mid-day central California sun the faded red bandana she wore as a filter wasn't enough to keep her from retching at the rotting corpse stench from the nearby lake of decomposing manure that was large enough to encompass about six football fields.[20]

FARM-FRESH CYANIDE

According to the EPA, U.S. farm animals generate about half a billion tons of manure, which is more than three times the amount of waste produced by the country's human population.[21] As animal waste decomposes, it releases hundreds of compounds, many of which can harm and kill people and animals. There are too many dangerous compounds to profile here, but hydrogen sulfide and ammonia lead the human health–threat pack.

Hydrogen sulfide, one of the primary CAFO airborne threats, is a chemical asphyxiant that impacts the human body like a dose of cyanide.[22] According to a medical doctor and University of Minnesota professor, "[p]aralysis of the respiratory center is the primary lethal toxic effect and results in immediate 'knockdown' at high concentrations."[23] Moving and dumping massive quantities of manure can release lethal amounts of hydrogen sulfide, and it can and has killed farm workers.[24] Even at low levels, the gas can cause chest pains, breathing difficulty, and irritation of the respiratory tract and eyes.[25]

Along with hydrogen sulfide, the EPA considers ammonia an extremely hazardous gas. In the United States, farm animals are the largest source of ammonia emissions.[26] As the National Association of Local Boards of Health put it, the gas can cause "chemical burns to the respiratory tract, skin, and eyes, severe cough, chronic lung disease."[27] The more you're in it, the deeper it is in you. In the words of one expert, "tolerance develops with continued exposure. This will lead to deeper and greater respiratory exposure as deeper breaths will occur when the person adapts to the irritant effects of ammonia."[28] In the long run, ammonia can lead to chronic bronchitis.[29] It's particularly hard on children because, compared to adults, their young lungs take in much more air with each breath. Studies of kids attending schools near CAFOs show that they are much more likely to have asthma compared to other kids. Unsurprisingly, the schools located near CAFOs tend not to be the schools of rich kids.[30] Every week, several hundred *pounds* of ammonia seeped out of the manure lake at Olivera.

For years, Olivera's neighbors complained to local and state agencies but did not receive any meaningful help. To test the complaints about pain and discomfort, Olivera's lawyers hired a doctor to examine the neighbors. The strategy was to show that there was nothing wrong with them, or if there was, it had nothing to do with the ammonia they spent so much of their lives in. This doctor had the neighbors drive more than an hour north to be examined in an office in Sacramento.

The flaw in this arrangement was that the case was entirely about the impact caused by living next to an ocean of manure. There was no manure in the doctor's office, and that was a critical misstep, as our expert physician and toxicologist pointed out. Removing the neighbors from the alleged cause of their symptoms would obviously mean the examination might not find any. Additionally, the Olivera doctor said these neighbors were only exposed to low-levels of ammonia, which, according to OSHA workplace standards, were not unhealthy. Our expert pointed out that the workplace standard is the wrong standard as it's geared toward young healthy workers, not vulnerable populations. Moreover, the workplace standard didn't fit because this was not just 40-hour-a-week workplace exposure; for many of the neighbors, it was around-the-clock chronic exposure. Ultimately, the case didn't hinge on establishing some medical injury caused by the factory farm.

The neighbors' nuisance claim is one that has centuries-old roots. Indeed, more than 500 years ago in England, some idiot who put his pigsty too close to his neighbors found himself on the business end of a nuisance claim in *William Aldred's Case*.[31] The case made clear that one can be liable "for erecting a hogstye so near the house of the plaintiff." Hundreds of years later in the late-nineteenth century, the U.S. Supreme Court observed that it has been the settled law both of this country and of England that a man has no right to maintain a structure upon his own land which by reason of disgusting smells, loud or unusual noises, thick smoke, noxious vapors, the jarring of machinery, or the unwarrantable collection of flies, renders the occupancy of adjoining property dangerous, intolerable, or even uncomfortable to its tenants. No person maintaining such a nuisance can shelter himself behind the sanctity of private property.[32]

So, the Olivera case presented an ancient problem amplified by the industrialization of egg farming. The neighbors' case against Olivera, like those stretching back for centuries before it, focused on intolerable, uncomfortable conditions, not proof of a medical injury caused by the defendant.

Three years after my boss and I first visited the cesspool, a jury returned a verdict in favor of the neighbors, finding the egg factory farm was in fact a nuisance.[33] That verdict obliged Olivera to pay just over a half-million dollars in damages to the neighbors.[34] Ultimately, as part of a post-trial settlement process, the factory farm agreed to stop using the cesspool. This was an improvement but not a complete cure. In the years since the verdict, Olivera's neighbors have continued fighting the facility in court, alleging the same sort of nuisances that prompted the 2008 lawsuit.

By the end of the Olivera trial in the spring of 2011, Larry David had thoroughly trashed the pad we rented together in Sacramento. Quit fanning yourself—it's not what you think. We slept in separate beds in a bleak midtown motel room.

Larry is the black-and-white cat who bookends the conclusion of the Olivera case. From day one, he was big, difficult, and wicked smart, the kind of cat who learns how to work a doorknob just from watching you use one a few times. He got me through that trial. When it began, he turned up at Jennifer Fearing's home in Sacramento. Initially, he stayed with me in her guest room. Since her hen-rescuing work at the Gilroy Olivera facility in 2005, Jennifer had gone on to become a peerless animal protection lobbyist.

During the trial, I worked long into the night, sitting on the bed with my back against the wall and with Larry sitting on me. He stretched from my lap to my face, purring and squinting up at me, his cotton-ball forepaws on my collarbones. I could barely reach the laptop around him. After a few days, we checked into a motel because Larry was steadfastly disassembling Jennifer's guest room. I took the queen bed near the door, and Larry took the one by the window. He slept through those warm Sacramento nights sprawled diagonally on the rumpled white sheets of his own giant bed.

Not Evel, Evil

The relationship between factory farms and the communities surrounding them is a quintessential example of economic and political bullying. As noted earlier, you will rarely find three-quarters of a million hens and an ocean of their feces in a rich white neighborhood.

In the last few days of the Obama administration, the EPA sent an excoriating letter to the Acting Secretary of the North Carolina agency responsible for protecting the state's environment and regulating CAFOs.[35] The letter stemmed from an ongoing EPA civil rights investigation requested by attorneys with the University of North Carolina's Center for Civil Rights and Earthjustice on behalf of The North Carolina Environmental Justice Network, Rural Empowerment Center for Community Help, and Waterkeeper Alliance.[36] The investigation focused on alleged racially discriminatory impacts of the Department of Environmental Quality's regulation of pig CAFOs.[37]

The letter is extraordinary because the EPA's investigation hadn't even reached a conclusion. However, the timing also makes sense, as EPA investigators must have known that the Trump regime would immediately scuttle the investigation. The letter expressed the EPA's "deep concern about the possibility that African-Americans, Latinos, and Native Americans have been subjected to discrimination" as a result of how the state administers environmental permitting for pig CAFOs.[38]

Relying on a demographic study, the EPA concluded that there is a "linear" correlation between minority population counts and the number of pigs in North Carolina.[39] In other words, in any given part of the state, for every 10 percent increase in the populations of Native American, African-American, and Latino people, you will find a corresponding and significant increase in the number of pigs within three miles.[40] The EPA noted that North Carolina did not dispute that correlation and thus didn't dispute that pig CAFOs are disproportionately impacting those communities.[41] It's not immediately obvious to the layperson that on a statewide basis CAFOs are disproportionately wrecking the quality of life of minorities. That's all the harder to see because, as mentioned earlier, the government generally doesn't know where, or how many, CAFOs are scattered across the country. New Jersey U.S. Senator Cory Booker aptly summed up what's happening to North Carolina's minority communities as "evil."[42]

THE GROCERYCYCLE X-2

As mentioned earlier, the transition from backyard flocks to caged hens inside massive warehouse-like buildings completely escaped my grandmother's notice. It hid in plain sight from her as it did for many. Likewise, industrialized animal agriculture and its pollution is everywhere, yet most never truly see it.

My entire life I've been going to grocery stores. I never once thought about the beat-up electric scooters charging by grocery store entrances. That changed after my grandmother had an incident with one near the end of her life. A few times a week, a woman helped grandma with chores and shopping. One afternoon, when she was an even one century old, Grandma was paying for her groceries with ApplePay. I'm kidding—of course she was writing a check. For reasons best known to himself, a man driving an electric scooter rammed her as she paid. Then he backed up and hit her again, this time knocking her down. Miraculously, she didn't break a hip, but she did break a few bones in her foot. Even more astoundingly, the guy made a clean, three-mile-per-hour getaway on the Grocerycycle X-2 he had borrowed from the store.

It took Grandma many months to recover from the 2014 Grocery-cycle attack. She was never a strong walker again. A top-notch attorney in nearby San Luis Obispo took Grandma as a client and he sent a letter threatening a lawsuit to the giant corporate entity that owned the grocery store. The grocery store had supplied the weapon: the electric scooter. The mega-corporation essentially told Grandma's lawyer: *Her fight is with the guy on the scooter not us, and by the way, we don't know who that guy is and have no way of figuring that out since he fled the scene at three miles per hour.* This seemed to really put the brakes on what looked to me like a fantastic lawsuit. I went down to visit Grandma during this deadlock.

I decided to investigate. I went to the store and saw two dented half-ton scooters by the entrance. No matter how drunk a person might be, he or she only had to walk through the front door, hop on a scooter, and start mowing down grandparents. There were no employees supervising the scooter loan out. There wasn't even a sign-in sheet. As a five-year-old, if I had understood how lax this loan out process was, I would have driven one of those scooters directly to the woods and off a jerrybuilt ramp into a creek.

I looked at the store's check-out area. Over every cash register I saw a mirrored bubble. The cameras in those bubbles are there so the store can record its employees as they handle cash. I took pictures of all of this and emailed them to my uncle who passed them on to Grandma's attorneys.

Presumably what happened next was this: Grandma's attorneys asked for all the camera footage on the day of the incident, and rather than doing that, the grocery store put the tiniest bit of effort into figuring out who the slow-motion daredevil was. Once found, that guy was brought in to the impending lawsuit. What happened next stunned me.

Somehow that dude had a form of insurance that covered him in the event he repeatedly rammed a borrowed grocery-scooter into a century-old lady. His insurance company promptly settled for six figures before the case even really began. Shortly after the settlement, he died.

There's nothing wrong with a store providing a scooter, but they could certainly do it in a more reasonable way—for instance, by making sure they are not easily accessible to any and all topless frat boys on acid. I had never noticed these electric scooters in stores before. Ever since my grandmother's run-in, I always notice them, and my eyes dart from side to side each time I'm paying for groceries.

If next week every hardware store started willy-nilly loaning out forklifts to shoppers, I would notice that because it's not something my eyes are accustomed to. The grocery store scooter loan-out situation is not much different: It is a heavy piece of equipment that stores let anyone hop onto, despite incidents like my grandmother's. I never saw those scooters before because I never tried to focus on them and, as George Orwell famously observed, "To see what is in front of one's nose needs a constant struggle."[43]

You've been watched by hundreds if not thousands or even tens of thousands of pairs of cows', pigs', and chickens' eyes peering down from trucks, through wooden slats or metal openings. The trucks move billions of them every year to pens and cages, and sooner or later to a gruesome death. This is everywhere, but it largely goes unnoticed.

ALWAYS ACCEPTING NEW MEMBERS

Grandma lived at home right through the end of her life at age 101. She outlived the grocery store daredevil. She had in-home care partly paid for, and partly required by, the grocery store hit and "run." The people who looked after Grandma in her last year were sweet, attentive, and thoughtful. After she died, the nurse who had been with her on that last night contacted me about a recording of Grandma's last words. She texted me the audio recording. For days, I was afraid to play it. I finally did. Later, I played it again for her children and my cousins gathered around Grandma's dining room table after her funeral. She spoke about life and her love for her children, grandchildren, and great-grandchildren. She knew she hadn't always been her best self, but she had tried to be.

Until the last bit of the recording, her last words were touching, but not uniquely personal or beautiful. Her voice cracks and wavers, but she doesn't sound scared or forlorn. Yes, she could be hard to read, but I really don't think she was worried or sad. Her very end would have made Groucho proud. Her final words were "adios" and "too-da-loo."

7

HURRICANE HUSBANDRY

Factory Farms Speed Climate Change, Which Makes Those Facilities Deadlier

"Maybe I'll just sit and burn. Flames will come off my head so high that God's ass will burn, and every time he sits down, he'll remember me."—"My Name," Interlude #1, Megacrush[1]

One sweaty summer night in 1980s Seattle, my friend Nate, and I and three hundred strangers wedged ourselves into a concert at the OK Hotel, a venue that should have held no more than one hundred. It reeked of cigarette smoke and dudes with no interest in showering. We'd driven up from Tacoma to see NoMeansNo from Canada and Tacoma's own My Name, a band I did not yet appreciate because I was an idiot.

What happened that night is like one possible climate change reality we're heading toward. While NoMeansNo played, Nate found himself immobilized by crowd gridlock. As was the style at summer-night punk shows of that era, many shirtless men thrashed around. One of these bare-torsoed guys, looking like a bearded manatee, reeled backward at Nate. His arms were down at his sides as he backpedaled at a high speed toward my friend.

For some reason, Nate's index finger pointed toward the approaching topless lumberjack. Nate looked at the guy falling backward at him; then he looked down at his extended finger. By the time he looked back up, it was too late: He watched his index finger enter a hot, naked armpit—penetrating it to the hilt, as it were. Nate was never the same.

Whether it's an armpit attack or something more consequential, I'm interested in the moment of divergence of the possible from the impossible, the instant in which one realizes something terrible is impending and unavoidable. As with Nate and the speeding armpit, it's already too late to avert many climate change calamities; they're happening now and cannot be stopped. In other cases, we might yet mitigate environmental and humanitarian disasters. There may still be time to retract our fingers.

Whatever enjoyment-potential industrial animal agriculture provides is not worth its climate-changing price of admission. Although we didn't consciously analyze it, Nate and I chose to go to that show that night because the potential for fun outweighed the risks—even improbable armpit risks. If we hadn't been at that show, Nate wouldn't have ended the night attempting to burn his finger clean with a lighter under the Alaska Way Viaduct, but that was a risk we assumed.

In contrast, by supporting the farm animal industry, if you have no real need to, you're not only assuming personal health risks, you're helping to wreck the lives of people on the other side of the planet who have nothing to do with your choice. Climate change and its attendant ills are already dispossessing poor and indigenous people around the world. Its droughts and extreme weather drive small farmers to destitution. That extreme weather likewise spurs six-year-olds to abandon school for full-time work. Animal agribusiness is a primary force in this, and the industry is thriving thanks to support from well-to-do people in places like the United States, Europe, and China who support it daily even though they have no need to. Like many teenaged males, Nate and I were self-centered idiots, but if we knew our night out was somehow going to harm innocent third parties, then I'm sure we would have stayed home and watched *Fletch II.*

GATHERING THE PERFECT SHIT STORM

There is a mutually re-enforcing relationship between industrial animal agriculture, climate change, and the spread of disease. Looking at the whole supply chain involved in the farm animal sector, the FAO concluded that the total greenhouse gas (GHG) emissions were equivalent to about 14.5 percent of all human-induced emissions.[2] In addition to driving climate change, animal agriculture creates conditions in which diseases thrive. As this 2010 joint World Bank and U.N. report explains:

> [K]ey drivers for the emergence of disease include increased density and mobility of animal and human populations, decreased diversity of ecosystems, intensification of agriculture, trade, people movement, global warming and/or variability, and environmental degradation.[3]

The common practice of transporting farm animals by the millions over vast distances is a fantastic means of spreading disease. Finally, the environmental degradation brought on by industrial agriculture makes overcrowded factory farms more susceptible to the climate change–driven extreme weather events that are becoming far more common and severe.

A PERMANENT HURRICANE

An elevator pitch for my movie idea:

Fade in:

INTERIOR: WEATHER CHANNEL CONTROL ROOM

The room is dark except for the blue green light of dozens of LED screens. A young intern in thick, black-rimmed glasses says: "Well, hang on a tick! That just cannot be right. . . ." (He's a Brit, on loan from the Oxford meteorology Ph.D. program.) He waves his boss over, a 51-year-old with a tumescent red nose between two sad eyes. The dark circles under his eyes have their own dark circles, and his hair retreats from these features into Larry David–pattern baldness. He wears a faded blue, short-sleeved collared shirt untucked from his Dockers. Stooping to squint at his intern's screen, the boss says, "Jesus Horatio Sans Kee-rist!"

The screen shows the projected route of an approaching category nine hurricane hitting land right at the border between Texas and Louisiana, and then accelerating northerly inland. But, on day two, instead of fizzling out into a rainstorm, the projection has it taking a hard left.

By day five, the weather software predicts it will not have lost any strength as it charges further inland from the Gulf of Mexico. By day seven, it's expected to slam into the Rocky Mountains, somehow going over the range and down the other side. On day ten, it looks like it'll do a few donuts all over Los Angeles County, then head toward the Pacific. At Venice Beach, it suddenly breaks due north, hitting Santa Barbara, Lompoc, San Francisco, and then Portland, Tacoma, and Seattle before taking a hard right and heading to Boise. It just keeps going.

With the orange glow from the spiraling storm on his screen reflecting on his glasses, the intern says, "Well, I guess that's curtains for North America."

"Think so? I've gotten used to shit storms *way* worse than this."

The boss is right. After a couple months of this, we somehow adjust to living with a permanent hurricane, a *Permacane* (trademark pending) ricocheting around North America.

I'm still toying with how to shape the second and third acts.

I know what you're thinking: *Sure, this is a brilliant idea for a film franchise, and I'm eager to invest in it, but what does it have to do with farm animals?*

Everything. Animal agriculture is a major driver of climate change and, at the same time, it will increasingly be pummeled by it. Human-driven climate change will cause more frequent and more severe weather events, including droughts, heat waves, typhoons, and hurricanes like the 2017 hurricanes in Texas and Florida and 2018's Hurricane Florence that hit the Carolinas.[4] If you set out to design a perfect system for incubating and spreading influenza strains that could kill millions, you would end up with the standard industrialized pig, chicken, or turkey facility. The already frightening threat of pandemic influenza will only be amplified as the climate warms. In short, the favorite practices of industrialized animal agriculture make it ideally suited to spreading pathogens and disgorging millions of gallons of manure during hurricanes and tornadoes brought on by climate change.

AN ARMPIT OF OUR OWN MAKING

If you've made it this far in this book, you're not the type to believe that Earth is flat or that human activity is not changing the global climate. Maybe you do, though. Maybe you're flipping through this book at a friend's house or you picked it out of a pile of wet textbooks and empty CD jewel cases on an Oakland sidewalk under a hand-written FREE sign. If you do have doubts along these lines, it's probably best you put this book down now. Look for an adult coloring book, and please remember crayons are *not* for eating no matter how pretty they are. Here are the basics, as explained in 2014 by the Intergovernmental Panel on Climate Change (IPCC):

Human influence on the climate system is clear, and recent anthropogenic emissions of greenhouse gases are the highest in history. Recent climate changes have had widespread impacts on human and natural systems. . . .Warming of the climate system is unequivocal, and since the 1950s, many of the observed changes are unprecedented over decades to millennia. The atmosphere and ocean have warmed, the amounts of snow and ice have diminished, and sea level has risen.[5]

In 2019, another body, representing 130 national governments observed that,

Climate change is a direct driver that is increasingly exacerbating the impact of other drivers on nature and human well-being. Humans are estimated to have caused an observed warming of approximately 1°C by 2017 relative to pre-industrial levels, with average temperatures over the past 30 years rising by 0.2°C per decade. The frequency and intensity of extreme weather events, and the fires, floods and droughts that they can bring, have increased in the past 50 years, while the global average sea level has risen by between 16 and 21 cm since 1900, and at a rate of more than 3 mm per year over the past two decades.[6]

Additionally, "[t]he scientific consensus concerning climate change may soon rival heliocentrism and natural selection. However, as with earlier examples public understanding and acceptance of these revolutions lags far behind that of science."[7] That's a very formal way of comparing those who deny humanity's role in changing the global climate to those who deny any evolutionary connection between humanity and other primates and to those who refuse to believe Earth orbits the sun.

Carbon dioxide (CO_2) is well known as the primary global warming culprit. Since the industrial age, this gas and the loss of forests and wild grasslands that absorb it have accounted for most of global warming.[8] The leading sources of CO_2 emissions are the use of fossil fuels for producing electricity and transportation.[9]

As mentioned earlier, the global supply chain involved with our use of farm animals is responsible for a large share of all human-driven (anthropogenic) climate-warming emissions.[10] CO_2 makes up about one-third of those emissions (27 percent) with nitrous oxide (N_2O) about matching that (29 percent).[11] Nearly half of the farm animal sector's emissions are in the form of methane (CH_4).[12] Summarizing recent research, one expert explained in 2018 that,

> Plant-based protein sources—tofu, beans, peas and nuts—have the lowest carbon footprint. This is certainly true when you compare average emissions. But it's still true when you compare the extremes: there's not much overlap in emissions between the worst producers of plant proteins, and the best producers of meat and dairy.[13]

In terms of their contribution to global warming, after carbon dioxide, methane is the most significant culprit.[14] Estimates vary but consistently indicate that methane is to blame for about 16 to 20 percent of global warming over roughly the past 150 years.[15] It gets worse: Methane combines with other compounds in the atmosphere, and those combos are responsible for about another 17 percent of global warming.[16]

As a first-date icebreaker, I recommend this conversation starter: "What do you think is one of the largest sources of anthropogenic methane emissions?" The answer? Animal agriculture. Between about 35 to 50 percent of methane emissions have nothing to do with human activities; they naturally seep from things like wetlands.[17] Methane also seeps out of natural gas and petroleum operations, landfills, and coal mining.[18] I've always loved the way flooded rice paddies look. Unfortunately, those are the second largest source of agricultural methane emissions.[19] There are ways to grow rice that do not involve the long-term flooding of paddies, which can cut rice methane emissions by up to 90 percent while also conserving water.[20] There are practical impediments in many parts of the world to implementing these water-conserving and climate-protecting adaptions, but as a further bonus, these improved practices also reduce arsenic levels in rice.[21]

It's true that animal agriculture is responsible for a disproportionately large amount of GHG emissions, but that doesn't fully describe its role in the problem. This is because the gases differ widely in their warming potency and in how long they hang around trapping heat. Methane is among the most potent, with about 86 times the global warming potential of carbon dioxide.[22] But methane breaks down relatively quickly, taking only about a decade or two compared to carbon dioxide, which lingers for at least a century.[23]

Farm animal protein production's supply chain seems designed to damage the climate as much as possible: We lose the cooling capacity of forests and wild grasslands as they are plowed under to grow farm animal feed, a practice that typically uses fertilizer often made up of petroleum products that emit climate warming gases both in their production and as they break down on fields.[24] The feed makes its way, often across oceans and continents, wasting natural resources on the way, to factory farms. The animals who consume the feed emit methane and other gases simply by digesting it. Then there are the emissions of methane and hundreds of other compounds, some lethal to humans and animals, from massive piles and lakes of manure and urine that are, judging by weight and volume, the primary product of industrialized farm animal production. And, of course, ultimately, those farm animals are forced onto semi-trucks to begin harrowing journeys that end in evisceration at slaughter facilities.

It may surprise you that of all the links in this supply chain, the top emitter is "[e]missions from the production, processing and transport of feed." This alone is responsible for about 45 percent of emissions from farm animal protein production.[25] So, not only is production of feed crops for animals to be kept and killed for meat, eggs, and milk wasteful in terms of land and water use, and inefficient in terms of addressing global hunger, it's driving climate change.

After feed production, a digestive process in ruminants (think cud-chewers, like cows) called enteric fermentation is animal agriculture's second largest emitter, weighing in at about 40 percent of the sector's total emissions.[26] Thanks to enteric fermentation, cattle emit more of animal agriculture's greenhouse gas emissions than other animals.[27] The stockpiling, spraying, or spreading of huge quantities of manure accounts for about 10 percent of animal agriculture's emissions.[28]

The solution is not a return to grazing all cattle on grass rather than the modern practice of transporting feed to barren feedlots. The pro-grazing crowd sees potential for grazing cattle in ways that do less damage to the land and thus protect or even enhance pastures' capacity to absorb and store carbon, offsetting the animals' emissions. The problem with this approach is that any carbon sequestration benefits from grazing—*i.e.*, enhancement of land's ability to hold onto (sequester) carbon rather than emit it—would offset "only 20–60% of annual average emissions from the grazing ruminant sector" and thus it "makes a negligible dent on overall livestock emissions."[29] So carrying on with grazing or convincing the industrialized cattle feedlot interests to shift production back to hooves on pastures will not do the trick. As a group of Oxford experts put it in their excellent 2017 overview, *Grazed and Confused?*:

> Expansion or intensification in the grazing sector as an approach to sequestering more carbon would lead to substantial increases in methane, nitrous oxide and land use change-induced CO_2 emissions.[30]

Just because the cattle industry is the leader in methane emissions does not mean that the pork, poultry, and other farm animal industries' emissions are negligible. Globally, the supply chains involved with producing pork, poultry (meat and eggs), buffalo (meat and milk), and other forms of small ruminant meat (think lambs) contribute about 7 to 10 percent of the greenhouse gases emitted by the animal protein sector.[31]

A recent U.N. trade report paints a depressing prognosis. It states that "[p]revailing trends toward further industrialization of agriculture, along with landless, large-scale livestock production, are likely to contribute to an increase in greenhouse gas by more than a third by 2030."[32] By 2030, "without additional policies . . . [animal agriculture's] N_2O [nitrous oxide] and CH_4 [methane] emissions are projected to increase by 35–60% and 60% respectively."[33] Farm animals are not the only climate-change drivers, but their contribution has to be controlled and limited because, as one study explained, "by 2050, the livestock sector alone may either occupy the majority of, or significantly overshoot, recently published estimates of humanity's" climate change "'safe operating space.'"[34] The study goes on to suggest that "reining in growth of this sector should be prioritized in environmental governance."

TAKING FROM THE POOR

The impacts of climate change fall heaviest on the poor, their children, and farmers of all sorts, but especially farmers of animals who will have to deal with thriving parasites and animal diseases.[35] The U.S.

Department of Defense sees global warming as a multiplier of threats because it destabilizes societies as they increasingly suffer extreme weather, droughts, and food shortages.[36] That destabilization hits vulnerable agrarian communities especially hard:

> [s]ome forecasts anticipate that by 2050, as a consequence of climate change, an additional 120 million people will be at risk of undernourishment, of which 24 million will be children; almost half of the increase would be concentrated in sub-Saharan Africa.[37]

The risk of undernourishment stems from a reduction in fish populations, threats to animal health generally, and extreme weather damage to crop farming.[38] All of this can decrease incomes, and it directly takes food off the plates of people who are already impoverished.[39] The poor in cities as well as in the country spend more of their income on food than others.[40] Flooding, droughts, and hurricanes can destroy assets, causing immediate and long-lasting damage to incomes.[41]

Those of us who are relatively well-off have signed up for the impacts of climate change by virtue of our lifestyles. It's one thing to buy a ticket to a show and risk a damp armpit attack. The armpit might not have been specifically foreseeable, but Nate and I knew we were signing up for some potential unpleasantness simply by driving to that show in Seattle. What if we had not gone and instead just kicked back in Nate's basement, watching *Spies Like Us*? If so, and if in the blue glow of the TV-lit basement, a topless stranger dove armpit first at us from a dark corner, we'd be justifiably upset about that. We didn't sign up for that.

The poor of the world, roughly one-seventh of the population, contribute the least to climate change, yet they will be the ones disproportionally hammered by it. As one scholar, Jonathan Lovvorn (who happens to be my boss) put it, "the collective top 10% of the world financially emit more than half of all global GHG emissions, whereas the bottom 50% collectively emit just 10%" of such emissions."[42]

As global warming upends agrarian life, an increasing number of children are forced into adult work. That work often endangers them in the short term and diminishes their long-term prospects. Human Rights Watch (HRW) estimates that about a quarter of a billion children are affected by armed conflicts now, and 70 million children are affected by natural disasters.[43] As noted earlier, climate change's extreme weather and other destabilizing effects can spur armed conflicts. As HRW explains, the result is often less education and foreclosed opportunities as children are pressed into labor because "parents may lose their jobs, and schools may be destroyed. With few other options, children often begin working."[44]

In a 2016 report, the U.N.'s International Labor Organization pointed out the "strong correlation between child labour and situations of conflict and disaster."[45] Children in such countries are also 50 percent more likely to be doing dangerous work as compared to the global rate of hazardous child labor.[46] Avoiding animal-derived foods is not only a boon to animals and the environment, it's a way to help impoverished children and their families.

CHOKING ON CRONUTS

The smart people who look for solutions to climate change typically stress that the best strategy for getting the planet out of the fine mess we've cooked up is to reduce emissions from both carbon dioxide and short-term warmers like methane.[47] There's nothing wrong with that as a strategy, but if you take a close look at *why* we're emitting CO_2 and methane, some important distinctions are apparent. We've already established that in the United States, the top two sources of CO_2 emissions are the use of fossil fuels for producing electricity and for transportation.[48]

Sure, a lot of transportation and electricity use is frivolous. For example, I won't try to defend my penchant for driving to the record store while blow-drying my permed mane. Yet not all applications of transportation and electricity are so frivolous. Ambulances, hospitals, fire trucks, and jets dropping food and medical supplies in disaster-stricken areas are a few examples of frivolity-free usage.

Also, we can reduce, and are reducing, some detrimental aspects of electricity generation and transportation, like with the development of electric cars charged by solar panels. As *National Geographic* reported, in 2014, about 27 percent of Germany's "electricity came from renewable sources such as wind and solar power, three times what it got a decade ago. . . ."[49] Modern transportation and electricity use have important, often life-saving uses. They are also not inherently inseparable from their currently damaging contribution to global warming: it is feasible to shift transportation away from fossil fuels, for example.

On the other hand, there is no bacon cheeseburger analog to the ambulance or fire truck. Industrialized animal agriculture expensively undermines public health, is an environmental catastrophe, and harms billions of animals just by churning out products that millions buy despite having no need for them. A huge number of hamburgers eaten in the United States serve the same role as the cronut: a frivolous treat displacing better foods.

In addition to being better for consumers, a shift to plant-based eating is better for national healthcare costs and the planet. Recently, several studies have looked at the co-benefits of shifting to a plant-based diet. In other words, they look at the impacts of such a shift on both national health care costs and global warming. One recent study concluded that "[t]ransitioning toward more plant-based diets that are in line with standard dietary guidelines could reduce global mortality by 6–10% and food-related greenhouse gas emissions by 29–70% compared with a [business as usual] reference scenario in 2050." The study estimated the "economic benefits of improving diets to be 1–31 trillion US dollars, which is equivalent to 0.4–13% of global gross domestic product (GDP) in 2050."[50]

Certainly not everyone is able to regularly shop at places offering healthy plant-based options, but there are tens of millions of people who not only can, but already do, and those are the people for whom meat, dairy, and eggs are inessential treats that do massive, unjustifiable damage.

No Billy Joel, We *Did* Start the Fire

There is some good news, though. Because methane has such a short life span, unlike carbon dioxide emissions, to the extent we can knock off our methane-generating activities, the methane generated by human activities would break down in about ten to twenty years. With carbon dioxide, once it's emitted, it sticks in the atmosphere for likely more than a century.[51] Thus, a recent study comparing 2011's global methane emissions to 2011's carbon dioxide emissions concluded that methane emissions "have a comparable or even larger impact on global temperatures over the next couple of decades than 2011 CO_2 emissions," but methane's "impact decays rapidly, whereas the impact of current CO_2 emissions persists throughout the 21st century and for many centuries beyond."[52]

Comparing two primary drivers of climate change, methane and carbon dioxide, pulls into focus a dilemma like this one: Imagine you're in charge of your county's only fire truck and you get a call that a small farmhouse is on fire. As you're heading off in the fire engine, another call comes in about a fire at a chemical plant a quarter mile from the burning farmhouse. The farmhouse fire is simple, and you know the water in your truck will extinguish it, while the chemical plant fire would take all your truck's water, and, even then, it's highly likely you won't be able to stop it before the facility collapses in cinders and maybe spreads to other buildings. You also know that a neighboring county is already sending several trucks and dozens of fire fighters to the chemical plant fire, but even those trucks may not be enough to contain the fire in the next three hours. If you went to the farmhouse fire, you know you could quickly extinguish it and then head over to help out with the chemical plant fire. On the other hand, if you focused your finite water and time on the chemical plant fire, the farmhouse will burn down and its flames may spread to the dry wheat fields and ultimately turn into an inferno that forces an evacuation of a nearby town. So, on which fire should you first direct your limited time and resources?

The threat of pandemic influenzas is terrifying enough on its own, but as mentioned earlier, climate change increases the risk of outbreaks and enhances conditions that allow viruses to spread like wildfires. Industrialized pig and poultry facilities around the world are already ideal spots for flu viruses to multiply and mutate into catastrophically contagious forms. A 2013 U.N. report warned that "uncontrolled further development of livestock causes a major threat to human health given that zoonotic diseases transmitted between animals and humans account for 60 per cent [*sic*] of all human pathogens."[53] The warming climate has caused changes to weather patterns like El Niño, the warming of vast areas of the atmosphere and the water beneath it around the equator in the Pacific Ocean.[54] Experts link those changes to increased transmission risks for several menacing diseases, including influenza and malaria.[55]

As with other aspects of global warming, this amplified disease risk disproportionately threatens the world's most vulnerable. In addition to coping with the direct impacts of extreme weather, including loss of shelter, income, and food, the world's most "marginalized populations" face indirect health risks from a warming planet.[56] According to the U.N.'s World Health Organization,

> Marginalized populations are more likely to face elevated health risks from environmental change. These include lower-income communities and indigenous communities that are coping with environmental changes driven largely by economic processes in other parts of the world. They are often especially vulnerable to disease risk as a result of multiple stresses, have few resources for combating global environmental change, and have little voice in the decision-making processes of local, regional, national or global policy institutions.[57]

As the Food and Agriculture Organization points out, the parasites and diseases that climate change helps to thrive "will have disproportionately large impacts on the most vulnerable men and women in the livestock sector."[58] The disease threat is another global warming fire fanned by the wealthy but disproportionately burning the poor and innocent.

HOMERIC BLAME SHIFTING

Homer Simpson's heart softened as he looked, by match light, at an old family photo in the farmhouse of his childhood. Then he inadvertently set the room ablaze. Simultaneously, in another room, Homer's father ruefully tossed a love potion into a fireplace setting another room on fire. The flames converged, and the farmhouse burned to the ground.[59] Who is to blame?

As a matter of tort law, they both are, because either father's or son's negligence on its own would have been enough to incinerate the farmhouse. Since a single disaster may have many causes, it is important to determine which causes depend on one another and which can independently lead to catastrophe. It's equally important to focus preventative energy on the causes we can mitigate or hopefully eliminate.

Speaking of the potential for a human influenza pandemic, Dr. Margaret Chan, when she was Director-General of the World Health Organization, said, "there is a chance we can smother the spark of a fire before it catches on."[60] If that fire does catch, WHO predicts it may cause millions of human deaths as it rapidly spreads worldwide, overwhelming healthcare systems and causing trillions of dollars' worth of damage worldwide.[61] To extend the metaphor, the spark for a human pandemic may come from avian influenza and, more specifically, from a sick wild bird.[62] Or the spark may come from a pig factory farm as it did in the U.S. swine flu outbreak that killed thousands of Americans in 2009, as described in more detail in Chapter 8.[63] But for that spark to catch, it must land in influenza-friendly conditions.

In the spring of 2017, the U.S. Government Accountability Office (GAO) reported on the USDA's responses to recent avian influenza outbreaks.[64] The avian influenza threat to human health is a danger with causes we can control and causes we cannot. Yet the GAO and

USDA focused almost exclusively on the causes we cannot control, like the movements of wild birds, which may drop the spark, and they elide causes we can control, such as not arranging factory farms like clustered-together pandemic bonfires waiting to be lit.

The GAO identified 308 lessons the USDA claims to have learned from the recent outbreaks, along with the USDA's steps to fix problems related to those lessons.[65] Yet of those lessons, only six relate to preventing outbreaks and none of those six asks the poultry industry to make a single change in their operations or practices. The remaining 302 lessons and action items are simply about damage control—what to do after the spark of the virus has become an uncontained wildfire.

Yet, as two generations of Simpson men realized too late, it's far better to prevent a fire than it is to try to extinguish it once it's raging. In studying the costs of preventing an outbreak as compared to the costs of an outbreak happening, the World Organisation for Animal Health reported that prevention is much cheaper and that investments in prevention pay off well.[66]

A 2016 Indiana outbreak of avian influenza puts these issues into context. Wild migratory birds are one apparent cause of that outbreak, but in fixating on wild birds as flu-carriers, which is as uncontroversial as it is unfixable, the GAO's report missed this salient point: However the virus got inside that factory farm, it entered as a not-so-dangerous, low pathogenic strain. Only once it was inside and spreading rapidly among intensively confined turkeys did it mutate into a never-before-seen highly pathogenic strain.[67] That rapid mutation into a novel, highly lethal form, involving a process called amplification, doesn't always happen. It happens when conditions favor it—conditions like miserable, damp, dark confinement with tons of decomposing feces.

A year before, another U.S. bird flu outbreak was far more alarming. North of the border, in the spring of 2015, Canadian authorities also found highly pathogenic avian influenza at three Ontario farms, but they were able to quickly contain the outbreak, killing fewer than 80,000 birds. Unlike the limited cost, killing, and economic fallout Canada experienced, U.S. taxpayers footed the bill for killing about 50 million birds across 15 states in 2015 in what the USDA called the largest animal health emergency in U.S. history.[68] The 2017 GAO report failed to even note the contrast between the U.S. and Canadian outbreaks.

The differences between U.S. and Canadian poultry industry practices teach important lessons about how changing our practices in the United States could be better for just about everyone.[69] According to Canadian government experts, differences in how Canadian farms are set up explains why the Ontario outbreak was not the nationwide bird-killing wrecking ball that the U.S. 2015 outbreak was. Conditions at U.S. poultry factory farms are ideally adapted for the rapid spread and mutation of influenza viruses. In the United States, birds are locked inside warehouse-like barns" (sheds, really), and the feed mills that supply them are often affiliated with one of a few major corporations. So, they tend to cluster together, sharing trucks and workers. Canadian farms, on the other hand, tend to be independent of each other, reducing human biosecurity risks. Another key difference is that compared to the U.S.'s massive facilities, Canadian farms are smaller. If a virus is detected at a Canadian farm, there are generally far fewer birds to kill, upping the likelihood of swiftly containing outbreaks.

The USDA focuses its biosecurity energy on scrubbing workers' boots and otherwise dealing with human-centric problems. That is not enough to overcome inherent problems in the farm animal industry status quo. Clearly it didn't stop the 2015 outbreak before it spread to fifteen states, leaving 50 million dead chickens and turkeys in its wake. The U.S. standard practice of packing tens or even hundreds of thousands of birds into windowless sheds where their waste piles up for months on end attracts and supports armies of flies and rodents. The virus travels by fly wings and mouse paws within buildings and to other nearby confined bird facilities. Until we persuade mice, rats, and flies to bathe between visits and don tiny HAZMAT suits, this virus conduit will remain heavily trafficked. The virus even spreads on water particles blown out of each building's massive exhaust fans, fans made necessary by all those tightly packed bodies treading over tons of their own accumulated waste.

Stocking farms with fewer birds limits the virus's opportunities to mutate as it spreads from one feathered friend to another. Think of it this way: Would you rather spend the night locked in a half-full Carnegie Hall knowing that one audience member has a nasty flu, or would you rather be stuck in the concert hall's elevator overnight and shoulder to shoulder with the flu victim and twenty other people? In the elevator, you are more likely to pick up the flu and to get a version that has mutated dangerously as it hops from one sad concertgoer to another. The chances of a deadly mutation increase as the number of virus hosts increases. So, if you set out to design the perfect flu factory, you'd lock 140,000 egg-laying hens in cages, wing-to-wing, and never let them feel the sun on their backs as they live among rats, flies, and tons of feces.

It is as myopic as it is idiotic for the GAO and USDA to fixate on the wild birds that can drop the spark of influenza into the tinderboxes that are U.S. industrial farms rather than focusing on the fixable problems. The GAO acknowledges, as it must, that we have never been able to control wild birds' movements. Wild birds were migrating for millennia before we figured out how to make a campfire work. Yet, wild birds do not tend to devastate their populations with influenza. This has a lot to do with how they live. Unlike factory farmed birds, wild birds feel the sun on their feathers, and in general, influenza viruses can only survive about thirty minutes in sunlight.[70] The virus does wildly better in damp feces, which pile up by the ton in factory farms. Depending on temperature, the virus can survive for weeks in crap.[71]

When a wild bird comes down with the flu, the chances of her spreading that virus to another is slim because she doesn't live perpetually crammed wing to wing with other birds. Thus, when a deadly strain of flu does emerge in a migrating duck, for example, that bird may die before she can pass it to even a single other bird, let alone thousands or hundreds of thousands. That chance all but vanishes when you force her to live in perpetual close contact with fellow birds.

In the end, *The Simpsons'* farmhouse analogy is too charitable to the GAO and USDA's current thinking about how to react to avian influenza. Either Homer or Grandpa Simpson acting alone would've burned that farmhouse to cinders. But in the avian influenza context, our relationship to the virus and wild birds is more akin to that of someone who douses his house in kerosene and then blames the fire entirely on an ember inadvertently cast off a passerby's cigarette.

There are immediate steps the USDA could take that would begin to make poultry factory farms less horrific for birds, less dangerous, and less costly for taxpayers. According to the GAO report, the outbreak punched a hole in the U.S. economy that was between one to 3.3 billion dollars in size.[72] Additionally, the USDA spent more than $900 million cleaning it up. Much of that USDA outlay reimbursed owners of the millions of "depopulated" (*i.e.*, killed) birds.[73] Current federal law requires the USDA to make those payments, but it sensibly allows the agency to require indemnification-seekers to agree to make improvements that will make recurring outbreaks less likely and less dangerous if they do occur.[74]

In comments to the USDA, the HSUS suggested the agency should condition future indemnification agreements on a requirement that facilities agree to reduce their bird-stocking densities.[75] This approach makes devastating multi-state outbreaks less likely and would also save taxpayer money on the USDA outbreak response.

In responding to those comments, the USDA acknowledged that high stocking density was the problem that the HSUS said it was, but decided on a hazy, open-ended approach of trying to convince the poultry industry to fix this problem.[76] Leaving the fixing to industry is imprudent because industry created the problem, and, in the short term at least, it profits from it. This USDA plan is worse than my initial Permacane sequel idea, "Permacane and Abel," in which scientists create Abel, a hurricane rotating in the opposite direction of the Permacane, and then a salty four-star general tries to make Abel collide with and cancel out the Permacane.

If you choose to live in a kerosene-soaked farmhouse, you should not expect others to underwrite your rebuilding when it explodes. This is especially true if you are on your third or fourth kerosene-imbued house. As WHO Director-General Chan puts it, "[i]nfluenza viruses are notorious for their rapid mutation and unpredictable behaviour" and they "have the great advantage of surprise on their side. But viruses are not smart. We are."[77] She may be over-estimating us.

PERMACANE II: PERMACANE VERSUS SHARKNADO: THIS TIME IT'S DORSAL[78]

INTERIOR, HOTEL ROOM:

A vibrating iPhone 5 serving as a coaster tips over an open extra-large can of Manwich's Original Sloppy Joe Sauce. A reddish meaty landslide slowly rolls out of the blackness of the half-empty can, flowing over a silver-flecked, black countertop strewn with dirty take-out containers and drained bottles of bottom-shelf tequila. This extended-stay hotel room looks like the home of alcoholic possums.

Jack, the Weather Channel meteorologist boss, sleeps with his now-even-balder head resting on the countertop in the path of the slowly approaching Manwich-slide. He is half sitting on a bar stool, with his left foot on the floor as if he had been clubbed unconscious as he started to stand up. He grabs the phone and, without lifting his head, hits the speaker icon and mumbles: "Fuck off and die."

"Jack, it's Nigel. You need to get down to the station straight away! The Permacane is going to hit eastern North Carolina."

"So?"

"Well there's only a hundred bloody million gallons of liquefied pig manure in the four-county area it's heading for and most of them are in a floodplain."

"Who put all that shit in a floodplain?"

"That's where the pig farms are—hundreds of the bloody things with lagoons full of feces and urine."

SMASH-CUT, EXTERIOR, RURAL NORTH CAROLINA: The Permacane's whirring black funnel snaps trees, yanking them from their roots like dandelions. It rips through the forest, lowering rivers to sand, sucking in turbid water, moving at 110 miles per hour. It is closing in on an adobe-colored rectangular lake. That manure lagoon is already cresting over its berms as torrents of rain darken everything in front of the approaching Permacane.

A Cresting Brown Wave

Extreme weather will exacerbate disastrous shit spills that are already occurring. A 2015 joint U.K.–U.S. Taskforce on Extreme Weather and Global Food System Resilience report predicted that an extreme food production shock "what we would have called 1-in-100-years over the period 1951–2010 may become as frequent as a 1-in-30-year event before the middle of the century."[79] These increasingly common extreme weather disruptions will obliterate the cesspools holding hundreds of millions of gallons of untreated farm animal waste. A 2004 report on the risks of manure spills noted, "[o]ne of the most serious concerns facing North Carolina agriculture is the ever-present threat of livestock waste spills and lagoon failures."[80]

Since the 1990s, millions of gallons of waste from pig and chicken manure lagoons have clogged streams and rivers throughout the Tarheel state.[81] These spills were glaringly foreseeable as many of the factory farms sit on land where the water table is essentially at ground level, and about 170 of the state's CAFOs are in the hundred-year flood plain.[82] So, of course, these tend to spill manure when hurricanes hit the counties that are essentially converted to multi-acre pig, chicken, and turkey toilets. It isn't rocket science.

Nationwide, these lagoons and the people responsible for them have proven adept at spewing millions of gallons of shit year after year even without the help of hurricanes. Every year in the United States, about twenty-five manure lagoons spill,[83] as far as we know, and sometimes with catastrophic results. As brown waves of liquefied shit and piss overrun streams and rivers, they choke out the oxygen in the water, killing fish and doing lasting habitat damage. The decomposing manure in these lagoons hosts deadly pathogens like *Salmonella*, insecticides, pharmaceuticals, antibiotics, and microorganisms resistant to powerful antibiotics.[84] Despite the dangers and their financial ability to do better, some of the largest and wealthiest factory farm producers of the latter part of the twentieth century have long rap sheets of environmental duncehood, like building manure lagoons *below* the water table, for example.[85]

The Federal Emergency Management Agency (FEMA), charged with responding to extreme weather disasters like hurricanes, warns about the threats posed by factory farms. It explains that many of the farms

> operate manure pits and lagoons that are susceptible to flooding. Consult with your State departments of environmental management or natural resources on how to prevent overflow of these waste treatment facilities into local streams, rivers, or even the drinking water supply.[86]

That last bit about asking states to remedy the threat posed by flooding manure lagoons is a model of delusional optimism. If it were as easy as just asking various state agencies—in states like Oklahoma and Idaho—to come up with a better way to manage the hundreds of millions of gallons of liquefied manure and urine dumped into pits and lagoons every day, we probably wouldn't be in this mess today. If I'm not mistaken, both Oklahoma and Idaho are in the process of designating manure as their new state birds.

PART III

IN THE END

8

A Convoy 150 Years Long

Trucking Farm Animals Is an Ideal Way to Spread Disease

"All animals, it should not be forgotten, require rest and sleep as well as man; and no man could stand in one of those stock cars for twenty-four hours without refreshments, enduring the jolting, without sickening and falling from exhaustion and suffering."
—Zadok Street, October 9, 1879[1]

As a kid, I fell asleep to the fading whistles of trains arcing around the bay below our house on a hill. I never considered that cows were locked in some of those train cars. About a century before, an Ohio man named Zadok Street traveled thousands of miles along railroad tracks following farm animals to document what happened to them after days on end of transport without rest, water, or food.[2] Thanks to Street and other investigators, people in the late-nineteenth century may have been more aware of the suffering endured by farm animals on long journeys than most of us in the 1980s, or even today.

As a teenager, I briefly hung around Tacoma's railyards as a novice upper-middle-class hobo. My pals and I were high school sophomores seeking that unique sort of excitement born of risking a waistline bisection. We needed that thrill because Tacoma's primary industry has long been tedium. My first encounter with farm animal transport happened during this idiotic period of my life in the '80s, on a train rolling through the dark over a dirty river. I wish I could say that the moment had been revelatory, that it had made me an activist. That wouldn't happen until years later. But what did happen in my hobo days stays with me, like an absurd haunting.

GOOD AT BUSINESS ECONOMICS

I had a plan about how to figure out where the best spots were to jump onto moving trains. I made my pitch right after geometry class, knowing that Randy wouldn't bite.

"There's no class where you do a report on freight trains," he said, responding to the pitch.

"Business Economics."

"That isn't a class, and we wouldn't take it."

"You think some old dude will know that? Why would they know that?"

Adopting his thinking pose, Randy tilted his head like a yellow lab listening for a train whistle several zip codes away. With his shaggy blond hair and Van Halen Monsters of Rock tour t-shirt, Randy looked as if his brain was steeped in bongwater. However, he was uncommonly sharp and, more importantly, the only one of my friends with the balls (*i.e.*, lack of judgment) to go for Project Tinker, Tailor, Hobo-Spy. I certainly lacked the balls to go at it alone. It was a two-clown job. After a long thoughtful pause, he said, "Get us an interview, and I'll do it."

He called my bluff. At that point, as required by the international code of adolescent males, I was strapped into this caper. Almost all of me had hoped it would die when spoken aloud. Had it died, I could have impressed Randy with my moxie and told myself, *Well, I gave it a shot, but Randy said, "Get the fuck out of here," so that's that. Hey, instead, maybe we should brew our own beer in Mike's bedroom.* Instead, he threw down the gauntlet. I stared deep into my locker, stifling a prescient pants-shitting.

That afternoon, I called the railyard office from the telephone in the kitchen at home. I was connected to Herb, who, I was terrified to learn, was not a low-level railyard drone. He ran the whole place, which he boasted was part of one of the busiest ports on the entire west coast. But not so busy as to keep him from chatting with this young fraud for a torturous ten minutes.

"Business Economics, huh? Yeah, I'm happy to help you guys out. How about you come by 4:30 this Friday?"

Thursday night, I scratched away on a legal pad I'd pinched from Dad's office, thinking it would look more Business Economical than my spiral notebook. Within an hour, I had at least forty detailed questions about container ships, grain from eastern Washington, and cars from Korea. They came to me so easily that I feared on some unconscious level I might actually be interested in business economics. I fought the urge to pat myself on the back about how well I did at asking thoughtful questions about matters I did not give one tepid crap about.

Horseshit and The House That Herb Built

Friday, as the sky faded from iron to black, Randy and I crunched across large-rock gravel along railroad track margins. We approached our meeting place, which we later dubbed The House That Herb Built. It was less an office than a mobile home encased in cinder blocks with floodlights framing its door.

Herb greeted us without getting up. He looked exactly like the boss of Tacoma's trains should: a Donkey Kong–era Mario with a black push-broom mustache docked on a wide face atop a hint of a neck squeezed into the collar of a denim shirt. All he needed was some gorilla-thrown speeding barrels to jump over.

After the introductory chitchat, I shut up and let Randy take over. He'd glance down at my yellow legal pad of filler questions then lob one at Herb. "So, is it mostly corn from the Midwest that comes through here?" Herb's wooden swivel chair creaked as he leaned back, choosing his words carefully. He was enjoying this. I looked on mutely for forty-five more minutes. I watched Randy, who many thought couldn't find his way out of a drained bong, con a full-on adult and right in the seat of all adult power: the office. Randy was perfectly executing a campaign of sustained deception.

He was nearly to the key question: "So, do you ever catch guys trying to get on trains?" This was one of the only non-horseshit questions on my notepad. It should have stuck out like a hundred-dollar bill in a stack of RC Cola coupons, but Herb went for it. He chuckled. "Yeah, sometimes. Pretty rare though."

Years later, I realized that Herb was invested in our con. Even if he had a doubt or two about whether we were interviewing him in earnest for a high school class, I'm pretty sure he wouldn't have derailed it. By the time Randy got to our last question—the subtle "When you catch guys trying to get on the trains, where do you find them hanging out?"—Herb should have kicked us out. What could that possibly have to do with business or economics? But people love to be interviewed, to be asked for their expert opinions. For many middle-aged men, and possibly Herb, the job may be the only aspect of life going halfway decently. Add to that the fact that the interviewers are composing an academic report—something for posterity—and ego overwhelms the sandbags of skepticism.

After our afternoon at The House That Herb Built, we were the toast of our fellow high-school newspaper staff members. Put another way, we dazzled other unpopular kids. We couldn't relax in our sort-of-cool-kid glory, though, because we didn't have time for it. Now, we had a posse who wanted to test the intelligence we had gathered as soon as possible. They expected Tacoma's answer to Tom and Huck to promptly hoist themselves onto moving trains and help others do the same.

About three decades later, in 2019, as I rolled through Tacoma's railyards on an Amtrak, I saw that our train-hopping spot, the one Herb had told us about, had been decommissioned. A razorwire-topped chain-link fence blocked access to what we had called Ten Mile Corner, so named because the turn was acute enough that trains had to slow to ten miles per hour—which is coincidentally about as fast as a gaggle of rain-dampened high-school-newspaper staffers can run.

I didn't realize it until I was much older, but The House That Herb Built caper showed me the value of investigating things myself, like Zadok Street did when he chased and peered between the slats of 1870s cattle cars. As an attorney, there are limits to how far I can go in this regard, but when possible, I still like to get out there, poke around, and ask questions.

You Guys Going to Reno?

Two weeks after our Herb interview, Randy and I skidded on our heels down a steep dirt bank to the edge of the tracks, right where they arc sharply at Ten Mile Corner. After slowing for that tight turn, southbound trains would continue to make their way down past huge, concrete grain silos.

At Ten Mile Corner, Randy and I sat under an overpass that barely kept us out of the drizzle. "This is boring as shit," Randy said. Then things got worse.

Two dudes slid down the bank to join us. "Hey, you guys going to Reno?" Thanks to hard living, these guys looked awful: gaunt as Iggy Pop; their faces worn by wind, sun, and rain. They could have been thirty or fifty. One was super-eager to get out of town because of an outstanding warrant that Tacoma's finest were aggressively following up on. What was it for? We didn't want to find out, and we edged away soon after hearing about the active manhunt.

The following weekend, a gang of our pals went with us to the railyard. I'd been shaken by the company at Ten Mile Corner, so we settled on a different spot. Seven of us trudged across the north side of the railyard on another starless winter night. We were hoping to hop a train before it crossed the Puyallup River and ran north through the light industrial areas and the remaining scraps of forest on the way to Seattle. We knew we had a dog-who-catches-the-car problem. What if we did manage to get on a train? When and where would it slow down enough for us to jump off without powderizing our femurs? And what was the plan after that? Say we jumped off where the tracks run along Seattle's downtown waterfront. That's thirty miles north of Tacoma. There was no Lyft or even a bus that would take us home at one in the morning. At that time, thanks to a robust economy rooted in malt liquor, heroin, and misery, most of downtown Seattle was terrifying at night.

At the time, I would have rather walked home from Seattle than get my parents on the horn at 1:45 a.m. to catch them up on my new hobo hobby and my need for them to come fetch me. It could be much worse, of course. Rather than nearby Seattle, the train might not slow down until Twin Falls, Idaho. If so, that is where you'd find me and my friends today, making a go of it under assumed names. Better that than what we feared our parents would do to us.

These concerns were beginning to seem moot that night. Most of the trains wobbled quietly along sidings and weren't heading across the short metal bridge over the polluted Puyallup River. To stay out of view of The House That Herb Built, we reclined on a wet gravel bank by the tracks. We waited on those sharp wet rocks for forever. I had to spin a long-form sales pitch to keep these future teachers, fire fighters, and Microsoft programmers hunkered down like entrenched World War I soldiers, but hunker they did.

Then everything lit up as a headlight swung over us and a train creaked off a siding down our tracks. The first ten or so cars passed by slowly. They were all boxcars. Contrary to Hollywood's depictions, the boxcar is not the best car to hop on. For starters, they are difficult to climb into. I was about six feet tall at the time, and the floors of those boxcars rattled by me at just below my shoulders. The train was picking up speed as we struggled to run on the gravel bank next to it. With legs swinging under the train, we hoisted ourselves up and in. To state the obvious, this is an ideal way to part company with a pair of legs. It is also impossible, even in daylight, to know what, or whom, you'll be joining as you wriggle onboard.

But wriggle we did. I flattened my upper body on the boxcar's floor and managed to pull myself inside, powered by a fear of bleeding out in the rain downhill from the Tacoma Dome. In the darkness, I could see my pal, a future teacher, also making it in. Then I noticed the smell. Three out of the seven of us made it into my boxcar, and I craned my neck out the massive sliding door to see the rest of the gang beaching themselves safely in the car behind.

The train crossed over the Puyallup. In addition to the now overpowering, horrid stench, a dark, slick, liquid covered us from our collarbones down. As we struggled to keep our footing, those of us in my boxcar unanimously concluded that the floor was coated with about one part diesel and nine parts cow manure. The future Microsoft programmer piped up, "I'm getting off this shit box." He spoke for us all. Once the train cleared the river, we jumped off and doubled back across the bridge. We drove home in separate cars, each of us sulking and reeking. The gang's interest in weekend hoboing nose-dived after our communal fecal baptism.

WHAT TAKES PLACE ON THE GREAT HIGHWAYS OF COMMERCE

That night in Tacoma, the disgusting patina of an ancient problem coated us. Until the early 1950s, all long-distance transport of farm animals in the lower forty-eight states happened in train cars like the one my friends and I climbed into.[3] By the late 1980s, moving farm animals by train was more rare.[4] My friends and I barely kept on our feet during our 500-foot journey over a narrow river, so, it's no surprise that farm animals routinely slip, collapse, and shatter bones during long-distance transport.

Until that drizzly night in the railyards, I hadn't thought about how animals must always be moving, like billions of hooved or beaked apparitions around me, on their way to being fattened or slaughtered. It would be nearly two decades before I worked on farm animal transport issues as a new lawyer. But I often thought, as I still do, of the silent, unseen animals locked in that boxcar before I climbed into it. It was such a clownish way to learn about something painful and sad—like a lost *Three Stooges* episode in which Moe puts Curly's head through the door of a dark cannery and as he blinks the sawdust from his eyes, rag-bandaged five-year-old workers look back at him.

In the latter part of the nineteenth century, decades before federal law banned child labor or allowed women to vote, President Ulysses S. Grant signed into existence the first federal animal welfare law.[5] Known as the Twenty-Eight Hour Law, it was aimed at protecting animals, then chiefly cattle, on trains.[6] In general, all that law has ever required was offloading animals in transit so they could be fed, given water, and allowed five hours of rest after every twenty-eight hours of confined travel.[7] The law imposed no requirements for the duration of the twenty-eight hours animals could spend locked in train cars. They could be denied—and almost always were denied—food, water, and protection from extreme cold and heat for twenty-eight straight hours.

The law was born of years of lobbying by early animal protection activists like Caroline Earle White of the Women's Pennsylvania Society for the Prevention of Cruelty to Animals and Henry Bergh, the founder of the American Society for the Prevention of Cruelty to Animals (ASPCA),[8] who would go on to also fight on behalf of abused children. Bergh's 1870 letter to the editor of *The New York Times* on the problem of farm animal transport conveyed his frustration at New York State's legislative inaction despite his "three consecutive winters" lobbying in Albany.[9] Bergh and his compatriots wanted a law to address the serious humane and public health problems created by an unregulated farm animal transportation industry that he took a dim view of:

> The prisons of the state are filled with felons whose crimes are white as snow compared with these infernal deeds knowingly and deliberately perpetuated by corporations, who, defying all law, state and municipal, regard the public as well as the helpless brute as mere ministers to their greed of gain.[10]

According to Bergh, ASPCA's lobbying for a New York State law failed in part because of "potent railroad influence."[11] Unable to spur action at the state level, activists pushed for a federal law.

It's tempting to think the U.S. Congress had strong support from business and industry in passing the Twenty-Eight Hour Law. But ranchers and the powerful railroad barons opposed the law before it was enacted in 1873 and repeatedly sought to weaken or repeal it in the decades that followed.[12] The law was amended in 1906 to allow the twenty-eight-hour limit to be extended to thirty-six hours in some cases. Of the latter battle, in his part of the agency's 1907 report to the President, the USDA's Solicitor George P. McCabe explained: "The passage of the act was vigorously sought by the livestock and railroad interests and as vigorously fought in committee and on the floor by members of the various humane societies throughout the United States."[13]

During a long debate one June 1872 evening, some lawmakers' remarks about the need for protecting animals were far ahead of their time.[14] Senator Lot Myrick Morrill of Maine, for example, pushed for the bill's passage, arguing:

> And when we know what takes place on the great highways of commerce, I think it a very provident thing, and one of very high expediency, that the Government of the United States should interpose its authority, and at least in some way give an admonition which shall teach men that even dumb animals have rights which are not to be violated.[15]

Ohio Senator Allen Granberry Thurman noted:

> There is no man more anxious than I am to see some remedy provided. I have witnessed with my own eyes the torture of these beasts until I turned away because I could not look at it any longer. I have seen them where they were lying dead, smothered by the heat and I know what it is. . . . It is not simply mercy to the poor brute although that of itself is sufficient with any right hearted man; it is mercy to ourselves, mercy to the people who eat the flesh of these animals, which, when improperly transported is unhealthy at its place of destination, and almost or quite unfit for food.[16]

Today, you might hear sentiments such as these from the likes of a man trying to keep his ponytail from getting in the way as he fills a hemp sack with hulled hemp seeds at the bulk bins of a Santa Cruz food co-op. But in 1872, Senator Thurman said all that, even though he didn't even support the bill as written.[17] He claimed to be worried that racing against the twenty-eight-hour time constraints of the law might force trains to injure animals by speeding.[18]

As meager as the law was in 1873, it was better than nothing. Before and after it was enacted, the American Humane Association and other animal protection groups sent agents like Zadok Street to follow tightly packed train cars and observe their unloading at stockyards and slaughterhouses.[19] Their reports were used on the floors of Congress and, later, to spur U.S. Attorneys to bring lawsuits based on documented violations.[20] A 1918 USDA bulletin reported that between 1906 and 1917, the agency received almost 9,000 reports of violations and collected $426,818.08 in fines, which is about $8 million in 2020 dollars.[21]

The courts took these cases seriously. One court, for example, refused to let a railroad company off the hook for not offloading animals in time, even though the pens that would've been used were engulfed in flames.[22] In the court's view, that didn't excuse the company's failure to make other arrangements for getting those animals the rest, food, and water they were legally due.[23]

Yet, enforcement notwithstanding, the threat of a $500 fine was simply not a deterrent to the absurdly wealthy railroad interests.[24] At the transition between the nineteenth and twentieth centuries, a $500 fine would sting for most—but not for the very wealthy. To put it in context, $500 in the early years of the twentieth century more than covered three years of tuition at the University of Pennsylvania's Law School.[25] The problem was, the railroads were the only ones that had to worry about paying that fine, and they swam in oceans of cash. They generally chose not to comply with the law, treating the fines as a cost of doing business.[26] That the USDA knew of 9,000 violations between 1906 and 1917 indicates that this was not an overly complied-with law.[27] In 1908, the USDA reported to Congress and the President that "a large number of railroads have disregarded the law."[28] Overcrowding rail cars and subjecting animals to days without water and food in extreme weather cost ranchers in the form of dead animals and the loss of meat due to bruising and muscle loss, but those losses were also just written off and absorbed.[29]

Today, the Twenty-Eight Hour Law is still the only federal law covering the transport of tens of millions of farm animals per year. A typical semi-truck is packed with about 165 pigs.[30] The industry fully expects that every year tens of thousands of pigs trucked to slaughter will die along the way or will be so sick, worn out, or injured upon arrival at the slaughtering plant that they will never stand again. The National Pork Board industry group estimates "that 0.7% of those transported to market either die (~0.22%) or become non-ambulatory (0.44%)."[31] Thus, of the more than 124 million pigs trucked to slaughter in the United States in 2018, about 27,280 of them walked onto a truck then died during transport, overcrowded on a urine-soaked floor.[32] That's about one pig dying every nineteen minutes.

The value of those pigs fluctuates, currently ranging between about $36 to $53 each.[33] So, weighing the vanishingly slim chance of getting caught and incurring a $500 fine on a truckload of animals worth up to about $8,745 is not a tough business call.[34] In 1915, $500 bought you an Ivy League law school education. Today, $500 is less than multinational meat corporations pay for an hour of a law firm partner's time.

Beginning in the early 1950s, trucks increasingly eclipsed trains as the means for moving farm animals.[35] As that transition happened, the USDA, which had helped enforce the law, decided that it did not apply to trucks at all. The USDA explained that because the law never mentions trucks, that meant that "[t]ruck shipments are not subject to the legislation mentioned above [the Twenty-Eight Hour Law] and stops en route for feed, water, and rest are discretionary."[36] A little wrinkle: Trucks did not exist in 1873 and, when the law was amended in 1906, trucks had only recently arrived and were not widely used.

Yet, that is not how federal statutes work. Since 1952, for example, it has been a federal crime, punishable with a long prison sentence, to commit fraud by "wire, radio, or television."[37] Though the law has been amended in recent years, it still doesn't mention fax machines, the Internet, or email. Nevertheless, the U.S. Department of Justice and courts agree that the law's broad prohibition on "wire" fraud covers these newer technologies.[38] Statutes often speak in general prohibitions precisely so they don't need to be amended every other day to account for what didn't exist before.[39] But in this case, the USDA's weird and tragic reasoning carried the day for the next five decades as animals were overcrowded into semi-trucks instead of train cars, and the agency quietly stopped enforcing the only federal law that offered them any protection at all.

The Pickle

In 2005, I worked on a rulemaking petition challenging the USDA's bizarre abandonment of the Twenty-Eight Hour Law. Rulemaking petitions essentially ask agencies to alter their regulations. Partly for fun and partly because we needed to keep it under wraps until the big reveal, we code-named the petition the Pickle. In the Pickle, the HSUS and other animal groups explained why the USDA's conclusion that the law did not apply to trucks was wrong. The petition also discussed the public health dangers that farm animal transport poses, as it injures and kills thousands of farm animals every year.

My boss, Peter Petersan, went with me as we delivered a paper copy of the Pickle by bicycle to the USDA's D.C. headquarters. Petersan delighted in this opportunity to combine two of his loves: the law and cycling. I was peddling the same beat-up mountain bike that I rode during my high school hobo phase. The Pickle was sixty-five pages long with hundreds of additional pages of studies and other supporting documents, making it about a ten-pound chunk of paper. The weight of it snapped off a metal part of my bike rack on the way over. A gracious and pleasant older woman at the USDA accepted the Pickle and gave us a written receipt. Riding back, it dawned on me that, like Herb in his railyard office, she might have thought I went to her office as part of some sort of school project, maybe a college-level Biz Econ 101.

In a strange move, the USDA responded to the petition a year later, claiming it had known for years that the Twenty-Eight Hour Law applied to trucks. Yet, the agency had never publicly said so. Instead, the USDA had repeatedly said things like "the Twenty-Eight Hour Law does not apply to transport by truck."[40] Sadly, the law remains essentially unenforced more than a decade after our USDA petition, despite compelling reasons to aggressively enforce the law or, better yet, abandon trucking farm animals *en masse*. Those reasons are the very reasons U.S. Senators articulated in 1872.

IDEALLY SUITED FOR SPREADING DISEASE

In his famous essay "Politics and the English Language," George Orwell observed:

> [A]n effect can become a cause, reinforcing the original cause and producing the same effect in an intensified form, and so on indefinitely. A man may take to drink because he feels himself to be a failure, and then fail all the more completely because he drinks.[41]

So it is with farm animals on trucks. To begin with, the industry's preferred genetic strain of pig predisposes every one of those animals to stress.[42] That, coupled with exhaustion caused by transport, weakens immune system responses and can cause a pig to collapse, which distresses her and suppresses her immune system all the more.[43] Collapsing in a moving truck with 164 other pigs packed in around you is not at all restful.

Once down, a pig can be crushed by others tightly confined in the semi and she is also more likely to pick up nasty pathogens like *Salmonella*, *E. coli*, and herpes viruses. This is not just because her immune system is impaired, but also because she's forced to wallow in manure and urine for hours.[44] A collapsed pig is not only more likely to pick up a dangerous infection; she, more than a standing pig, is more likely to shed that pathogen, increasing the infection's chances of spreading widely.[45] It's a painful disease-and-misery feedback loop. Although none of this is common knowledge, intuitively it makes perfect sense. If I were forced to put my face down on that boxcar's cold, wet floor and feel the eye-stinging ammonia for twenty hours while 164 clog-wearing strangers stomped and urinated on me, I'd be powerfully distressed.

According to the FAO, the transport of farm animals is "ideally suited for spreading disease":[46]

The animals commonly originate from different herds or flocks and they are confined together for long periods in a poorly ventilated stressful environment, all of which will favour the transmission within the group of infectious disease should sick animals be present.[47]

Like many of the pathogens animals pick up and spread in transport, *Salmonella* and influenza are zoonotic, meaning that one way or another they can jump from infected animals to infect humans.[48] Not long ago, the Director of the U.N.'s World Health Organization ranked pandemic influenza as one of the three greatest "looming" global threats to human health.[49] The ability of the virus to spread and mutate quickly makes it a threat of the most serious order.[50] It is one of the most common causes of respiratory disease in North American pig farms.[51] Influenza spreads directly from host to host or with the help of flies, manure, and rodents.[52] When a new virulent strain emerges, it has the potential to quickly kill millions of people.[53]

We saw this terrifying dynamic at work in a recent swine influenza outbreak at U.S. pig farms in the late nineties: a never-before-seen strain comprised of bird, pig, and human DNA. In 2009, this virulent hybrid rapidly spread throughout North America and then globally. The CDC estimates that the 2009 swine-origin flu pandemic sickened 60.8 million Americans, hospitalized 274,304, and killed 12,469, including more than a thousand kids.[54]

The trans-continental reach of this flu strain was likely facilitated by long-distance pig transport.[55] Most pigs are raised in the Midwest or North Carolina, but they may be trucked vast distances before slaughter.[56] For example, in recent years, one slaughter facility just miles from downtown Los Angeles has killed pigs from several states, including Nebraska.[57] Additionally, because transport leaves thousands of pigs unable to walk, it creates a subclass of individuals who we know are much more likely to be infected with influenza, even if we don't know precisely why that is.[58]

Cramming a bunch of terrified and immunosuppressed animals into a semi-truck generates public health threats that are categorically distinct from threats posed by plant-based foods. Grains, fruits, nuts, and vegetables may become contaminated due to poor packaging or conditions of transit, but these are not intrinsic risks in producing and shipping those products. They are instead preventable missteps between production and consumption. In contrast, collapsing, dying, and getting and spreading illnesses are all inherent aspects of trucking animals to become food—they are built in to the business model. More importantly, however it happens, contamination of plant-food products poses, at most, food safety risks. *Salmonella*-tainted peanut butter has sickened and killed people, but tainted plant foods have yet to intensify them and then spread a novel, deadly strain of an influenza virus—like, say, the 2009 swine flu.[59]

The pork industry bemoaned the "swine flu" name that stuck to the 2009 flu outbreak. But it was essentially ginned up and spread from pig farms, so, tough luck. Trucking pigs, chickens, and other animals *inherently* increases the chances of developing a virulent flu strain. Transport itself also *inherently* provides the means for spreading that potential mass killer continent-wide in a matter of months. With those dual inherent risks in mind, the key question becomes not, *How can we limit the frequency and duration of farm animal transport?* but rather, *Why are we transporting them anywhere at all?*

Though relatively few of us ever take notice of it, every week pigs are panting in lung-burning, ammonia-filled trucks stuck in Los Angeles traffic. And, in winter, patches of bright white fur on the face of a month-old calf darkens with wet manure as he freezes to death on the metal floor of a truck speeding down a Wisconsin highway.

RETIRING

One Saturday morning, weeks after our disappointing late-night boxcar ride, Randy and I ran after a train along the gravel bank at Ten Mile Corner. I'd nearly caught up to the powder-gray ladder leading to a sort of porch on the back of a grain car. I managed to climb up, joining Randy on the porch as the train accelerated around Commencement Bay, through the shuttered Asarco Smelter. A few miles later, our train slowed as it pulled out of a long tunnel under Point Defiance Park. As it stopped, we watched foam-frosted waves break against the faded green pillars holding up the Tacoma Narrows Bridge.

Sensing a fleeting chance to hop off while still in our native area code, we scurried off and hiked up a steep hillside of ferns and fir trees.

That was the end of our hobo phase. Maybe someone had radioed the engine after seeing us hop on and the conductor chose to give us a shot at bailing out before the Port of Los Angeles. We could not have traveled more than four miles total.

Zadok Street, on the other hand, followed trains hauling farm animals over more than 18,000 miles so he could witness and build a case for reform of a great cruelty. He did this right up until his death at the age of seventy-one. From what we know of the man, it's fair to say that he would be crushed to see the fight to which he devoted so much of his life fizzle and recede from public concern in the twentieth and twenty-first centuries. The same suffering and abuse Zadok Street documented still happens daily.

He worked to soften the impact of that first cresting wave of industrial animal agriculture. In 1870, he got a patent for a more humane "stock car," with water and food troughs as well as increased air circulation.[60] Describing the design, he said, "By my improved cars stock of all descriptions may be transported to any distance without suffering and without loss of health or flesh."[61] Even though he was up against railroad barons, among the richest and most powerful interests of his day, he thought he could improve the lot of animals raised for food. But his stock car never caught on. He overestimated industry's interest in transporting animals without causing them to suffer.

If anything, Street's fight is more winnable today than it was in the 1870s. Science confirms beyond reasoned dispute that there's no meaningful benefit, and plenty of disastrous downsides, to transporting farm animals. And the humane concern animating the

1872 Senate debate on the bill that became our first federal humane law has never been more widely shared. Remembering him shortly after his death, Street's colleagues remarked:

> [I]n his zeal he went beyond his strength. Through the intense heat of the summer he voluntarily underwent such exposures that would have severely tried the strength of younger men. . . . Those of us who were associated with him will never forget his earnestness. We miss to-day, also, his kindly face.[62]

9

Rendered Insensible in the End

Slaughter Remains Cruel and Dangerous

Hot, fevered, frightened, trampled, bruised, and torn;
    Frozen to death before the ax descends;
We kill these weary creatures, sore and worn,
    And eat them—with our friends.
—Charlotte Perkins Gilman, *The Cattle Train*, 1915[1]

If you carefully consider consequences and are empathetic, there is a chance that you might someday introduce strangers to a puppet on your hand. On the other hand, there is probably zero chance you'll run a self-destructive company that wrecks lives. This is what I learned from an older animal activist, and a slaughterhouse millionaire.

As my mid-twenties came and went during the late 1990s, I was broke and living in West Hollywood trying to figure out my future. At the time, one of my favorite *Simpsons* episodes was about Frank Grimes, "the man who had to struggle for everything he ever got." One scene in the episode's newsreel account of his life struck me. Under a blue sky, Grimes sprints across green pasture toward a grain silo. Right when he reaches it, the silo explodes. As a 24-year-old, I thought I was at a unique stage of life. The decades ahead were open like Frank Grimes' field, but I couldn't know, until it was too late, if I was running to a silo rigged to blow me to pieces.

Hoping to sort out which silos to run from, I studied older people around me who shared my passion for helping animals. One of these was an activist named Mary. In the late '90s, I didn't yet know of Mary's polar opposite, Steve Mendell. Back when I was riding L.A. city buses to work, Mendell was beginning a prosperous career slaughtering cows not far from where I lived. My life didn't intersect with his until a decade later, when the HSUS released undercover video of cruelty at his slaughter facility.

A WOLF ENTERS

In 1997 and 1998, after a series of soul-crushing temp jobs, I landed an entry-level position with a campaign working to pass a California ballot initiative to ban cruel wildlife traps and poisons. (That measure passed by a comfortable margin in November of 1998.) My job entailed answering the phone and doing other entry-level stuff. I encountered some animal activists who were grating, odd people. Those people, especially the ones who had been activists for decades, made me worry about who I might become if I stayed in the activism game.

At that time, the positive, older role models I met probably outnumbered the walking-cautionary-tales ten to one, but of course life is more fun when you fixate on the negative and frightening. Those disconcerting activists were torn people. They couldn't live in a world where animals are killed in protracted, painful ways for no good reason, yet they hung in there, fighting as best they could.

Mary was the most memorable of this sort. She was in her seventies. I didn't learn her history, because I couldn't ask many questions: she was a monologist, not a conversationalist. She regularly trapped my boss and me on the phone, retelling a twenty-minute story about her "hero" dog. According to Mary, her dog jumped into a river and saved a flailing child. Each time she told it, her voice cracked with emotion as the story progressed.

Sitting at his desk, a thrift-store folding table, my boss would be on the phone consoling her as he reheard the tale of the long-dead hero.

"I know . . . oh, I know."

"No! No, you don't know!" Mary snapped. "He was a hero!"

Mary was sane and lucid, but sad and angry. We heard from her by phone for weeks without ever seeing her, but one afternoon Mary followed through on her threat to "pop into the office." Though we expected weirdness, her stunner of an entrance put us far back on our heels. She entered in a wheelchair pushed by a blond, spikey-haired man with earlobes that were more earring than lobe. He wore a black turtleneck tucked into black slacks. He looked like a 50/50 blend of Billy Idol and Steve Jobs. We weren't introduced to him, and he said nothing. As we greeted her, however, Mary said, "Now say hello to Wolfy!" as she raised from her lap a gray wolf puppet on her right hand.

I smiled and waved to the hand puppet. I'm pretty sure she was just being quirky with the puppet and that she didn't think of it as an animate hand covering, but I'm not positive. Still, that is a colossal quirk. She and Wolfy didn't stay long (and neither did Billy Jobs), and I never saw them again. I can't remember anything about what she looked like *sans* Wolfy. If you want people to forget everything about your appearance just introduce them to a puppet on your hand.

At twenty-five, I knew I didn't want to be like Mary in my later years, and I feared I might. I don't know why, but I had a feeling that she had been like me when she was younger, so I wondered if a cause-driven life of frustration, anger, conflict, and few victories would taper off with me shopping for my own Wolfy.

On the other hand, as I got older, I saw firsthand that a disproportionate amount of what is awful in life is the puppet-free handiwork of dignified, unimaginative, forgettable people. The banal sort who are on a perpetual ascent to mediocrity.

IT MAKES YOU ILL

Not long after Mary came to our office, I rode my dented white mountain-bike home from work, my back damp against a backpack carrying only a printed-out *Los Angeles Times* article. At the top of a Sunset Boulevard hill, where Beverly Hills blurs into Hollywood, I waited in candle-dim twilight for the light to change. I squinted down the half-mile-long hill glowing with two lanes of red brake lights. Just as the light turned green, I flew between the lanes down Sunset, inches from barely moving cars on either side. I did this five nights a week. If I made one mistake or if any of the hundreds of drivers made a move I couldn't react to, I easily could have died. If this were a fair world, then, at minimum, I would have dictated this book from within a permanent full-body cast.

Later that evening, I lounged on a futon in my West Hollywood kitchen nook, reading the *Los Angeles Times* article. I was not relaxing in the kitchen nook of *my* apartment. I rented *only* the nook from my sister and her two roommates in an apartment at the foot of Runyon Canyon. The *LA Times* article was about non-ambulatory—*i.e.,* "downed"—farm animals and a recently enacted California law called the Downed Animal Protection Act. That law criminalized the abuse and neglect of immobilized, collapsed farm animals.

At twenty-five, I knew that slaughter was ugly and cruel, but I didn't realize that people were beating and dragging animals to get them up and lurching to the kill floor. To put this in context, in the United States, we cut the throats of about nine billion land animals every year, with chickens making up about 99 percent of that total.[2] We slaughter about 33,000,000 mature cattle a year, along with over 600,000 calves.[3]

In a nutshell, here's how cattle slaughter works. They arrive by semi-truck at one of the few hundred federally inspected cattle-slaughter facilities and are held in pens until USDA employees can inspect them.[4] It's a stretch to call it an inspection, as the USDA employee typically just looks for obvious maladies as dozens of cattle walk past. After this, the animals are pushed and prodded through a chute onto the kill floor where someone shoots a steel bolt through their forehead, which is supposed to be a knockout blow, rendering them insensible to pain. When it works, and it often doesn't, the stunned animals fall, a chain is looped around a back foot, and they're lifted from a blood-sticky floor and moved down a dis-assembly line. Death is supposed to happen quickly; after the cattle are stunned and hoisted, their throats are cut and they bleed to death.

It's well known that at any of the stages between arrival and death, much can go horribly wrong. Federal regulations allow the line to move at speeds that would allow shackling and hoisting a cow about every thirty seconds.[5] So, although it's illegal, it's not uncommon for an animal to be conscious while hanging and being cut and bled. Unfortunately, the USDA is remarkably timid about punishing violations, even violations as serious as consciousness during the dismembering process.

I knew some of this back in 1998, but what I didn't realize was that so much of the cruelty at slaughter happens as animals are unloaded from trucks and shunted to and from slaughter facility pens. So, I was surprised that California even needed a law to protect animals who collapse at slaughter and on the way there. Abuse of these animals was a common enough problem that California specifically made it a crime.

That law was prompted by an undercover video shot from a van parked across the street from the low white wall bordering Chino, California's Hallmark slaughter plant. Farm Sanctuary, one of the first groups to focus solely on farm animal cruelty and suffering, made the recording. California State Senator David Roberti, who championed the bill that became law, described the video to *The Los Angeles Times*: "When you watch the videos of those animals, it's impossible not to be affected. . . . It makes you ill."[6] The video showed a man torturing cows too sick or injured to stand and walk to slaughter. That video spurred the law that made such abuse a crime punishable with jail time.

A ROCKING CHAIR, A CAT, AND A LAPTOP

In late 1998, I left my Hollywood kitchen nook for Seattle. Not long after that, I went to law school in Portland before becoming an animal protection lawyer working in Washington, D.C. In 2007, I moved to San Francisco.

In November 2007, I was dreading watching a DVD that the HSUS had overnighted to my grim and costly Lower Haight apartment. It was hours of footage that an HSUS undercover investigator had recorded while working at Hallmark, that same slaughter plant in Chino that provided the video-recorded impetus for California's downed animal law. The HSUS investigator was at Hallmark by chance. He had been in the area, saw they were hiring, and got the job. When the time came to watch it, I steeled myself in a wicker rocking chair. At the time, for some reason that chair was the only place I was comfortable working. Our cat, Shoo, always jumped in my lap when I worked in the rocker.

It was the worst stuff I had ever seen. Years later, a Federal District Court judge summed up what was going on for a quarter of a century at Hallmark. The judge based her summary on undisputed facts gleaned from a long-time Hallmark employee, Daniel Navarro:

> He testified that the police showed him portions of the HSUS's undercover video of the Facility. He explained what he saw in the video accurately portrayed the workers'—and his own— treatment of cattle at the Facility while he worked there. He specifically testified that he and other workers at the Facility slaughtered non-ambulatory cattle throughout his 25-year tenure, as well as frequently used forklifts and chains to move non-ambulatory cattle. He also testified that he and his co-workers used electric shocks, called a "Hot-Shot," on the cattle regularly during his 25-year tenure. Also, he sprayed a water hose into the nostrils of the cattle to force the cattle to stand up. Finally, he testified that he and his co-workers would use their cellular telephones to warn each other of the location of the government inspectors to evade detection of the inhumane treatment and slaughter of non-ambulatory cattle.[7]

It's significant that the court described this account as undisputed. That means that the attorneys defending the slaughterhouse owners and operators failed to point to sufficient evidence to refute any of it.

In that boxcar-gray living room, with a black-and-white cat on my lap, I cried as I watched hours of horrific footage. The cows were caked in mud, but in places you could see unsoiled, sunlit white fur. They looked a lot like Shoo curled up in my lap. I promised the confused Shoo that we were going to land on these people with both feet and from off-of-the-top rope of the wrestling ring of life, but I didn't tell her what I knew: that this was a long shot. What often happens is the handful of people caught on video get blamed for everything. They're fired, the scandal dies down, and in a few months, it's as if the investigation never happened.

This would be the sort of massively frustrating situation I worried about since meeting Mary and Wolfy years earlier. I was looking at stellar evidence of cruelty that could be charged as dozens of separate felony counts. We had made this as easy as possible for the district attorney. Prosecutors are rarely lucky enough to know the identity of a person who also happens to be caught on video committing crimes. Yet, while watching the footage, I knew there was a strong chance we'd never even get charges filed against the company or those who ran it, or anyone else. Moments like that made me worry about what a lifetime of this sort of flattening sadness, anger, and high-stakes disappointment might do to me.

THE HARD SELL

A few days after watching the video, I met the undercover HSUS investigator and another colleague, a lawyer, in a hotel bar near LAX. This was my first time seeing our guy who managed to get inside Hallmark, but I spotted him immediately. He had a small bushy mustache and thick black eyebrows that almost seemed glued to the top of his black-rimmed glasses, and his nose was a hue that didn't match the color of his cheeks. He told us about his grueling, ten-hour shifts at Hallmark. Starting at 6:30 a.m. six days a week, he had worked unloading cows from double-decker semi-trucks so Hallmark could kill about 500 of them a day.

What made the work difficult, dangerous, and cruel was Hallmark's penchant for slaughtering cows the dairy industry calls "spent." As mentioned earlier, a "spent" cow is one who is sent to slaughter because her milk production has waned. According to a driver who transported cows to Hallmark in the 1980s and 1990s, "[t]he dairyman would get the last gallon of milk, the last cent out of the cow and then take it to auction. . . . But those were the ones [Hallmark] could get the most profit off of. It was advantageous for them to buy those cows."[8]

Male farm animals endure severe cruelty, but we seem to have gone out of our way to devise ways to make life painful and miserable for the females. The hooves of most U.S. dairy cows spend almost their entire time on concrete, not grass.[9] This encourages painful lesions. These in turn can lead to injury, collapse, and lameness; the last is a major killer of cows on farms.[10] A life spent on concrete and, in many cases, in near-constant confinement within a stall is not what cows need or prefer. They like softness, to walk on grass, and to lie down on soft straw bedding or grass.[11] Concrete breaks their bones when they fall on it, and falling is common because hooves work better on earth than on urine-slick concrete.[12]

In August 2019, there were about 8.8 million U.S. dairy cows, and each one produced about 1,987 pounds of milk that month.[13] Thirty years earlier, in August 1989, cows produced far less milk, about 793 pounds less per cow.[14] The extra quarter ton of milk that each of today's cows produces each month is the result of decades of selective breeding aimed solely at boosting milk production.[15] That myopic, profit-driven focus on radically increasing each animal's milk yield produces a wide variety of chronic and acutely painful conditions.

If you're built like me (*i.e.*, current-day Steven Seagal), the idea of jogging six hours a day, every day for weeks on end is not appealing. That's the level of metabolic work the modern dairy cow has to go through during lactation, thanks to the bonkers, high-milk-producing genes we've given her.[16] It pulls every bit of fat out of the animal and can leave her permanently unable to consume enough calories, which can lead to neurological damage. Excessive milk production and milking by machine are to blame for a painful, very common mammary gland infection called mastitis, a leading killer of dairy cows.[17] Cows can live to be more than twenty years old, but they're often deemed spent and sent to death at around age five. Not surprisingly, even the best of the "spent" cows are in terrible shape—worn out by a lifelong cycle of milking by machine, insemination, and anguishing separation from their calves right after birth. Slaughter facilities have caught on, and most won't take "spent" cows because they are disproportionately more likely to be dead or nearly dead on arrival or lying with a broken leg on a semi-truck's manure-covered metal floor.[18]

Even though fewer and fewer facilities will take them, slaughtering "spent" cows is not an anomalous practice. This means that "spent" cows are increasingly on trucks for longer periods between dairies and the few places that will still accept and kill them. The income from slaughtering "spent" cows is built into the dairy industry's business model. Dairies depend on it to contribute between three to nine percent of their total income.[19]

USDA slaughter inspectors "condemn" cows who are "spent" more frequently than cattle bred and raised strictly to produce beef.[20] Condemnation is USDA-speak for "this cow is in such a frighteningly awful condition that no part of the animal should enter the human food supply."

Because Hallmark was the only plant in that corner of the United States that would take "spent" cows, it pulled them in from hundreds of miles away, from about six states.[21] The circumstances create a cruel synergy: Because most slaughter facilities don't want these worn-out females, they travel much farther crammed in trucks *en route* to slaughter. And as the time spent in trucks increases, so does the number of cows who arrive dead, with broken legs, or too sick or exhausted to even try to stand up.

So, when he opened the metal door at the back of these trucks, the HSUS investigator often found cows unable or unwilling to stand. A 1,500-pound animal who can't stand can't be easily or humanely moved. This is why Hallmark workers used the panoply of evil methods described above to force them up. The cows would struggle to rise just to escape the man twisting their tails or shocking their faces. These practices are essentially unchanged at least since the 1870s, as evidenced by an 1877 humane society investigative report:

> Shippers use the goads upon their cattle until their blood runs. They wring and twist the tails of the cattle until the joints are dislocated, the poor creatures moaning piteously from the horrible cruelty. The animal, when down, would use in vain all his power to rise, which he often could not do, and in that condition was trampled to death by his fellows.[22]

Our investigator documented this cruelty with his hidden camera, but he never participated in it.

The investigator described his days at Hallmark to us in that nearly empty hotel bar as we prepared to make a hard sell for filing felony animal cruelty charges against the guys captured in his video footage. We were meeting the next day with Debbie, a thirty-something deputy district attorney. We knew Debbie a little and knew she was committed to prosecuting animal cruelty, whether the victim was a puppy or a cow. California, unlike many states, generally treats cruelty to a farm animal just as it treats cruelty to any other animal: It's a crime, and depending on circumstances it is one that can be prosecuted as a felony. In addition to violating California's general animal cruelty proscription, the abuse violated the Downed Animal Protection Act, which I'd read about a decade ago in my rented nook.

Debbie watched less than half of the three-minute video we'd prepared for her. She stopped it after the scene where Navarro rams a screaming cow with a forklift. "I'll charge them," she said.

Not long after the meeting, that forklift clip was on the national *CBS Evening News*. We had climbed the turnbuckle and were balancing on the top rope, nearly in position to launch. So began the uniquely unlikely beat-down I had promised Shoo in the rocking chair.

A few weeks later, Daniel Navarro, one of the two men blamed and then fired for Hallmark's systemic cruelty, sat in an interview room at the San Bernardino Police Department headquarters. A sergeant asked him why he kept spraying water up the nose of a cow he had already killed. This is something he had done to living cows repeatedly, but it made no sense to do this to a dead animal. Navarro replied only, *"Tontería."*

The sergeant's report translates this as "foolishness."

Navarro didn't say more about why he went out of his way to torture and degrade doomed cows. His role in this scandal always reminded me of the father in James Joyce's short story "Counterparts," who, disrespected by his boss, passes that along to his son: "The little boy looked about him wildly but, seeing no way of escape, fell upon his knees."[23]

Debbie needed her supervisors to sign off on filing charges, and that took several weeks. During that time, my colleagues and I worked on legal memos she could use as she lobbied her bosses to proceed. Charges were filed after *The Washington Post* broke the story, and the D.A.'s office was flooded with calls asking for prosecution.[24]

Ultimately, it wasn't middle management's decision; Michael Ramos, the Republican District Attorney, made the call to press charges against Navarro and another man. When he announced the charges, he said, "The facts of this case are horrendous. . . . It makes your stomach turn to see what they did to the cows."[25] He went further in his written statement on the filing of charges:

> I need the public to understand that my office takes all cases involving animal cruelty very seriously. It doesn't matter whether the mistreated animal is a beloved family pet or a cow at a slaughterhouse. Unnecessary cruelty will not be tolerated and will be prosecuted to the fullest extent allowed by law.[26]

In the end, both of the men charged were convicted. Rafael Sanchez Herrera pled guilty to three misdemeanor counts of violating the Downed Animal Protection Act. After Sanchez served his six-month sentence, he was deported to Mexico, because he hadn't been in the United States lawfully. Months earlier in my rocking chair,

I watched footage of him pushing a downed cow out of a truck, sending the two-ton animal slamming down onto her side on the concrete four feet below. That wasn't an isolated incident; the video showed him doing many similar gratuitously horrid things.[27]

Regardless, I never felt good about his deportation. As awful as what he did was, I knew Sanchez wasn't calling the shots at Hallmark. He wasn't getting rich there, and the suits who were doing both would never be at risk of deportation. According to an August 2008 newspaper article:

[T]he mother of Sanchez's three children said she has not seen Sanchez or spoken with him since his last court appearance. The children ask about their father. She said she does not think it was fair that only Sanchez and Ugarte [Navarro] received punishment for what occurred at the Chino plant.[28]

She wasn't wrong, but the story wasn't over either.

The other man, Navarro, pled guilty to two felony animal cruelty counts and two misdemeanor counts of violating the Downed Animal Protection Act.[29] He was sentenced to 270 days in jail, but that time may have been served doing community service or under house arrest.[30] Navarro was the very guy Farm Sanctuary had filmed abusing downed cows at Hallmark in the early 1990s in the video that inspired legislators to make that abuse a crime. And two decades later he was convicted under the same law his earlier misconduct had inspired.

In addition to the two criminal convictions, the USDA shut down Hallmark in early 2008. Within a day of the first *Washington Post* story about HSUS's investigation, the USDA pulled its five inspectors from the plant. Without USDA inspectors present, it was illegal for Hallmark to slaughter a single animal. As is the standard practice, the USDA told Hallmark that the inspectors would return to work only after Hallmark could satisfy the agency that there would be no more violations of the federal Humane Methods of Slaughter Act and USDA regulations. Hallmark wasn't able to do this.

A few words on the Humane Methods of Slaughter Act, which reaches back to the earliest days of humane work in this country and to the passage of federal legislation in the 1950s. Since the enactment in 1978 of some important amendments to the act, every U.S. commercial cattle-slaughter operation has had to comply with this federal law. It bans inhumane animal handling at slaughterhouses. That humane handling requirement applies everywhere at a slaughter facility, including on farm animal transport trucks and in holding pens—the very places where much of the Hallmark abuse happened. The law applies to pigs and other hooved animals, but the USDA has long insisted the act's term *livestock* was not meant to include any poultry. As a result, there is no federal poultry humane handling requirement, which leaves about nine billion animals, mostly chickens, without even the modest protection of the federal law that Hallmark skirted for decades.

A few weeks after the forced shut down, the USDA also insisted on a recall of more than 143,000,000 pounds of Hallmark beef and the agency made Hallmark cover the cost.[31] This was, and remains, the largest meat recall in U.S. history. Hallmark never recovered from the recall, the USDA-forced shut down, and the scandal that started it all.

NEURODEGENERATION ON C-SPAN

I first saw Steve Mendell, president of Hallmark, in a C-Span video, filmed a few weeks after the HSUS released its Hallmark investigation video. He was like a lot of middle-aged white men: earnest, jowly, and convinced by his own story. Unlike Mary and Wolfy, if I didn't know him, I wouldn't have minded sitting next to him on a cross-country flight. But the video was of him testifying before a Congressional subcommittee that had subpoenaed him to come in and explain his role in what remains arguably the country's biggest slaughterhouse scandal. [32]

At that hearing, Mendell read a prepared statement to the subcommittee.[33] He testified that the cows the HSUS undercover investigator documented as they were being abused should have been "treated humanely. They were not. . . ." But, he claimed, "these cows were not harvested and they did not enter the food supply."[34] This is a key issue, because slaughter of a downed cow—or, as he euphemistically put it, the harvesting of such a cow—violated federal food safety regulations.

When he finished reading his statement, subcommittee chairman Representative Bart Stupak of Michigan played a short HSUS video clip showing Hallmark employees prodding and dragging a downed cow to try to get her through a chute to the kill floor. When they couldn't force her to stand, the video shows them dragging her in to be bolted through her skull and killed. After seeing the video, which had been posted on the HSUS website, Mendell admitted that it looked like that downed cow had in fact gone into the human food supply.[35]

Across the continent, I was back in the wicker rocker with Shoo on my lap, watching the live feed and as happy as I was nervous. Every day since I first watched the footage, my emotional investment, dread, and excitement about how this story would end had been ratcheting up. And here was a decisive victory playing out in flat tones and pallid C-Span colors. By this point, Shoo would've been asleep, but I was riveted. The regulations that ban the slaughter of downed cattle are in place because those animals are more likely to carry bovine spongiform encephalopathy (BSE), also known as mad cow disease. Consuming meat from a cow carrying BSE leads to Creutzfeldt-Jakob disease, a human neurodegenerative disorder that can take up to twenty years to manifest. Once it does kick in, however, it is always fatal. Because of that long dormant stage, Representative Stupak challenged Mendell's repeated claims that the meat from abused downed cows posed no food safety threat: "So, the statement that there's been no illness because of this recall. We don't know that until on an average thirteen years later, because of the incubation period. Correct?"

"That would be correct," Mendell replied.

Mendell's admission and the USDA's conclusion that Hallmark had illegally slaughtered downed cows had implications that Mendell could not have foreseen while he testified.

FALSE CLAIMS

Despite Navarro's and Sanchez's criminal convictions, and all the blame heaped upon them, it wasn't enough to spare Mendell and the companies running Hallmark. The final hit took shape as the HSUS quietly filed a lawsuit in a Riverside, California, federal district court, just as *The Washington Post* was breaking the Hallmark investigation in early 2008. False Claims Act lawsuits, like ours, target individuals or companies who defraud the federal government. Such lawsuits are initially only shared with a federal district court and the U.S. Attorney's office. Not even the defendants, the people accused of defrauding the federal government, get to know that the lawsuit has been filed. After it's filed, the U.S. Attorney has several months to investigate the case and decide whether to join the lawsuit against the alleged defrauders. The feds join less than 25 percent of these lawsuits, and when they do not join, the lawsuit's chances of success plummet. Conversely, the chances of winning go up if the feds do join. They joined our lawsuit.

The complaint we filed alleged that Hallmark broke conditions in its contracts to sell ground beef to the USDA for the federal school lunch program and other federal food programs. In the years before the scandal broke, Hallmark had sold upwards of $150 million of ground beef to the USDA pursuant to contracts that all mandated that the company treat cows humanely. Those federal contracts also specifically prohibited selling beef from any downed cows to the USDA. The False Claims Act imposes some crushing financial penalties, the most significant of which is that whatever damages a court determines the feds suffered are multiplied by three.[36] So, if the court determined the feds were ripped off to the full extent that the HSUS alleged (about $150 million), that becomes a liability of more than half-a-billion dollars.[37]

Those behind Hallmark, including Mendell, fought the lawsuit until 2013, when they agreed to settle before a trial. As *The New York Times* described it, "The parties settled the lawsuit for $155 million, but the Justice Department determined the defendants could only afford to pay a total of about $3.1 million because they were financially devastated by the recall."[38] This remains the single largest animal cruelty–related U.S. court judgment.

THE UPSHOT

While writing this book in the summer of 2017, I stayed for a bit in West Hollywood a few blocks from my former kitchen-nook-home. I woke up at six on my first Hollywood morning and happily hiked up the hills toward my old nook on my way to Runyon Canyon. As I waited for the light on Hollywood Boulevard, cars roared by at about 50 m.p.h. on that residential street. Then a guy with an apparently weak will to live rolled by on a bike amid the speeding and texting drivers. I thought, *What kind of idiot bikes down Hollywood Boulevard?* Then I smiled, realizing that I had been *precisely* that idiot twice a day, five days a week in 1998. I like to think my foolishness was the victimless kind because it didn't get me smeared into the side of a speeding Land Rover. Also, I was a *young* idiot. Mendell was in his forties when his *tontería* came to light.

My luck held out night after night biking down Sunset's faded lane lines before turning up and onto Hollywood Boulevard. Mendell's luck gave out in the Hallmark scandal despite his life's outward appearance of quiet sensibleness.

When the 2013 settlement was inked, I wasn't completely satisfied, which is ridiculous because I'd always known it was likely that Mendell and the other suits would come out of all of this unscathed. I'm not in a full-body cast caused by my late 1990s Sunset Boulevard biking idiocy, and Mendell wasn't left wearing nothing but a barrel, because this isn't a fair world. Ask the cows.

The criminal penalties borne by the two men caught on video are categorically far worse than the financial and reputational penalties that hit the likes of Mendell. This was never lost on those of us that worked on the Hallmark investigation and its aftermath. We worked hard to get the district attorney to pursue the company and its executives criminally, and not just Navarro and Sanchez. One afternoon as I stayed at a dear friend's house in L.A., I grew tired of trying to schedule a call about this with a middle-management prosecutor. So, in the late afternoon, I told his secretary I was just going to drive out and hang out at his office until he would talk to me about charges against those at the top. I was halfway out to Chino when the prosecutor called me. I pulled off the freeway into a community college parking lot. I paced around as I tried to explain why it was not just feasible to charge these people, but that it was important to do so, and that such a prosecution had a high likelihood of success. There were horses in the pasture bordering the parking lot where I took this call. They came over to me and we shared a moment. They looked at me hoping for a treat as I tried to reason with a lawyer. The call ended and I was sure this guy would never file the charges we asked for.

On the drive back to my friend's house, I realized the scene with the horses and me was reminiscent of my favorite moments in *Michael Clayton*, one of my favorite movies. George Clooney (who coincidentally looks a fair bit like me) plays the eponymous character, a mightily stressed out big firm lawyer. Just after dawn, he leaves his big black Mercedes idling on the side of a two-lane rural New York road and walks up a hill to spend a few quiet moments with three horses. As it was for Clooney's Michael Clayton, things did not work out as I wanted them to, but it could've been a hell of a lot worse.

In addition to cratering Hallmark, the 2008 scandal hurt the entire U.S. meat industry. Some of that damage is hard to measure, and it may continue for decades. A 2010 Purdue and Kansas State University study examined grocery store sales of beef, pork, and poultry before and after extensive news coverage of the Hallmark scandal. The authors concluded that "[a]s a whole, media attention to animal welfare has significant, negative effects on U.S. meat demand."[39] They also recognized that "[i]ncreasing media attention to animal welfare issues triggers consumers to purchase less meat rather than reallocate expenditures across competing meats."[40]

In 2008, total U.S. beef consumption dropped from about 28 billion pounds to roughly 27 billion pounds—that's a billion pounds of cattle no longer going into Americans' mouths—and consumption continued to decrease, dropping further to 24.8 billion in 2015.[41] It has since trended back up, but as of 2018 (the latest figures available) it hadn't yet reached the highs it was at before Hallmark.[42] That decrease in beef consumption is, of course, not all due to the Hallmark investigation. There are likely many explanations for it, including increasing evidence connecting meat to climate change, heart disease, and cancers. But Hallmark and the wave of subsequent investigations played a role. The investigations are recurring reminders that however far we might be from the transport trucks, holding pens, or kill floors, there is someone like Daniel Navarro, Rafael Sanchez Herrera, or Steve Mendell acting on our behalf.

A lot changed because of Hallmark, but not enough. In the scandal's wake, the USDA improved its humane handling rules for calves and mature cattle, but, so far, the agency has not extended those improvements to other species. The USDA eliminated loopholes in its regulations that had incentivized slaughter plants to keep downed calves and mature cattle alive, as well as to abuse and torment them in an effort to get them up and walking to slaughter. The agency reasoned that the Humane Methods of Slaughter Act's command that all handling of animals at slaughter facilities must be humane required a bright-line rule for prompt, humane euthanasia. Anything less would increase the chances of downed cows being dragged, shocked, and clubbed, as was the case at Hallmark. Relatedly, changing this rule for calves and mature cattle would improve animal welfare at farms and in transport by removing any financial incentive to send weak, injured, and sick animals to slaughter.

I'm not satisfied with these modest rule improvements for a couple of reasons. First, transport is harder on a pig than it is on nearly any other farm animal. Pigs regularly collapse on trucks, often more quickly than mature cattle do. In huge numbers, they arrive at slaughter facilities unable to stand or they've died en route. The USDA has yet to improve its rules and remove the incentives to abuse downed pigs the way cows were abused at Hallmark.

Secondly, the rules don't matter if the USDA is too weak in the knees to meaningfully punish rule-breakers. For more than forty years, the USDA has failed to use its power to press for federal criminal charges for even the most horrific of Humane Methods of Slaughter Act violations. Obviously, Congress created those criminal penalties because the prospect of a multi-year stint in federal prison is a powerful deterrent. The USDA has only pushed for criminal humane handling charges on three occasions, each against tiny backyard slaughter operations in Florida. To put this in perspective, imagine how it would look if, in a forty-year span, the IRS only ever sought criminal penalties against a few immigrant-run roadside fruit stands.

On a more fundamental level, I'm not satisfied with what happened after Hallmark, because I see no need for operations like Hallmark in the first place. They exist to make products our federal nutrition experts tell us we don't need to eat. And a "spent" dairy cow bleeding on the dirt of a slaughter pen drank thousands of gallons of water on the way to this stupid, tragic end. Over her truncated lifespan, she consumed even more water in the form of alfalfa grown just to cycle through her, with the overwhelming majority of that feed becoming manure. And the methane and other gases generated by farm animals is a strong and growing driver of climate change. In the years since Hallmark's collapse, more people are beginning to do what I did in 1998 as I read that *LA Times* article in my nook: They are beginning to connect these dots and are choosing to skip meat, dairy, and eggs.

There are other, less quantifiable ways to value what happened at Hallmark. The investigation and its findings generated a lot of news attention and put the slaughtering industry on notice that groups like the HSUS actually could land on upper management with both feet even when the USDA wouldn't. The False Claims Act case made clear that there would be consequences beyond blaming and firing low-level workers caught on undercover video. As my boss Jonathan Lovvorn put it, "The meat industry should take notice that if they defraud federal agencies and the American taxpayers by abusing animals, there will be serious consequences for their inhumane and reckless actions."[43]

The Hallmark media coverage also inspired activists, something that hasn't been measured and probably can't be. In 1998, a single *Los Angeles Times* article about California's Downed Animal Protection Act made an immediate, and probably permanent, impression on me, despite the fact that I was dim enough to bike down the middle of Sunset Boulevard at twilight. Because of the Hallmark investigation and all that it precipitated, *The Los Angeles Times* printed more than ten articles, including three editorials, covering the scandal, spanning from the day the video was posted online in February 2008 to the 2013 inking of Mendell's and others' settlement of the False Claims Act lawsuit. *The New York Times* also published several articles and editorialized on the issue. All the major news wire services ran multiple stories that were printed in large and small newspapers across the country, and the video footage was on national evening news programs and CNN.

Before I read that article in 1998, I had no idea that people clubbed prone farm animals. I never forgot that as I went through law school and became an animal protection attorney.

In the End the Wolf Wins

In their different ways, both Mary and Mendell taught me to err on the side of looking a fool because you care. A life that depends on *not* caring about suffering must dull you emotionally, and, as far as I can tell, it makes you a dull person. Or maybe the callous, exploitative life attracts people like Mendell as much as it repels people like me, Mary, and Wolfy. You can be dull and still end up looking a fool, remembered—if at all—for your fuck-ups.

I wish I could say that Mary and her gray wolf alter ego were our best volunteers, but they weren't. Other volunteers in her age bracket did more than she did, donated more, and required far less of my attention. Mary was what some people incorrectly think of as a typical animal activist: eccentric, abrasive, and prone to tears. But wheelchair-bound and approaching her eighth decade, she was passionately doing what she could to help, which is more than I can say about long stretches of my adult life.

I may bow out before my sixties, but it won't be because I'm afraid of becoming like Mary. I wouldn't be confident in that conclusion had it gone differently with Hallmark. It would have been far more plausible for Hallmark to have rolled out from under every atomic knee drop and elbow slam we directed at them. If they had, my rocking-chair tears falling on Shoo's black-and-white fur would have marked nothing but the first of dozens of furious, futile afternoons spent running full tilt at a silo set to explode.

My colleagues and I worked intensely all day, every day, to hit Hallmark as hard as possible, and we knew we might not even leave a bruise. Some of my colleagues worked through the night, sleeping in shifts on yoga mats pulled out of their office filing cabinets. I'm inherently lazy, so I'm never happy about having to work through the weekend. I can't speak for all of my colleagues, but since Hallmark, when I do work those long hours, it's partly because I know it can pay off. If it hadn't gone down the way it had, I might not be able to hang in there through the inevitable defeats that come with litigating for farm animals. A setback like that, coming just a couple of years into my life as a lawyer, might have had me faking my own death and then popping up as a maladjusted Silverlake barista.

As far as I can tell, Steve Mendell's adult life before the Hallmark scandal was dignified, quiet, and comfortable. He financed that comfort with systemic, self-destructive exploitation. Hallmark sought out "spent" dairy cows because therein lay the greatest profits. Some may wonder if Mendell was truly surprised by the HSUS video footage, as he claimed to be. Maybe, despite his daily work at Hallmark for over a decade and his position of control over the operation, he never saw the abuse the HSUS documented in just a few weeks. If somehow he didn't know, he certainly could and should have.

In the end, whatever dignity and privacy he had quickly burned off, like a coastal morning fog. During the scandal, the *Press Enterprise* newspaper repeatedly sent reporters to his home. Writing about one visit, the paper reported that Mendell

> also declined to comment when contacted one recent morning at his oceanview Newport Beach home, where he was watering his flowers while wearing an In-N-Out Burger T-shirt.[44]

Months before, on the same day that the HSUS released its undercover video, In-N-Out dropped Hallmark as a supplier.[45]

ACKNOWLEDGMENTS

Thanks to Harvard Law School's Animal Law and Policy Program, which gave me the fellowship that made this book possible. Chris Green, the Rick Wakeman of animal law, at Harvard provided key guidance and help from the beginning. Martin Rowe, Emily Lavieri-Scull, and Lantern Publishing & Media took a chance by publishing this odd book, and it wouldn't have happened otherwise. I'm very grateful for Martin's patient, excellent editing.

Thanks to my brilliant and generous friends who edited and punched up: Becky Jenkins, Sue Coe, Jon Lovvorn, Boo Davis (who also helped with the cover), Lida Husik, Matt Hayek, Jen "NBH" Gannett, Jessie Brockway, Adrienne Craig, Danielle Elefritz, Erin Williams, Nick Arrivo, and especially Camila Cossio and Miyun Park. Michael Greger and Sara Shields gave me helpful advice and content and I'm very gratful for their help. Thank you also to my sister, Claire Brandt, for the illustrations.

My Tacoma friends, especially Randy "concert pants" Tonkin who let me use his real name.

Thank you to Jet Black, and Oracle and the other cafes where I wrote, stared out of windows, and rewrote.

I owe a lot to my my HSUS colleagues and friends, particularly the lawyers past and present, and to Bruce "three scoops" Wagman. Bernie Unti's research and writing was a huge help to me, as was his excellent, committed editing.

A second, huge thank you to Sue Coe for the cover art. If any animal activists will be remembered from our era it should be Sue. She has no equal when it comes to talent, vision, intelligence, compassion, humor, and making the most of free continental breakfasts at affordable London hotels.

NOTES

All URLs were accessed as of May 19, 2020.

APHIS: Animal and Plant Health Inspection Service
CDC: Centers for Disease Control and Prevention
DHHS: Department of Health and Human Services
DOJ: Department of Justice
EPA: Environmental Protection Agency
FAO: United Nations Food and Agriculture Organization
FDA: Food and Drug Administration
GAO: Government Accountability Office
FSIS: Food Safety and Inspection Service
HSUS: Humane Society of the United States
USDA: United States Department of Agriculture
WHO: World Health Organization

Preface

1. Taylor Telford and Kimberly Kindy, "As They Rushed to Maintain U.S. Meat Supply, Big Processors Saw Plants Become Covid-19 Hot Spots, Worker Illnesses Spike," *Washington Post*, April 25, 2020.

2. Peter Waldman, Lydia Mulvany, and Polly Mosendz, "Cold, Crowded, Deadly: How U.S. Meat Plants Became a Virus Breeding Ground," *Bloomberg*, May 7, 2020.

3. Sarah Rieger, "3rd Death Linked to Canada's Largest COVID-19 Outbreak at Alberta Slaughterhouse," *CBC*, May 11, 2020.

4. LULAC, LULAC Responds to Trump Administration Declaring Meat Plants "Critical Infrastructure" And Treating Essential Workers As Disposable, n.d., https://lulac.org/news/pr/LULAC_Responds_To_Trump_Administration_Declaring_Meat_Plants_Critical_Infrastructure.

Introduction
1. *Katko v. Briney*, 183 N.W.2d 657 (Sup. Ct. IA. 1971).
2. David Brown, "USDA Orders Largest Meat Recall in U.S. History," *Washington Post*, February 18, 2008.
3. Associated Press, "Government Bans 'Downer' Cows from Food Supply," *The Star Online*, March 15, 2009.
4. National Institute of Neurological Disorders and Stroke, "Creutzfeldt-Jakob Disease Fact Sheet," https://www.ninds.nih.gov/Disorders/Patient-Caregiver-Education/Fact-Sheets/Creutzfeldt-Jakob-Disease-Fact-Sheet.
5. DHHS, "2015–2020 Dietary Guidelines for Americans," 8th Edition, December 2015, https://health.gov/dietaryguidelines/2015/guidelines.
6. Nat Bearman, "The 10 Biggest Food Recalls in U.S. History," *Money Inc.*, http://moneyinc.com/biggest-food-recalls-u-s-history/.
7. Michael Winter, "Calif. Meat Packer to Pay $317M Over Abuse, Recall," *USA Today*, November 16, 2012.

Chapter 1: Diet and the Upper and Lower Primates
1. Sandi Doughton, "Aged, Beloved Ivan the Gorilla from Tacoma Dies at Atlanta Zoo," *The Seattle Times*, August 22, 2012.
2. Barbara King, "Ivan Dies at 50: A Gorilla Life, Remembered," *National Public Radio*, August 23, 2012.
3. Jon Osterberg, "Tacoma's Ivan the Gorilla Dies in Atlanta," Pemco, August 24, 2012, https://pemco.com/blog/tacomas-ivan-the-gorilla-dies-in-atlanta.
4. Allison Argo, "Ivan the Gorilla Lived Alone in a Shopping Mall for Over 20 Years (The Urban Gorilla)," YouTube Video, 1992, https://www.youtube.com/watch?v=OYYL2LxotA8.
5. *Ibid.* at 2:58.
6. Doughton, "Aged, Beloved Ivan,"
7. Special to *The New York Times*, "A Gorilla Sulks in a Mall as His Future Is Debated," *New York Times*, October 17, 1993.
8. Ted Nugent, The Endangered Species Act, the EPA, Humane Society of the US Are All Rotten Frauds & Scams from Hell. Facebook, December 29, 2013, https://www.facebook.com/tednugent/posts/10151883537692297.
9. *David Mikkelson, "Ted Nugent Dodged the Draft?" Snopes.com (last modified April 20, 2012), https://www.snopes.com/fact-check/the-artful-dodger/.*
10. For background on the history of federal endangered species statutes, see "A History of the Endangered Species Act of 1973: Timeline," U.S. Fish and Wildlife Service, n.d., https://www.fws.gov/endangered/laws-policies/timeline.html.

11. For the U.S. Fish and Wildlife Service's Endangered Species Act listing information on gorillas, see "Gorilla: Species Profile," U.S. Fish and Wildlife Service, n.d., https://ecos.fws.gov/ecp0/profile/speciesProfile?sId=4080. The Lacey Act, enacted in 1900, created civil and criminal penalties for interstate and international commerce in protected species. See, "Lacey Act: International Affairs," U.S. Fish and Wildlife Services, n.d., https://www.fws.gov/international/laws-treaties-agreements/us-conservation-laws/lacey-act.html. In 1975, gorillas were protected by the Convention on International Trade in Endangered Species of Wild Fauna and Flora (CITES) as well. See "Gorilla: Species Plus," CITES, n.d. https://www.speciesplus.net/#/taxon_concepts/7116/legal.

12. Scott Weathers and Sophie Hermanns, "Open Letter: Open Letter: Why WHO Should Address Industrial Animal Farming," Grain.org, May 25, 2017, https://www.grain.org/article/5729-open-letter-why-who-should-address-industrial-animal-farming/.

13. FAO, *World Agriculture: Toward 2015/2030: An FAO Perspective* (2003), 85 fn. 20, http://www.fao.org/tempref/docrep/fao/005/y4252E/y4252e.pdf.

14. FAO, *Global Livestock Production Systems* (2011), 43, http://www.fao.org/docrep/014/i2414e/i2414e05.pdf.

15. Tianrui Poultry Equipment, "Tianrui Automatic H Type Poultry Battery Cages for Layers," 1, https://farmingport.en.made-in-china.com/product/WXIxbFRdZPrY/China-Tianrui-Automatic-H-Type-Poultry-Battery-Cages-for-Layers.html.

16. Michael Pollan, "Big Food Strikes Back: Why Did the Obamas Fail to Take on Corporate Agriculture?" *New York Times Magazine*, October 5, 2016. I used this source for information on the political and economic power of the feed, meat, dairy, and agriculture sectors.

17. *The Mighty Boosh*, "Eels," Season 3, Episode 1. Directed by Paul King; written by Julian Barratt and Noel Fielding. BBC, November 15, 2007; Elizabeth Kolbert. "Flesh of Your Flesh," *New Yorker*, November 9, 2009.

18. *Fresh Air*, "'Tales' of Pig Intelligence, Factory Farming and Humane Bacon," interview of Barry Estabrook by Dave Davies, *National Public Radio*, May 5, 2015, http://www.npr.org/sections/thesalt/2015/05/05/402584436/tales-of-pig-intelligence-factory-farming-and-humane-bacon.

19. Kolbert, "Flesh of Your Flesh,"

20. Michael Gross, "The Paradoxical Evolution of Agriculture," *Current Biology* 23, no. 16 (August 2013): 667–670, https://doi.org/10.1016/j.cub.2013.08.001. For an overview of prehistory and agriculture, see Kent Flannery and Joyce Marcus, *The Creation of Inequality: How Our Prehistoric Ancestors Set the Stage for Monarchy, Slavery and Empire* (Cambridge, MA: Harvard University Press, 2014).

21. *Assoc. des Éleveurs de Canards v. Harris*, 729 F.3d 937 (9th Cir. 2013), oral argument at 5:00, https://www.ca9.uscourts.gov/media/view.php?pk_id=0000010793.
22. *Assoc. des Éleveurs de Canards et d'Oies du Québec v. Becerra*, 870 F.3d 1140, 4 (9th Cir. 2017), http://cdn.ca9.uscourts.gov/datastore/opinions/2017/09/15/15-55192.pdf.
23. *Ibid.*
24. *Assoc. des Éleveurs de Canards v. Harris*, 729 F.3d 937 (9th Cir. 2013), oral argument at 5:20, https://www.ca9.uscourts.gov/media/view.php?pk_id=0000010793.
25. Maura Dolan, "California's Foie Gras Ban Is Upheld by Appeals Court," *Los Angeles Times*, August 30, 2013.
26. Kolbert, "Flesh of Your Flesh,"
27. Leo Tolstoy, *On Civil Disobedience and Non-Violence* (New York: Signet Classic: 1967), 170–171. Tolstoy placed this text in quotations, but did not attribute the quote to anyone, and he makes clear he agrees with the point.
28. Kolbert, "Flesh of Your Flesh,"
29. *Ibid.*
30. Elizabeth Kolbert, "Congress Moves to Sabotage the Paris Climate Summit," *The New Yorker*, December 4, 2015.
31. Fiona Harvey, "Eat Less Meat for Greater Food Security, British Population Urged," *The Guardian*, June 4, 2013.
32. DHHS, "2015–2020 Dietary Guidelines for Americans," 8th Edition, December 2015, https://health.gov/dietaryguidelines/2015/guidelines.
33. *Ibid.*, Q&A, https://health.gov/dietaryguidelines/2015/qanda.asp.
34. *Ibid.*, Appendix 14: Food Safety Principles and Guidance, https://health.gov/dietaryguidelines/2015/guidelines/appendix-14/.
35. WHO, "Q&A on the Carcinogenicity of the Consumption of Red Meat and Processed Meat," October 2015, http://www.who.int/features/qa/cancer-red-meat/en/.
36. DHHS, "2015–2020 Dietary Guidelines for Americans," 8th Edition, 25.
37. *Ibid.*
38. *Ibid.*, 15.
39. *Ibid.*: 32, 90. See also, Healy, Melissa. "New Dietary Guidelines for Americans: Watch Your Sugar, but Enjoy the Eggs and Coffee," *Los Angeles Times*, January 7, 2016, http://www.latimes.com/science/sciencenow/la-sci-sn-dietary-guidelines-eggs-coffee-20160107-story.html.
40. DHHS, "2015–2020 Dietary Guidelines for Americans," 8th Edition, 24.
41. Stacy Simon. "World Health Organization Says Processed Meat Causes Cancer. American Cancer Society," Cancer.org, October 26, 2015, https://www.cancer.org/latest-news/

world-health-organization-says-processed-meat-causes-cancer.html; "Cancer Stat Facts: Colon and Rectum Cancer," National Cancer Institute, n.d., https://seer.cancer.gov/statfacts/html/colorect.html.

42. Jennifer Singleterry, *The Costs of Cancer: Addressing Patient Costs.* The American Cancer Society Cancer Action Network, April 2017, https://www.acscan.org/sites/default/files/Costs%20of%20Cancer%20-%20Final%20Web.pdf.

43. Simon, "World Health Organization."

44. CDC, "Smoking & Tobacco Use," n.d., https://www.cdc.gov/tobacco/data_statistics/fact_sheets/fast_facts/index.htm.

45. Personal correspondence with author.

46. Associated Press, "Ivan the Gorilla May Have Found Romance in Atlanta," *Seattle Times*, April 18, 2005.

47. Doughton, "Aged, Beloved Ivan."

Chapter 2: Having a Life Span Is Not the Same as Having a Life

1. J. P. Felt, *Hostages of Fortune: Child Labor Reform in New York State* (Syracuse, NY: Syracuse University Press, 2015), 175.

2. Jane Addams, *Twenty Years at Hull-House with Autobiographical Notes* (New York: Macmillan 1912, http://digital.library.upenn.edu/women/addams/hullhouse/hullhouse.html, 86–87.

3. *Ibid.*

4. Diane L. Beers, *For the Prevention of Cruelty: The History and Legacy of Animal Rights Activism in the United States* (Athens, OH: Swallow Press/Ohio University Press, 2006), 227, n. 4.

5. Howard Markel, M.D., "Case Shined First Light on Abuse of Children," *The New York Times*, December 14, 2009.

6. *Ibid.*

7. *Ibid.*

8. *Ibid.*

9. Beers, *For the Prevention of Cruelty*, 93.

10. *Ibid.*

11. *Ibid.*

12. International Labor Organization, *Global Estimates of Child Labor: Results and Trends 2012–2016*, September 2012, http://www.ilo.org/wcmsp5/groups/public/---dgreports/---dcomm/documents/publication/wcms_575499.pdf.

13. *Ibid.*, 34.

14. *Ibid.*

15. *Ibid.*

16. *Ibid.*, 2.

17. Jack Healy, "5-Year-Olds Work Farm Machinery, and Injuries to Follow," *The New York Times*, January 29, 2018.
18. CDC: The National Institute for Occupational Safety and Health, "Child Labor Research Needs," n.d., https://www.cdc.gov/niosh/docs/97-143/ default.html; and Healy, "5-Year-Olds Work Farm Machinery."
19. Anthony Schick, "Child Farm Labor in Oregon and the U.S.: Big Dangers, Little Change," *The Oregonian*, September 29, 2012.
20. *Ibid.*
21. *Ibid.*
22. James D. Schmidt, *Industrial Violence and the Legal Origins of Child Labor* (Cambridge: Cambridge University Press, 2010), 86.
23. *Ibid.*
24. *Ibid.*
25. Jane Addams, "Child Labor and Pauperism," National Conference of Charities and Correction, *Proceedings* (May 9, 1903): 114–121, esp. 115, https://digital.janeaddams.ramapo.edu/items/show/1185.
26. Upton Sinclair, *I, Candidate for Governor: and How I Got Licked* (Berkeley: University of California Press, 1994), 109.
27. Stanford Encyclopedia of Philosophy, "Section 1.3.1: Rational Persons," n.d., https://plato.stanford.edu/entries/moral-animal/#RatiPers.
28. Stanford Encyclopedia of Philosophy, "Section 1.2: Human Exceptionalism," n.d., https://plato.stanford.edu/entries/moral-animal/#HumaExce.
29. *U.S. v. Oregon State Medical Society*, 343 U. S. 326, 333 (1952); *U.S. v. W. T. Grant Co.*, 345 U.S. 629, 633 (1953).
30. Gro V. Amdam and Anne Lene Hovland. "Measuring Animal Preferences and Choice Behaviour," *Nature Education Knowledge* 3, no. 10 (2011): 74, https://www.nature.com/scitable/knowledge/ library/measuring-animal-preferences-and-choice-behavior-23590718.
31. Hans A. M. Spoolder, *et al.* "Provision of Straw as a Foraging Substrate Reduces the Development of Excessive Chain and Bar Manipulation in Food Restricted Sows," *Applied Animal Behaviour Science* 43, no. 4 (July 1995): 249–262, esp. 250, https://doi.org/10.1016/0168-1591(95)00566-B; and J. J. McGlone and S. D. Fullwood, "Behavior, Reproduction, and Immunity of Crated Pregnant Gilts: Effects of High Dietary Fiber and Rearing Environment," *Journal of Animal Science* 79, no. 6 (June 2001): 1466–1474, esp. 1469–1470, http://doi.org/10.2527/2001.7961466x.
32. Spoolder, *et al.*, "Provision of Straw," 249–262, 250.
33. Temple Grandin, "Perspectives on Transportation Issues: The Importance of Having Physically Fit Cattle and Pigs." *Journal of Animal Science* 79, W Suppl. (July 2000), http://www.grandin.com/behaviour/perspectives. transportation.issues.html.

34. The Pig Site, "Basic Pig Husbandry—The Weaner," April 18, 2006, http://www.thepigsite.com/articles/1616/basic-pig-husbandry-the-weaner/.

35. M. A. Sutherland, *et al.* "Tail Docking in Pigs: Acute Physiological and Behavioural Responses," *Animal* 2, no. 2 (2008): 292–297, https://doi.org/10.1017/S1751731107001450.

36. American Veterinary Medical Association, *Literature Review on the Welfare Implications of Teeth Clipping, Tail Docking and Permanent Identification of Piglets* (July 15, 2014), 3, https://www.avma.org/sites/default/files/resources/practices_piglets_bgnd.pdf.

37. *Ibid.*

38. *Ibid.*; also Sutherland, *et al.*, "Tail Docking in Pigs."

39. A. Prunier, *et al.*, "A Review of the Welfare Consequences of Surgical Castration in Piglets and the Evaluation of Non-surgical Methods." *Animal Welfare* 15 (2006): 277–289, https://ec.europa.eu/food/sites/food/files/animals/docs/aw_prac_farm_pigs_cast-alt_research_inra_2006-prunier_castration-aw.pdf. See also Palmer J. Holden and M. E. Ensminger, *Swine Science*, 7th Edition (Upper Saddle River, NJ: Pearson Prentice Hall, 2005), 365–366. See also The European Food Safety Authority Scientific Panel on Animal Health and Welfare, *Opinion of the Scientific Panel on Animal Health and Welfare on a Request from the Commission Related to Welfare Aspects of the Castration of Piglets*, July 2004, https//doi.org/10.2527/2005.831216x.

40. A. Prunier, *et al.*, "Effects of Castration, Tooth Resection, or Tail Docking on Plasma Metabolites and Stress Hormones in Young Pigs," *Journal of Animal Science* 83 (2005): 216–222, https://doi.org/10.2527/2005.831216x.

41. American Veterinary Medical Association, *Literature Review on the Welfare Implications of Swine Castration* (May 29, 2013), https://www.avma.org/KB/Resources/LiteratureReviews/Documents/swine_castration_bgnd.pdf, 2.

42. *Ibid.*

43. Kitty Block, "HSUS Documents Animal Abuse at Major Pork Producers," January 31, 2012, https://blog.humanesociety.org/2012/01/pig-investigation.html.

44. *Ibid.*

45. *Ibid.*

46. *Ibid.*

47. *Ibid.*

48. HSUS, "The HSUS' Legal Complaints Force Seaboard Foods to Stop False Animal Care Claim," February 18, 2013, http://www.fao.org/ag/againfo/themes/animal-welfare/news-detail/en/c/169871/. See also "Seaboard Foods Settles HSUS Complaint,"

Meat + Poultry, February 2, 2013, https://www.meatpoultry.com/articles/9526-seaboard-foods-settles-hsus-complaint.

49. Block, "HSUS Documents."

50. Federal Trade Commission, "Advertising FAQ's: A Guide for Small Business," (last modified April 2001), https://www.ftc.gov/tips-advice/business-center/guidance/advertising-faqs-guide-small-business.

51. *Ibid.*

52. HSUS, "The HSUS' Legal Complaints."

53. Aerica Bjurstrom, "Opportunity in Value-added Dairy-beef Calves. Dairy Herd Management," October 18, 2017, https://www.dairyherd.com/article/opportunity-value-added-dairy-beef-calves; and Jamie Johansen, "Veal Myths Busted," Animal AgWired, January 22, 2018, http://animal.agwired.com/2018/01/22/veal-myths-busted/.

54. Bjurstrom, "Opportunity in Value-added Dairy-beef Calves."

55. USDA FSIS, "Veal from Farm to Table," August 2013, https://www.fsis.usda.gov/wps/portal/fsis/topics/food-safety-education/get-answers/food-safety-fact-sheets/meat-preparation/veal-from-farm-to-table/CT_Index.

56. American Veal Association, "Group Housing Goal Nears Reality," September 20, 2017, https://static1.squarespace.com/static/56b1263940261d30708d14b4/t/59c2a6e803596e6e8d4245e9/1505928937831/AVA+Group+Housing+Update+September+2017.pdf; Marian Burros, "Veal to Love, without the Guilt," *The New York Times*, April 18, 2007; HSUS, "Veal Crates: Unnecessary and Cruel," last modified July 2012, https://www.humanesociety.org/sites/default/files/docs/hsus-report-animal-welfare-veal-industry.pdf; and Abby Elizabeth Conway, "Mass. Voters Approve Question 3, Banning Certain Farm Animal Confinement Practices," *WBUR*, November 8, 2016.

57. USDA FSIS, "Veal from Farm to Table"; HSUS, "Felony and Misdemeanor Animal Cruelty Charges Filed in Vermont Dairy Calf Abuse Case," June 4, 2010, http://enviroshop.com/felony-and-misdemeanor-animal-cruelty-charges-filed-in-vermont-dairy-calf-abuse-case/.

58. USDA FSIS, "Veal from Farm to Table."

59. Dairy Herd Management, "Are We Headed for $5.00 Bull Calves?" n.d., https://www.dairyherd.com/article/are-we-headed-500-bull-calves.

60. Mary Bates. "The Emotional Lives of Dairy Cows," *Wired*, June 30, 2014; and Science Daily, "Early Separation of Cow and Calf has Long-term Effects on Emotional Behavior. University of Veterinary Medicine," April 28, 2015, https://www.sciencedaily.com/releases/2015/04/150428081801.htm.

61. Dale A. Moore, *et al.*, *Dairy Calf Housing and Environment: The Science Behind Housing and On-Farm Assessments*. Washington State University Extension, n.d., https://s3.wp.wsu.edu/uploads/sites/2147/2017/07/EM045E.pdf.

62. *Ibid.*, p. 2.

63. Bates, "The Emotional Lives of Dairy Cows,"

64. Sue Coe, *Cruel* (New York: OR Books, 2011), 39.

65. *Superseding Indictment, U.S. v. Castillo-Serrano et al.*, Case No. 3:15CR0024 p. 6, https://www.justice.gov/opa/file/625166/download; and DOJ, "Two Defendants Sentenced for Role in Forced Labor Scheme that Exploited Guatemalan Minors at Ohio Egg Farms," April 11, 2016, https://www.justice.gov/opa/pr/two-defendants-sentenced-role-forced-labor-scheme-exploited-guatemalan-minors-ohio-egg-farms.

66. *Superseding Indictment*, 7.

67. *Ibid.*, 6.

68. *Ibid.*, 7.

69. *Ibid.*, 7–8.

70. *Ibid.*, 8.

71. *Ibid.*, 9.

72. The DOJ. Two Defendants Sentenced,

73. *Superseding Indictment*, 10–11.

74. *Ibid.*, 11.

75. *Ibid.*

76. *Ibid.*, 12.

77. *Ibid.*

78. *Ibid.*

79. DOJ, "Fourth Defendant Charged in Ohio Trafficking Scheme Involving Immigrant Minors," December 27, 2017, https://www.justice.gov/opa/pr/fourth-defendant-charged-ohio-trafficking-scheme-involving-immigrant-minors.

80. DOJ, "Two Defendants Sentenced."

81. Austin Alonzo, "Top 20 US Egg Company Profiles," Watt Agnet, February 11, 2016, https://www.wattagnet.com/articles/25649-top---us-egg-company-profiles.

82. Eric Heisig, "Egg Producer Changed Protocol Following Labor-trafficking Raid, Company Says," *Cleveland.com*, January 27, 2016, http://www.cleveland.com/court-justice/index.ssf/2016/01/egg_producer_changed_protocol.html.

83. *Ibid.*

84. *Ibid.*

85. Eric Heisig, "Guatemalan Human Trafficker Sentenced for Forcing Laborers to Live in Squalor, on Egg Farms," *Cleveland.com*, June 27, 2016, http://www.cleveland.com/court-justice/index.ssf/2016/06/guatemalan_human_trafficker_se.html.

86. Raphael Guatteo, *et al.*, "Sources of Known and/or Potential Pain in Farm Animals," *Advances in Animal Biosciences* 5, no. 3 (2014): 319–332, esp. 325, https://doi.org/10.1017/S204047001400020X.

87. Ülkü Gülcihan Şimşek, *et al.*, "Effects of Conventional and Organic Rearing Systems and Hen Age on Oxidative Stress Parameters of Blood and Ovarian Tissues in Laying Hens," Ankara Universitesi Veteriner Fakultesi Dergisi 65, no. 1018: 85–91, https://doi.org/10.1501/Vetfak_0000002832.

88. Michael C. Appleby, *et al.*, *Poultry Behaviour and Welfare* (Wallingford, UK: CABI Publishing, 2004), 46; and Raphael Guatteo, *et al.*, "Sources of Known."

89. Lesley J. Rogers, *The Development of Brain and Behaviour in the Chicken*, (Wallingford, UK: CABI Publishing, 1995), 219.

90. Sara Shields and Ian Duncan, *A Comparison of the Welfare of Hens in Battery Cages and Alternative Systems*. HSUS Animal Studies Repository, 2009, http://animalstudiesrepository.org/cgi/viewcontent.cgi?article=1014&context=hsus_reps_impacts_on_animals, 5.

91. *Ibid.*, 5.

92. *Ibid.*

93. *Ibid.*, 1.

94. *Ibid*, 9.

95. *Ibid.*

96. Sara Shields and Michael Greger, "Animal Welfare and Food Safety Aspects of Confining Broiler Chickens to Cages," *Animals* 3 (May 13, 2013): 386–400, esp. 393; and Shields and Duncan, *A Comparison of the Welfare of Hens*, 3.

97. Shields and Duncan, *A Comparison of the Welfare of Hens*, 9.

98. Ivan Dinev, "Diseases of Poultry," The Poultry Site, n.d., http://www.thepoultrysite.com/publications/6/diseases-of-poultry/234/cage-layer-fatigue/; Unigwe, *et al.*, "Therapeutic Importance of Calcium Glconate-r in Cage Layer Fatigue (CLF), the Effects on Egg Production, Haematology and Serum Biochemistry of Commercial Layers," *International Journal of Research Studies in Science* (Engineering and Technology) 1, no. 1 (April 2014): 48, https://pdfs.semanticscholar.org/0bcc/47f3b03bf5f94777b6e4727e39ff1d034f53.pdf.

99. Shields and Duncan, *A Comparison of the Welfare of Hens*, 9.

100. Shields, Sara, *et al.*, "A Decade of Progress Toward Ending the Intensive Confinement of Farm Animals in the United States," *Animals* 7, no. 5 (May 7, 2017), https://doi.org/10.3390/ani7050040.

101. European Food Safety Authority, "Report of the Task Force on Zoonoses Data Collection on the Analysis of the Baseline Study on the Prevalence

of *Salmonella* in Holdings of Laying Hen Flocks of *Gallus Gallus*," *EFSA Journal* 97 (2007): 1–84, https://doi.org/10.2903/j.efsa.2007.97r; and Michael Greger, "Housing and Egg Safety Review Ignores Best Available Science on *Salmonella* Risk," *Poultry Science* 90, no. 3 (March 2011): 531.

102. J. J. Carrique-Mas, *et al.*, "Salmonella Enteritidis in Commercial Layer Flocks in Europe: Legislative Background, On-Farm Sampling and Main Challenges," *Brazilian Journal of Poultry Science* 10 (January–March 2008): 1–9, https://doi.org/10.1590/S1516-635X2008000100001; and Greger, "Housing and Egg Safety."

103. Greger, "Housing and Egg Safety"; J. J. Carrique-Mas, *et al.*, "Persistence and Clearance of Different *Salmonella* Serovars in Buildings Housing Laying Hens," *Epidemiology and Infection* 137 (2009): 837–846, https://doi.org/10.1017/S0950268808001568.

104. Greger, "Housing and Egg Safety."

105. *Austin DeCoster and Peter DeCoster v. United States of America*, Brief for the United States in Opposition, http://www.scotusblog.com/wp-content/uploads/2017/04/16-877-BIO.pdf, 4.

106. Tribune News Service, "Government Files Suit Against U.S. Firm on Behalf of Workers," *Chicago Tribune*, May 19, 1998.

107. *Ibid.*

108. *Ibid.*

109. Colin Woodward, "Maine Businessman 'Jack' DeCoster Gets Jail for Selling Tainted Eggs," *Portland Press Herald*, April 13, 2015.

110. Bob Link, "DeCoster Settles Rape, Sex Suit," *Globe Gazette*, October 1, 2002.

111. *Ibid.*

112. Associated Press, "Animal Cruelty Case Against Egg Farm Settled for $125,000," *Bangor Daily News*, June 7, 2010, http://bangordailynews.com/2010/06/07/news/animal-cruelty-case-against-egg-farm-settled-for-125000/.

113. Elizabeth Fuller, "Egg Recall: DeCoster-linked Farm Releases Contaminated Eggs. Again," *Christian Science Monitor*, November 9, 2010; and John Fassler, "Timeline of Shame: Decades of DeCoster Egg Factory Violations," *The Atlantic*, September 16, 2010.

114. Edward D. Murphy, "Judge Lets Egg Baron Jack DeCoster Serve Prison Time in New Hampshire," *Portland Press Herald*, August 14, 2015.

115. *State of Missouri. ex rel. Chris Koster v. Kamala D. Harris*, 847 F.3d 646 (2016), https://cdn.ca9.uscourts.gov/datastore/opinions/2016/11/17/14-17111.pdf.

116. *The State of Missouri v. Xavier Becerra*, Petition for a Writ of Certiorari, http://www.scotusblog.com/wp-content/uploads/2017/03/16-1015-cert-petition.pdf.

117. Dan Flynn, "DeCoster Sentencing in Sioux City Reveals Many Sides of the Story," *Food Safety News*, April 14, 2015, http://www.

foodsafetynews.com/2015/04/decoster-sentencing-in-sioux-city-reveals-many-sides-of-the-story/.

118. Dan Flynn, "Egg Man Starts 3-Month Term as 'Responsible Corporate Official,'" *Food Safety News*, November 24, 2017, http://www.foodsafetynews.com/2017/11/egg-man-starts-3-month-term-as-responsible-corporate-official/.

119. Appleby *et al.*, *Poultry Behaviour and Welfare*, 23–24; Claire A. Weeks, *et al.*, "The Behaviour of Broiler Chickens and Its Modification by Lameness," *Applied Animal Behaviour Science* 67, nos. 1–2 (2000): 111–125, https://doi.org/ 10.1016/S0168-1591(99)00102-1.

120. Appleby, *et al.*, *Poultry Behaviour and Welfare*, 23–24.

121. *Ibid.*

122. *Ibid.*

123. Weeks, *et al.*, "The Behaviour of Broiler Chickens."

124. Appleby, *et al.*, *Poultry Behaviour and Welfare*, 23–24.

125. USDA National Agriculture Statistics Service, "Poultry Slaughter 2019 Summary," Washington DC, February 2020, https://www.nass.usda.gov/Publications/Todays_Reports/reports/pslaan20.pdf, 5.

126. HSUS, "An HSUS Report: Welfare Issues with Selective Breeding for Rapid Growth in Broiler Chickens and Turkeys," n.d., https://www.humanesociety.org/sites/default/files/docs/hsus-report-breeding-chicken-turkeys-welfiss.pdf, 1; and Penn State Extension, "Small-Flock Turkey Production" (last modified February 11, 2005), https://extension.psu.edu/small-flock-turkey-production.

127. VCU Libraries Social Welfare History Project, "National Child Labor Committee by Catherine A. Paul" (last modified 2017), http://socialwelfare.library.vcu.edu/programs/child-welfarechild-labor/national-child-labor-committee/.

128. *The Simpsons*, "Homer vs. the Eighteenth Amendment," Season 8, Episode 18. Directed by Bob Anderson; written by John Swartzwelder, *et al.* Fox, March 16, 1997.

129. Jane Addams, "Child Labor and Pauperism," National Conference of Charities and Correction, *Proceedings* (May 9, 1903): 114–121, esp. 119, https://digital.janeaddams.ramapo.edu/items/show/1185.

130. *Ibid.*

Chapter 3: Rich, Not Famous, and Pushing Drugs

1. Jeff Simmons, "Keynote Speaker 87th National FFA Convention and Expo, November 7, 2014," YouTube Video, https://www.youtube.com/watch?v=zCXakXteZzE&t=319s.

2. *Ibid.*

3. Andrew Martin, "The Case for Juiced-Up Cows in the Organic Age," *Bloomberg*, October 29, 2015.

4. Carlos A. Monteiro, *et al.*, "The Snack Attack," *American Journal of Public Health* 100, no. 6 (June 2010), https://www.ncbi.nlm.nih.gov/pmc/articles/PMC2866614/pdf/975.pdf.

5. Hannah Ritchie and Max Roser, "Meat and Dairy Production," FAO: Our World In Data (last modified November 2019), https://ourworldindata.org/meat-production; and Philip K. Thornton, "Livestock Production: Recent Trends, Future Prospects," *Philosophical Transactions of the Royal Society of London. Series B, Biological Sciences*, September 27, 2010, https://doi.org/10.1098/rstb.2010.0134; and Yukiko Nozaki, "The Future of Global Meat Demand—Implications for the Grain Market," Mitsui & Co, September 9, 2016, https://www.mitsui.com/mgssi/en/report/detail/1221523_10744.html.

6. K. J. M. Varma, "More Chinese Turning Vegetarian," *Business Week*, February 25, 2018, http://businessworld.in/article/More-Chinese-turning-vegetarian/25-02-2018-141723/; and Nozaki, "The Future of Global Meat Demand."

7. Jeff Simmons, *Making Safe, Affordable and Abundant Food a Global Reality*, Range Beef Cow Symposium, University of Nebraska–Lincoln. DigitalCommons@University of Nebraska—Lincoln (2011), https://digitalcommons.unl.edu/cgi/viewcontent.cgi?article=1299&context=rangebeefcowsymp, 9.

8. American Egg Board, "U.S. Egg Industry Egg Facts—Q1 2014," http://www.aeb.org/farmers-and-marketers/industry-overview/69-farmers-marketers/market-data-trends.

9. United Nations, "At UN, Global Leaders Commit to Act on Antimicrobial Resistance," (last modified September 21, 2016), https://news.un.org/en/story/2016/09/539912-un-global-leaders-commit-act-antimicrobial-resistance.

10. *Ibid.*

11. Giorgia Guglielmi, "Are Antibiotics Turning Livestock into Superbug Factories?" *Science*, September 28, 2017, http://www.sciencemag.org/news/2017/09/are-antibiotics-turning-livestock-superbug-factories.

12. WHO, *WHO Guidelines on Use of Medically Important Antimicrobials in Food Producing Animals* (Geneva: 2017), http://apps.who.int/iris/bitstream/10665/258970/1/9789241550130-eng.pdf, xi.

13. *Ibid.*

14. *Ibid.*

15. Johns Hopkins Center for a Livable Future, *Congressional Briefing: Antibiotic Resistance: A Multi-Billion Dollar Health Care Crisis*, December 2, 2009, https://livablefutureblog.com/CLF%20Briefing%20Book.pdf, 1.

16. WHO, *WHO Guidelines on Use.*
17. Anthony So, *et al.*, "An Integrated Systems Approach Is Needed to Ensure the Sustainability of Antibiotic Effectiveness for Both Humans and Animals," *Journal of Law, Medicine & Ethics* 43, no. 3 (Summer 2015): 38–45, esp. 41, https://doi.org/10.1111/jlme.12273.
18. C. Lee Ventola, "The Antibiotic Resistance Crisis—Part 1: Causes and Threats," *Pharmacy & Therapeutics* 40, no. 4 (April 2015): 281, https://www.ncbi.nlm.nih.gov/pmc/articles/PMC4378521/pdf/ptj4004277.pdf.
19. Minnesota Department of Health, *Staphylococcus aureus,* February 2010, https://www.health.state.mn.us/diseases/staph/staph.pdf.
20. Ventola. "The Antibiotic Resistance Crisis."
21. Joan A. Casey, *et al.*, "High-Density Livestock Operations, Crop Field Application of Manure, and Risk of Community-Associated Methicillin-Resistant *Staphylococcus aureus* Infection in Pennsylvania," *JAMA Internal Medicine* 173, no. 21 (November 2013): 1980–1990, https://doi.org/10.1001/jamainternmed.2013.10408.
22. Guglielmi, "Are Antibiotics Turning Livestock into Superbug Factories?"
23. Casey, *et al.*, "High-Density Livestock Operations."
24. Jared S. Hopkins, "Why Big Pharma Wants to Switch Billions of Farm Animals to Vaccines from Antibiotics," *Bloomberg*, August 5, 2016.
25. Karen L. Tang, *et al.*, "Restricting the Use of Antibiotics in Food-producing Animals and Its Associations with Antibiotic Resistance in Food-producing Animals and Human Beings: A Systematic Review and Meta-analysis," *The Lancet Planet Health* 1, no. 8 (November 1, 2017) E316–E327, https://doi.org/10.1016/S2542-5196(17)30141-9.
26. WHO, *WHO Guidelines on Use.*
27. *Ibid.*
28. *Ibid.*
29. Maurice T. Washington, *et al.*, "Monitoring Tylosin and Sulfamethazine in a Tile-drained Agricultural Watershed Using Polar Organic Chemical Integrative Sampler (POCIS)," *Science of the Total Environment* 612 (January 15, 2018): 358–367, esp. 359, https://doi.org/10.1016/j.scitotenv.2017.08.090.
30. FDA, "Fact Sheet: Veterinary Feed Directive Final Rule and Next Steps" (last modified July 29, 2019), https://www.fda.gov/animalveterinary/developmentapprovalprocess/ucm449019.htm; and Danny Hakim, "At Hamburger Central, Antibiotics for Cattle That Aren't Sick," *New York Times*, March 23, 2018.
31. FDA, "Fact Sheet: Veterinary Feed Directive."
32. Expert Commission on Addressing the Contribution of Livestock to the Antibiotic Resistance Crisis, *Combating Antibiotic Resistance: A*

Policy Roadmap to Reduce Use of Medically Important antibiotics in Livestock (Washington, D.C., 2017), 16, http://battlesuperbugs.com/sites/battlesuperbugs.com/files/Final%20Report%208.25.17.pdf.

33. *Ibid.*, 16f.

34. *Ibid.*, 17.

35. Global Accountability Project, "More Information Needed to Oversee Use of Medically Important Drugs in Food Animals, GAO17-192" (last modified April 7, 2017), 1, https://www.gao.gov/products/GAO-17-192.

36. *Ibid.*

37. *Ibid.*

38. Hakim. "At Hamburger Central."

39. FDA, "2009 Summary Report Antimicrobials Sold or Distributed for Use in Food-Producing Animals (last modified September 2014), 11, Table 1, https://www.fda.gov/downloads/forindustry/userfees/animaldruguserfeeactadufa/ucm231851.pdf.

40. WHO, "Critically Important Antimicrobials for Human Medicine," (5th Revision 2016) 10, Table 1, https://apps.who.int/iris/bitstream/handle/10665/255027/9789241512220-eng.pdf.

41. Susan Chow, "Pneumonia History," News Medical Life Sciences, October 11, 2015, https://www.news-medical.net/health/Pneumonia-History.aspx.

42. WHO, "Critically Important Antimicrobials."

43. *Ibid.*

44. WHO, "Campylobacter" (May 1, 2020), https://www.who.int/news-room/fact-sheets/detail/campylobacter.

45. *Ibid.*

46. USDA APHIS, "Feedlot 2011, Part IV: Health and Health Management on U.S. Feedlots with a Capacity of 1,000 or More Head," (last modified September 2013), 68, https://www.aphis.usda.gov/animal_health/nahms/feedlot/downloads/feedlot2011/Feed11_dr_PartIV_1.pdf; Michael D. Apley, *et al.*, "Use Estimates of In-Feed Antimicrobials in Swine Production in the United States," *Foodborne Pathogens and Disease* 9, no. 3 (2012): 272–279, https://doi.org/10.1089/fpd.2011.0983.

47. Stacy R. Joy, *et al.*, "Fate and Transport of Antimicrobials and Antimicrobial Resistance Genes in Soil and Runoff Following Land Application of Swine Manure Slurry," *Environmental Science and Technology* 47, no. 21 (2013): 12081–12088, https://pubs.acs.org/doi/suppl/10.1021/es4026358/suppl_file/es4026358_si_001.pdf.

48. Dana Kolpin, *et al.*, "Pharmaceuticals, Hormones, and Other Organic Wastewater Contaminants in U.S. Streams, 1999–2000: A National Reconnaissance," *Environmental Science and Technology* 36 (March 13, 2002): 1202–1211, Table 1, http://digitalcommons.unl.edu/usgsstaffpub/68.

49. Archana Jindal, *et al.*, "Antimicrobial Use and Resistance in Swine Waste Treatment Systems," *Applied and Environmental Microbiology* 72, no. 12 (December 2006): 7813–7820, https://doi.org/10.1128/AEM.01087-06.

50. FDA, "Ractopamine and Tylosin Finishing Swine Feed: Type C Medicated Feed," n.d., https://www.fda.gov/media/90804/download.

51. *Ibid.*

52. SwineCast, Interview with Laurie Hueneke, podcast audio 0719 (July 6, 2012), http://www.swinecast.com/swinecast-0719-ractopamine-clears-the-codex-hurdle.

53. Lindsay Chichester, *et al.*, "Beta-agonists: What Are They and Should I Be Concerned?" UNL Beef Watch (last modified October 1, 2013), http://newsroom.unl.edu/announce/beef/2563/14863.

54. P. J. Huffstutter and Tom Polansek, "Special Report: Lost Hooves, Dead Cattle Before Merck Halted Zilmax Sales," *Reuters*, December 30, 2013; and Theopolis Waters, "Tyson Foods to Suspend Buying Cattle Fed Zilmax Additive," *Reuters*, August 7, 2013.

55. FDA: ADE [Adverse Drug Experience] Source Report PAYUS03040, July 26, 2003, p. 308 (Illinois zip code 61421).

56. FDA: ADE Source Report US200403294, March 24, 2004, p. 40 (Indiana zip code 46140).

57. FDA, "Ractopamine and Tylosin," 2.

58. Deena Shankar, "American Farmers Have to Stop Juicing Their Pigs to Meet China's Food Safety Standards," *Quartz*, August 11, 2015, https://qz.com/476232/American-farmers-have-to-stop-juicing-their-pigs-to-meet-chinas-food-safety -standards/.

59. European Food Safety Authority, "Scientific Opinion, Safety Evaluation of Ractopamine," April 2, 2009, 20–21, https://www.readcube.com/articles/10.2903/j.efsa.2009.1041.

60. *Ibid.*

61. *Ibid.*

62. J. M. Marchant-Forde, "The Effects of Ractopamine on the Behavior and Physiology of Finishing Pigs," *Journal of Animal Science* 81 (2003): 416–422, https://pdfs.semanticscholar.org/e359/c6537d71c73c73f18ac5eee6a568c77f6604.pdf; R. Poletto, *et al.*, "Aggressiveness and Brain Amine Concentration in Dominant and Subordinate Finishing Pigs Fed the β-adrenoreceptor Agonist Ractopamine," *Journal of Animal Science* 88, no. 9 (September 2010): 3107–3120, https://doi.org/10.2527/jas.2009-1876; and B. W. James, *et al.*, "Effects of Dietary L-Carnitine and Ractopamine HCI on the Metabolic Response to Handling in Finishing Pigs," *Journal of Animal Science* 91, no. 9 (2013): 4426–4439, https://doi.org/10.2527/jas.2011-4411.

63. Marchant-Forde, "The Effects of Ractopamine."
64. *Ibid.*
65. *Ibid.*
66. Saia Maraki, *et al.*, "*Myroides Odoratimimus* Soft Tissue Infection in an Immunocompetent Child Following a Pig Bite: Case Report and Literature Review," *Brazilian Journal of Infectious Diseases* 16, no. 4 (July/August 2012): 390–392, https://doi.org/10.1016/j.bjid.2012.06.004; I. Brook, "Management of Human and Animal Bite Wound Infection: An Overview," *Current Infectious Diseases Reports* 11, no. 5 (2009): 389–395, https://doi.org/10.1007/s11908-009-0055-x; Ph. Declercq, *et al.*, "Complicated Community-Acquired Soft Tissue Infection by MRSA from Porcine Origin," *Infection* 36, no. 6 (December 2008): 590–592; and F. Escande, *et al.*, "*Actinobacillus Suis* Infection after a Pig Bite," *The Lancet* 348, no. 9031 (September 28, 1996): 888, https://doi.org/10.1016/S0140-6736(05)64756-3.
67. Helena Bottemiller, "Ractopamine and Pigs: Looking at the Numbers," *Food & Environment Reporting Network*, February 23, 2012, https://thefern.org/blog_posts/ractopamine-and-pigs-looking-at-the-numbers/.
68. *Ibid.*
69. ADE Source Report US201000086, January 12, 2010 (Iowa zip code 52563).
70. *Ibid.*
71. FDA, "Final Rule; Technical Amendment," *Federal Register* 67(140) (July 22, 2002): 47679–48014, esp. 47691–47701.
72. H. S. Hurd, *et al.*, "*Salmonella Enterica* Infections in Market Swine with and without Transport and Holding," *Applied and Environmental Microbiology* 68, no. 5 (May 2002): 2376–2381, https://doi.org/10.1128/AEM.68.5.2376-2381.2002.
73. CDC, "Salmonella Questions and Answers," n.d., https://www.cdc.gov/salmonella/general/index.html.
74. Thomas Edrington, *et al.*, "Effects of Ractopamine HCl on Escherichia Coli O157:H7 and Salmonella In Vitro and on Intestinal Populations and Fecal Shedding in Experimentally Infected Sheep and Pigs," *Current Microbiology* 53, no. 1 (June 2006): 82–88, https://doi.org/10.1007/s00284-006-0019-4.
75. Pork.org, "Consumer Messaging for Modern Pork Production," Clint Sievers, Maslansky + Partners, 2013 Pork Management Conference, (June 18–21 2013), https://www.pork.org/blog/consumer-messaging-modern-pork-production/.
76. Jayson L. Lusk, *et al.*, "Consumer Preferences for Farm Animal Welfare: Results of a Nationwide Telephone Survey," Department of Agricultural Economics Oklahoma State University, August 7, 2007, ii, http://

cratefreefuture.com/pdf/American%20Farm%20Bureau-Funded%20
Poll.pdf; Sara Shields, *et al.*, "A Decade of Progress Toward Ending the
Intensive Confinement of Farm Animals in the United States," *Animals*
(Basel) 7, no. 5 (May 15, 2017), 16, https://doi.org/10.3390/ani7050040;
M. G. S. McKendree, *et al.*, "Effects of Demographic Factors and
Information Sources on United States Consumer Perceptions of Animal
Welfare," *Journal of Animal Science* 92 (2014): 3161–3173, https://pdfs.
semanticscholar.org/d75d/0cca22651173d14e54da874b2a6b3e5aac08.
pdf; and Rebecca Riffkin, "In U.S., More Say Animals Should Have
Same Rights as People," Gallup, May 18, 2015, http://www.gallup.com/
poll/183275/say-animals-rights-people.aspx.

77. Michael Pellman Rowland, "State Laws Are Creating Anxiety for Food
Producers" *Forbes*, May 19, 2017.

78. *Ibid.*

79. FDA, "Ractopamine and Tylosin Finishing Swine Feed: Type B
Medicated Feed," n.d., https://www.fda.gov/media/77607/download;
and FDA (Taiwan), "Freedom of Information Summary, Ractopamine
Hydrochloride," (2003), https://www.fda.gov.tw/upload/133/02%20
US%20FDA%20(evaluation%20of%20ractopamine%20for%20beef).pdf.

80. J. K. Wall, "Lilly Hopes Elanco Becomes Cash Cow," *International
Business Journal*, May 8, 2010, https://www.ibj.com/articles/19823.

Chapter 4: In the End the Coyote Wins

1. Mark Twain, *Roughing It* (Layton, UT: Gibbs M. Smith Inc., 2017) also
available online, https://www.gutenberg.org/files/3177/3177-h/3177-h.
htm.

2. Ian Sample, "DNA Research Identifies Homeland of the Domestic Cat,"
The Guardian, June 29, 2007.

3. Simon Worrall, "How the Most Hated Animal in America Outwitted Us
All," *National Geographic*, August 7, 2016.

4. Emily Zeugner, "Feline Geneticist Traces Origin of the Cat," *Associated
Press*, June 9, 2008.

5. Josh Gabbatiss, "Evidence of First Ever Humans to Colonise North
America Found by Scientists," *The Independent* (UK), January 3, 2018.

6. Todd Wilkinson, "Dog's Death Spotlights Use of Cyanide 'Bombs' to Kill
Predators," *National Geographic*, April 20, 2017.

7. Tom Knudson, "Long Struggles in Leg-Hold Device Make for Gruesome
Deaths," *The Sacramento Bee*, April 28, 2012; USDA Wildlife Services,
"The Livestock Protection Collar," (May 2010), https://www.aphis.
usda.gov/publications/wildlife_damage/content/printable_version/
fs_livestock_protection_collar.pdf; and Controlling Predators on Sheep

Farms (last modified, November 2013), http://www.sheep101.info/201/predatorcontrol.html.

8. USDA Wildlife Services, "The Livestock Protection Collar."

9. Melissa Waage, "Stop Predator Poisons from Killing Wildlife and Harming Ecosystems: There's No Place for These Deadly Poisons on American Lands," NRDC (last modified, February 2014), https://www.nrdc.org/sites/default/files/predator-poisons-FS.pdf.

10. Center for Biological Diversity, "Lawsuit Filed to Save Imperiled Native Carnivores From Deadly 'Cyanide Bombs," April 4, 2017, https://www.biologicaldiversity.org/news/press_releases/2017/m44s-04-04-2017.php.

11. Kathleen Fagerstone and Gail Keirn, "Wildlife Services—A Leader in Developing Tools and Techniques for Managing Carnivores," *Proceedings of the 14th WDM Conference* (2012): 44–55, esp. 46, https://www.aphis.usda.gov/wildlife_damage/nwrc/publications/12pubs/fagerstone122.pdf.

12. USDA APHIS, "2018 Program Data Reports," https://www.aphis.usda.gov/wildlife_damage/pdr/PDR-G_Report.php?fy=2016&fld=&fld_val.

13. Wilkinson, "Dog's Death Spotlights."

14. Michael McNutt, "Hunters Post Coyote Kills Along Fences," *News OK*, February 2, 1986, http://newsok.com/article/2136335; and Liza Gross, "Coyote Killings: A Complex Debate of Conservation and Cruelty," *KQED*, February 6, 2013.

15. Sue Coe, "Crucified Coyote", http://www.graphicwitness.org/coe/aa091099.jpg.

16. USDA Wildlife Services, "The Livestock Protection Collar"; Worrall, "How the Most Hated Animal in America Outwitted Us All" ; and Christopher Ketcham, "The Rogue Agency," *Harper's Magazine*, March 2016.

17. Robert Wielgus and Kaylie Peebles. "Effects of Wolf Mortality on Livestock Depredations," *PLoS ONE* 9, no. 12 (2014): 1, https://doi.org/10.1371/journal.pone.0113505.

18. Adrian Treves, *et al.*, "Predator Control Should Not Be a Shot in the Dark," *Frontiers in Ecology and the Environment* 14, no. 7 (2016): 380–388, http://faculty.nelson.wisc.edu/treves/pubs/Treves_Krofel_McManus.pdf (internal citations omitted).

19. *Ibid.*, 381.

20. *Ibid.*, 381.

21. *Ibid.*, 381.

22. *Ibid.*, 386.

23. *Ibid.*, 380.

24. Rachel Bale, "This Government Program's Job is to Kill Wildlife," *National Geographic*, February 12, 2016.

25. USDA National Agriculture Statistics Service, *2019 State Agriculture Overview: California* (last modified February 20, 2020), https://www. nass.usda.gov/Publications/AgCensus/2017/Online_Resources/County_ Profiles/California/cp99006.pdf (valuing sheep, goats, wool, mohair, and milk produced in California at $86,900,000); and Los Angeles County Economic Development Corporation, Otis College of Art and Design, *2019 Otis Report on the Creative Economy: California*, 2020, https:// www.otis.edu/creative-economy/2019 (reporting California's creative economy is worth over 227.8 billion dollars in direct labor income).

Chapter 5: Reaping Drought by Design

1. *The Young Ones*, "Bambi," Season 2, Episode 1. Directed by Paul Jackson; written by Ben Elton, Rick Mayall, and Lise Mayer. BBC, May 8, 1984.
2. Charles Dickens, "A Small Star in the East," *All the Year Round* Vol. I New Series, December 19, 1868, http://www.djo.org.uk/all-the-year-round/volume-i-new-series/page-62.html.
3. *Ibid.*
4. John Burnett, "A Toxic Century: Mining Giant Must Clean Up Mess," *National Public Radio*, February 4, 2010.
5. EPA, Region 10, *Five-Year Review Report: Commencement Bay Nearshore/ Tideflats Superfund Site Tacoma, Washington* (December 29, 2004), 4, 6, https://semspub.epa.gov/work/HQ/179200.pdf; Derrick Nunnally, "Three Decades After the ASARCO Smelter Shutdown, Its Toxic Legacy Surprises Tacoma Newcomers," *The News Tribune*, November 7, 2015; and Associated Press, "Suit Settled over Arsenic Fallout ASARCO to Pay $67.5 Million to People Near Tacoma Smelter," *The Spokesman Review*, February 2, 1995.
6. Their Mines, Our Stories, "Work, Environment and Justice in ASARCO-Impacted Communities, Ruston/Tacoma—Historical Images," n.d., http://www.theirminesourstories.org/?cat=4.
7. EPA, Region 10, *Five-Year Review Report*, 53.
8. *Ibid.*, 4.
9. Marianne Sullivan, "Contested Science and Exposed Workers: ASARCO and the Occupational Standard for Inorganic Arsenic," *Public Health Reports* 122 (July–August 2007): 541–547, https://www.ncbi.nlm.nih.gov/pmc/articles/PMC1888505/pdf/phr122000541.pdf.
10. *Ibid.*
11. *Ibid.*
12. Margaret Riddle, "The ASARCO Smokestack—Once the World's Largest—Is Demolished at the Company's Old Copper Smelter in Ruston, North of Tacoma, on January 17, 1993," History Link, August 26, 2008, http://www.historylink.org/File/8744.

13. Herbert L. Needleman, "History of Lead Poisoning in the World," 1999, http://www.biologicaldiversity.org/campaigns/get_the_lead_out/pdfs/health/Needleman_1999.pdf.
14. Burnett, "A Toxic Century."
15. Herbert L. Needleman, "The Persistent Threat of Lead: A Singular Opportunity," *American Journal of Public Health* 79, no. 5 (May 1989): 643–45, http://ajph.aphapublications.org/doi/pdf/10.2105/AJPH.79.5.643; and Burnett. "A Toxic Century."
16. David Wilma and Walt Crowley, "Tacoma—Thumbnail History," History Link, January 17, 2003, http://www.historylink.org/File/5055.
17. *Ibid.*
18. Their Mines, Our Stories, "Ruston/Tacoma—Historical Images," n.d., http://www.theirminesourstories.org/?cat=4.
19. Josef Elsinger, "Early Consumer Protection Legislation: A 17th Century Law Prohibiting Lead Adulteration of Wines," *Interdisciplinary Science Reviews* 16, no. 1 (1991): 61–68, https://doi.org/10.1179/isr.1991.16.1.61.
20. See Josef Elsinger, "Lead and Wine: Eberhard Gockel and the Colica Pictonum," *Medical History*, 26, no. 3 (August 1982): 279–302, https://www.ncbi.nlm.nih.gov/pmc/articles/PMC1139187/pdf/medhist00086-0053.pdf.
21. Needleman. "History of Lead Poisoning in the World."
22. *Ibid.*
23. Tacoma population, https://www.google.com/search?q=tacoma+population+1993&ie=utf-8&oe=utf-8, 4, 6; Nunnally, "Three Decades"; and Associated Press, "Suit Settled Over Arsenic Fallout."
24. Gadi Borkow, "Using Copper to Improve the Well-being of the Skin," *Current Chemical Biology* 8, no. 2 (August 2014): 89–102, https://doi.org/10.2174/2212796809666150227223857; and Lena H. Sun, "The Bacteria-Fighting Super Element That's Making a Comeback in Hospitals: Copper," *The Washington Post*, September 20, 2015.
25. Burnett, "A Toxic Century."
26. Gidon Eshel, *et al.*, "Land, Irrigation Water, Greenhouse Gas, and Reactive Nitrogen Burdens of Meat, Eggs, and Dairy Production in the United States," *PNAS* 111, no. 33 (August 2014): 11996–12001, esp. 11999, Fig. 4A, https://doi.org/10.1073/pnas.1402183111.
27. *Ibid.*
28. *Ibid.*
29. United Nations Convention to Combat Desertification, *Global Land Outlook* 2017, 126, http://www.unccd.int/sites/default/files/documents/2017-09/GLO_Full_Report_low_res.pdf.

30   J. Poore and T. Nemecek, "Reducing Food's Environmental Impact through Producers and Consumers," *Science* 360, no. 6392 (June 2018): 987–992, https://doi.org/10.1126/science.aaq0216.

31.   Tara Garnett, *et al.*, *Grazed and Confused? Ruminating on Cattle, Grazing Systems, Methane, Nitrous Oxide, the Soil Carbon Sequestration Question—and What It All Means for Greenhouse Gas Emissions. Food Climate Research Network*, 2017, 16, http://www.fcrn.org.uk/sites/default/files/project-files/fcrn_gnc_report.pdf; and Bojana Bajželj, *et al.*, "Importance of Food-Demand Management for Climate Mitigation," *Nature Climate Change* 4, no. 10 (October 2014): 924–929, http://sbc.ucdavis.edu/files/202364.pdf.

32.   FAO, *The Second Report on the State of the World's Animal Genetic Resources for Food and Agriculture* (2015), 180–183, http://www.fao.org/3/a-i4787e/index.html.

33.   Bajželj, "Importance of Food-Demand Management," 2.

34.   FAO, *Unlocking the Water Potential of Agriculture* (2003), 1, http://www.fao.org/docrep/006/y4525e/y4525e04.htm.

35.   Human Rights Council, Thirteenth Session, "Resolution 13/4: The Right to Food" (April 14, 2010), http://www2.ohchr.org/english/bodies/hrcouncil/docs/13session/A.HRC.RES.13.4_AEV.pdf.

36.   FAO, *The Future of Food and Agriculture, Trends and Challenges* (2017), 71, http://www.fao.org/3/a-i6583e.pdf.

37.   FAO, *The State of Food and Agriculture* (2016), 6, 8, http://www.fao.org/3/a-i6030e.pdf.

38.   Garnett, *et al.*, *Grazed and Confused?* 90, 122, 123; Bajželj, *et al.*, "Importance of Food-Demand Management."

39.   Carlos A. Monteiro, *et al.*, "The Snack Attack," *American Journal of Public Health* 100, no. 6 (June 2010): 975–981, https://www.ncbi.nlm.nih.gov/pmc/articles/PMC2866614/.

40.   P. W. Gerbens-Leenes, *et al.*, "The Water Footprint of Poultry, Pork and Beef: A Comparative Study in Different Countries and Production Systems," *Water Resources and Industry* 1–2 (March–June 2013): 25–36, esp. 26, https://doi.org/10.1016/j.wri.2013.03.001.

41.   United Nations Conference on Trade and Development, *Trade and Environment Review 2013: Wake Up Before It is Too Late*, 226, 228, http://unctad.org/en/PublicationsLibrary/ditcted2012d3_en.pdf.

42.   Bajželj, *et al.*, "Importance of Food-Demand Management."

43.   U.S. Department of Defense, *2014 Quadrennial Defense Review* (2014), 8, http://archive.defense.gov/pubs/2014_Quadrennial_Defense_Review.pdf.

44.   *Ibid.*

45. Colin P. Kelley, *et al.*, "Climate Change in the Fertile Crescent and Implications of the Recent Syrian Drought," *PNAS* 112, no. 11 (March 2015): 3241–3246, http://www.pnas.org/content/112/11/3241.full.pdf; and Jonathan Lovvorn, "Climate Change Beyond Environmentalism Part I: Intersectional Threats and the Case for Collective Action," *The Georgetown Law Review* 29, no. 1 (April 4, 2017): 1–67, esp. 39, https://gielr.files.wordpress.com/2017/04/zsk00117000001.pdf.

46. Office of the Under Secretary for Department of Defense for Acquisition and Sustainment, *Report on Effects of a Changing Climate to the Department of Defense* (January 10 2019), 8, 16, https://media.defense.gov/2019/Jan/29/2002084200/-1/-1/1/CLIMATE-CHANGE-REPORT-2019.pdf.

47. FAO, *The State of Food and Agriculture: Livestock in the Balance* (2009), 65, http://www.fao.org/3/i0680e/i0680e.pdf.

48. Bajželj, *et al.*, "Importance of Food-Demand Management."

49. *Ibid.*

50. *Ibid.*

51. FAO, *Livestock's Long Shadow: Environmental Issues and Options* (2006), 134, http://www.fao.org/3/a0701e/a0701e00.htm.

52. Bajželj, *et al.*, "Importance of Food-Demand Management"; Garnett, *et al.*, *Grazed and Confused*, 100; Eshel, *et al.*, "Land, Irrigation Water," 11998.

53. FAO, "2016 International Year of Pulses," http://www.fao.org/pulses-2016/news/news-detail/en/c/379385/; and FAO, "What Are Pulses?" (last modified October 15, 2015), http://www.fao.org/pulses-2016/news/news-detail/en/c/337107/.

54. FAO, "2016 International Year of Pulses."

55. *Ibid.*

56. Washington State Department of Agriculture, "Agriculture: A Cornerstone of Washington's Economy," n.d., https://agr.wa.gov/washington-agriculture.

57. Washington State Wine, "Washington State Wine Fast Facts," n.d., https://www.washingtonwine.org/wine/facts-and-stats/state-facts.

58. USDA National Agricultural Statistics Service, "2019 State Agriculture Overview: Washington," https://www.nass.usda.gov/Quick_Stats/Ag_Overview/stateOverview.php?state=WASHINGTON.

59. *Ibid.*

60. FAO, "2016 International Year of Pulses."

61. *Ibid.*

62. *Ibid.*

63. USDA National Agricultural Statistics Service, *Washington Soil Atlas* by Karl W. Hipple, n.d. 15, 19, 25, 31, 37, 39, 41, 63, 71, 103, 112, https://www.nrcs.usda.gov/Internet/FSE_DOCUMENTS/nrcs144p2_034094.pdf.

64. Eshel, *et al.*, "Land, Irrigation Water."
65. Daniel H. Putnam, *et al.*, "Long-term Hay Exports Have Increased Dramatically, But Are Dampened by Recent Trade Disputes," Alfalfa & Forage News, January 22, 2019, https://ucanr.edu/blogs/blogcore/postdetail.cfm?postnum=29204.
66. *Ibid.*
67. Nunnally. "Three Decades"; and EPA, Region 10, *Five-Year Review Report*, § 6.2.
68. *Federal Water Pollution Control Act, U.S Code* 33 (1972), §§ 1319(1) & (2) & 1321 (b)(3).
69. Natalie DeFord, "Tacoma's New Point Ruston," *South Sound Magazine*, July 20, 2016, http://southsoundmag.com/tacomas-new-point-ruston/.
70. FAO, *The Second Report on the State of the World's Animal Genetic Resources for Food and Agriculture* (2015), 158, http://www.fao.org/3/a-i4787e/index.html.
71. *Ibid*; and Philip K. Thornton, "Livestock Production: Recent Trends, Future Prospects."
72. Nozaki, "The Future of Global Meat Demand"; Varma, "More Chinese Turning Vegetarian."
73. *Ibid.*
74. Nozaki, "The Future of Global Meat Demand."
75. *Ibid.*
76. *Ibid.*
77. *Ibid.*
78. *Ibid.*
79. State of Washington Department of Ecology, "Tacoma Smelter Plume Project," n.d., https://ecology.wa.gov/Spills-Cleanup/Contamination-cleanup/Cleanup-sites/Toxic-cleanup-sites/Tacoma-smelter.
80. EPA, Region 10, *Five-Year Review Report*, 4, 6; Nunnally, "Three Decades."
81. EPA, "Basic Information about Lead Air Pollution," n.d., https://www.epa.gov/lead-air-pollution/basic-information-about-lead-air-pollution; and Needleman, "History of Lead Poisoning in the World."
82. U.S. General Services Administration, "Tacoma Union Station, Tacoma, WA," n.d., https://www.gsa.gov/historic-buildings/tacoma-union-station-tacoma-wa.

Chapter 6: If You Mostly Make Crap, Everywhere Looks Like Your Toilet

1. Associated Press. *"Congressman Says Evel Bad Influence on Kids," Spokesman-Review, September 4, 1974.*
2. EPA, "Proposed Rule: National Pollutant Discharge Elimination System (NPDES) Concentrated Animal Feeding Operation (CAFO) Reporting

Rule," *Federal Register* 76, no. 204 (October 21, 2011): 65431–65458, esp. 65431 and 65436, https://www.govinfo.gov/content/pkg/FR-2011-10-21/pdf/2011-27189.pdf; and EPA, "Final Rule: National Pollutant Discharge Elimination System Permit Regulation and Effluent Limitation Guidelines and Standards for Concentrated Animal Feeding Operations (CAFOs)," *Federal Register* 68, no. 29 (February 12, 2003): 7176–7274, esp. 7176, 7179, https://www.gpo.gov/fdsys/pkg/FR-2003-02-12/pdf/03-3074.pdf.

3. GAO, "Concentrated Animal Feeding Operations: EPA Needs More Information and a Clearly Defined Strategy to Protect air and Water Quality from Pollutants of Concern," (September 4, 2008), 30, https://www.gao.gov/products/GAO-08-944.

4. *Ibid.*, 48.

5. Donnelle Eller, "Iowa Uses Satellites to Uncover 5,000 Previously Undetected Animal Confinements," *Des Moines Register*, September 15, 2017.

6. *Ibid.*

7. Bill Leonard, "Iowa View: State has Turned into a 'Toilet' for Industrial Ag," *Des Moines Register*, October 13th, 2013.

8. Proposed Rule: National Pollutant Discharge Elimination System, Fed. Reg. 65434.

9. Oliver Milman, "Meat Industry Blamed for Largest-ever 'Dead Zone' in Gulf of Mexico," *The Guardian*, August 1, 2017.

10. Jennifer Colton, "Weiser Feedlot Neighbors Still Searching for Closure," *The Argus Observer*, August 6, 2006.

11. Carissa Wolf, "Dirty Water," *Boise Weekly*, February 1, 2006.

12. Colton, "Weiser Feedlot Neighbors Still Searching for Closure."

13. David Trigueiro, "County Doesn't Register Feedlot as CAFO," *Weiser Signal American*, June 28, 2006, http://www.ruralnetwork.net/~newsroom/story%2006064.htm.

14. Colton, "Weiser Feedlot Neighbors Still Searching for Closure."

15. *Ibid.*; and DHHS, "Sunnyside Area Ground Contamination: Evaluation of Antibiotic, Steroid Hormone & Nitrate Compounds in Groundwater Near a Confined Animal Feeding Operation (CAFO)," (March 19, 2007), 3, https://www.atsdr.cdc.gov/hac/pha/SunnysideAreaGroundwaterContamination/SunnysideAreaGroundwaterHC031907.pdf.

16. Lynda Knobeloch, *et al.*, "Blue Babies and Nitrate-Contaminated Well Water," *Environmental Health Perspectives* 108, no. 7 (July 2000): 675–678, https://www.ncbi.nlm.nih.gov/pmc/articles/PMC1638204/pdf/envhper00308-0137.pdf.

17. *Ibid.*

18. David Kruse, "The CommStock Report," *The Daily Reporter*, October 5, 2012, http://www.spencerdailyreporter.com/story/1900801.html.

19. Humane California, "Why I'm Voting Yes on Prop 2," YouTube Video, 2008, https://www.youtube.com/watch?v=RUYhKGifO5A.

20. Stack, "How Many Acres is a Football Field?" n.d., www.stack.com/a/how-many-acres-is-a-football-field.

21. Final Rule: EPA, National Pollutant Discharge Elimination System, 7176, 7179.

22. Steven R. Kirkhorn, "Agricultural Respiratory Hazards and Disease," *Partners in Agricultural Health*, Module IV (2002): 1–38, https://pdfs.semanticscholar.org/fd58/b0dcf5998e141780d5456ff143fca599f3af.pdf.

23. *Ibid.*, 5.

24. Grant Rodgers and Donnelle Eller, "Iowa Father, Son Die from Manure Pit Fumes," *The Des Moines Register*, July 28, 2015; and John M. Shutske, *et al.*, "Notes from the Field: Death of a Farm Worker After Exposure to Manure Gas in an Open air Environment—Wisconsin, August 2016," *Morbidity and Mortality Weekly Report* (MMWR) 66, no. 32 (August 18, 2017): 861–62, http://dx.doi.org/10.15585/mmwr.mm6632a6.

25. Kirkhorn, "Agricultural Respiratory Hazards and Disease," 5.

26. Natalie Anderson, *et al.*, "Airborne Reduced Nitrogen: Ammonia Emissions from Agriculture and Other Sources," *Environment International* 29, nos. 2–3 (June 2003): 277–286, https://doi.org/10.1016/S0160-4120(02)00186-1.

27. National Association of Local Boards of Health, "Understanding Concentrated Animal Feeding Operations and Their Impact on Communities" (last modified 2010), 6 Table 1, https://www.cdc.gov/nceh/ehs/docs/understanding_cafos_nalboh.pdf.

28. Kirkhorn, "Agricultural Respiratory Hazards and Disease,", 6.

29. *Ibid.*

30. *Ibid.*, 5–6.

31. Cordon M. Smart, "The 'Right to Commit Nuisance' in North Carolina: A Historical Analysis of the Right-to-Farm Act," *North Carolina Law Review* 94, no. 6 (2016): 2098–2154, https://scholarship.law.unc.edu/cgi/viewcontent.cgi?article=4880&context=nclr.

32. *Camfield v. U.S.*, 167 U.S. 518, 523 (1897).

33. Erin Fuchs, "Calif. Egg Ranch Emissions Are Nuisance, Jury Says," Law 360, May 26 2011, https://www.law360.com/articles/247513/calif-egg-ranch-emissions-are-nuisance-jury-says.

34. *Ibid.*

35. EPA, "Letter to William G. Ross, Jr. Acting Secretary of North Carolina Department of Environmental Quality by Lilian S. Dorka," (January 12, 2017), http://blogs.law.unc.edu/documents/civilrights/epalettertodeq011217.pdf.

36. North Carolina Environmental Justice Network, "DEQ in Bed with Big Pig" (last modified March 8, 2016), https://ncejn.org/2016/03/title-vi-update-deq-in-bed-with-big-pig/.
37. EPA, "Letter to William G. Ross, Jr."
38. *Ibid.*, 1.
39. *Ibid.*, 6–7.
40. *Ibid.*, 7.
41. *Ibid.*, 9.
42. Erica Hellerstein and Ken Fine, "A Million Tons of Feces and an Unbearable Stench: Life Near Industrial Pig Farms," *The Guardian*, September 20, 2017.
43. George Orwell, "In Front of Your Nose," *Tribune*, March 22,1946, http://orwell.ru/library/articles/nose/english/e_nose.

Chapter 7: Hurricane Husbandry

1. My Name, "Interlude #1," track 3 on Megacrush, C/Z Records, 1992.
2. FAO, *Tackling Climate Change Through Livestock—A Global Assessment of Emissions and Mitigation Opportunities* (2013), 15, http://www.fao.org/3/a-i6030e.pdf.
3. United Nations and the World Bank, *Animal and Pandemic Influenza: A Framework for Sustaining Momentum*. Fifth Global Progress Report (July 2010), 102, http://documents.worldbank.org/curated/en/880721468335983143/pdf/879300PUB0Box30Progress0Report02010.pdf.
4. David A. Relman, *et al.*, *Global Climate Change and Extreme Weather Events: Understanding the Contributions to Infectious Disease Emergence: Workshop Summary* (Washington DC: National Academies Press, 2008), xii–xiii, https://www.ncbi.nlm.nih.gov/books/NBK45747/pdf/Bookshelf_NBK45747.pdf; and Lu Liang and Peng Gong, "Climate Change and Human Infectious Diseases: A Synthesis of Research Findings from Global and Spatio-Temporal Perspectives," *Environment International* 103 (June 2017): 99–108, esp. 105, https://doi.org/10.1016/j.envint.2017.03.011 (internal citations omitted).
5. Intergovernmental Panel on Climate Change, *Climate Change 2014: Synthesis Report, Summary for Policymakers*, 2, https://www.ipcc.ch/pdf/assessment-report/ar5/syr/AR5_SYR_FINAL_SPM.pdf.
6. Intergovernmental Science-Policy Platform on Biodiversity and Ecosystem Services (IPBES), *The Global Assessment Report on Biodiversity and Ecosystem Services: Summary for Policymakers* (2019), 15, https://ipbes.net/sites/default/files/2020-02/ipbes_global_assessment_report_summary_for_policymakers_en.pdf (emphasis in original).

7. Colin D. Butler, "Infectious Disease Emergence and Global Change: Thinking Systemically in a Shrinking World," *Infectious Diseases of Poverty* 1 (October 2012), https://doi.org/10.1186/2049-9957-1-5.

8. Yadvinder Malhi, *et al.*, "Climate Change, Deforestation, and the Fate of the Amazon," *Science* 319, no. 5860 (January 2008): 169–172, https://science.sciencemag.org/content/319/5860/169; Richard J. Millar, *et al.*, "A Modified Impulse-response Representation of the Global Near-Surface Air Temperature and Atmospheric Concentration Response to Carbon Dioxide Emissions," *Atmospheric Chemistry and Physics* 17 (June 16, 2017): 7213–7228, https://doi.org/10.5194/acp-17-7213-2017; and *see* Scot M. Miller, *et al.*, "Anthropogenic Emissions of Methane in the United States," *Proceedings of the National Academy of Sciences* 110, no. 50 (December 2013): 20018–20022, https://doi.org/10.1073/pnas.1314392110.

9. EPA, "Sources of Greenhouse Gas Emissions," n.d., https://www.epa.gov/ghgemissions/sources-greenhouse-gas-emissions.

10. FAO, *Tackling Climate Change Through Livestock*, 15.

11. *Ibid.*

12. *Ibid.*

13. Hannah Ritchie and Max Roser, "Environmental Impacts of Food Production," FAO: Our World In Data (last modified January 2020), https://ourworldindata.org/environmental-impacts-of-food.

14. J. Su, *et al.*, "Expression of Barley SUSIBA2 Transcription Factor Yields High-Starch Low-Methane Rice," *Nature* 523 (July 2015): 602–606, https://www.nature.com/articles/nature14673.

15. Tara Garnett, *et al.*, *Grazed and Confused? Ruminating on Cattle, Grazing Systems, Methane, Nitrous Oxide, the Soil Carbon Sequestration Question— and What It All Means for Greenhouse Gas Emissions. Food Climate Research Network*, 2017, 16, http://www.fcrn.org.uk/sites/default/files/project-files/fcrn_gnc_report.pdf; and Su, *et al.*, "Expression of Barley," 602.

16. David Allen, "Attributing Atmospheric Methane to Anthropogenic Emission Sources," *Accounts of Chemical Research* 49 (June 2016): 1344–1350, https://doi.org/10.1021/acs.accounts.6b00081.

17. EPA, "Overview of Greenhouse Gases," n.d., https://www.epa.gov/ghgemissions/overview-greenhouse-gases.

18. *Ibid.*

19. J. H. Massey, *et al.*, "Reduced Water Use and Methane Emissions from Rice Grown Using Intermittent Irrigation," April 23, 2003. Paper presented at Proceedings of the 33rd annual Mississippi Water Resources Conference, Mississippi Water Resources Research Institute, https://www.ars.usda.gov/research/publications/publication/?seqNo115=149754.

20. Bruce A. Linquist, *et al.*, "Reducing Greenhouse Gas Emissions, Water Use, and Grain Arsenic Levels in Rice Systems," *Global Change* Biology 21, no. 1 (January 2015): 407–417, https://onlinelibrary.wiley.com/doi/abs/10.1111/gcb.12701; and Tim Searchinger, *et al.*, "Wetting and Drying: Reducing Greenhouse Gas Emissions and Saving Water from Rice Production," *World Resources Institute*, December 2014, http://www.wri.org/publication/wetting-and-drying-reducing-greenhouse-gas-emissions-and-saving-water-rice-production.

21. *Ibid.*

22. Gayathri Vaidyanathan, "How Bad of a Greenhouse Gas Is Methane?" *Scientific American*, December 22, 2015.

23. *Ibid.*; and USDA Agricultural Research Service, *Climate Change and Agriculture in the United States: Effects and Adaptation.* Technical Bulletin 1935 (February 2013) 182, https://www.usda.gov/oce/climate_change/effects_2012/CC%20and%20Agriculture%20Report%20(02-04-2013)b.pdf.

24. FAO, *Tackling Climate Change Through Livestock*, 7 Table 1.

25. *Ibid.*, 17.

26. *Ibid.*

27. FAO, *The State of Food and Agriculture: Livestock in the Balance* (2009), 65, http://www.fao.org/docrep/012/i0680e/i0680e.pdf.

28. FAO, *Tackling Climate Change Through Livestock*, 17.

29. Garnett, *et al.*, *Grazed and Confused*, 33.

30. *Ibid.*

31. FAO, *Tackling Climate Change Through Livestock*.

32. United Nations Conference on Trade and Development, *Trade and Environment Review 2013: Wake Up Before It is Too Late*, 226, 228, http://unctad.org/en/PublicationsLibrary/ditcted2012d3_en.pdf.

33. *Ibid.*, iv.

34. Nathan Pelletier and Peter Tyedmers, "Forecasting Potential Global Environmental Costs of Livestock Production 2000–2050," PNAS107, no.43 (October 2017): 18372, http://www.pnas.org/content/107/43/18371.

35. FAO, *The State of Food and Agriculture: Livestock in the Balance* (2009), 65.

36. U.S. Department of Defense, *2014 Quadrennial Defense Review*, 2014, 8, http://archive.defense.gov/pubs/2014_Quadrennial_Defense_Review.pdf.

37. FAO, *The Future of Food and Agriculture: Trends and Challenges* (2017), 137, http://www.fao.org/3/a-i6583e.pdf.

38. *Ibid.*

39. *Ibid.*

40. *Ibid.*

41. *Ibid.*

42. Jonathan Lovvorn, "Climate Change Beyond Environmentalism Part I: Intersectional Threats and the Case for Collective Action," *Georgetown International Environmental Law Review* 29, no. 1 (July 2018), 19, https://papers.ssrn.com/sol3/papers.cfm?abstract_id=2946120; and Oxfam International, "Extreme Carbon Inequality, Media Briefing" (last modified December 2, 2015), 1–2, https://www-cdn.oxfam.org/s3fs-public/file_attachments/mb-extreme-carbon-inequality-021215-en.pdf.

43. Susan Raqib, "How Wars and Disasters Fuel Child Labor," Human Rights Watch (last modified June 12, 2017), https://www.hrw.org/news/2017/06/12/how-wars-and-disasters-fuel-child-labor.

44. *Ibid.*

45. International Labour Office, *Global Estimates of Child Labour: Results and Trends 2012–2016*, 2017, 12, http://www.ilo.org/wcmsp5/groups/public/---dgreports/---dcomm/documents/publication/wcms_575499.pdf.

46. *Ibid.*

47. Kirsten Zickfeld, *et al.*, "Centuries of Thermal Sea-Level Rise Due to Anthropogenic Emissions of Short-Lived Greenhouse Gases," *Proceedings of the National Academy of Sciences* 114, no. 4 (September 2017): 657–662, https://doi.org/10.1073/pnas.1612066114.

48. EPA, "Sources of Greenhouse Gas Emissions."

49. Robert Kunzig, "Germany Could Be a Model for How We'll Get Power in the Future," *National Geographic*, November 2015.

50. Marco Springmann, *et al.*, "Analysis and Valuation of the Health and Climate Change Cobenefits of Dietary Change," *Proceedings of the National Academy of Sciences* 113, no. 15 (April 2016): 4146–4151, https://doi.org/10.1073/pnas.1523119113.

51. David Archer, *et al.*, "Atmospheric Lifetime of Fossil Fuel Carbon Dioxide," *Annual Review of Earth and Planetary Sciences* 37 (May 2009): 117–134, https://www.annualreviews.org/doi/full/10.1146/annurev.earth.031208.100206.

52. Myles R. Allen, *et al.*, "New Use of Global Warming Potentials to Compare Cumulative and Short-lived Climate Pollutants," *Nature Climate Change* 6 (August 2016): 775, https://www.nature.com/articles/nclimate2998.epdf.

53. United Nations Conference on Trade and Development, *2013 Trade and Environment Review*, 228.

54. U.S. National Oceanic and Atmospheric Administration, "What Are El Niño and La Niña? (last updated February 10, 2020), https://oceanservice.noaa.gov/facts/ninonina.html.

55. Lu Liang and Peng Gong, "Climate Change and Human Infectious Diseases"; and WHO, *Our Planet, Our Health, Our Future, Human Health and the Rio Conventions: Biological Diversity, Climate Change and Desertification* (2012), 8, 25, http://www.who.int/globalchange/publications/reports/health_rioconventions.pdf.

56. *Ibid.*, p. 4, 8.

57. *Ibid.*, 8.

58. FAO, *The State of Food and Agriculture: Livestock in the Balance*, 65.

59. *The Simpsons*, "Homer and Abraham Burn Down the Old Farmhouse," Season 6, Episode 10. Directed by Wesley Archer; written by Bill Oakley, *et al.* Fox, December 4, 1994.

60. WHO, *WHO Handbook for Journalists: Influenza Pandemic* (updated December 2005), 6, http://www.who.int/csr/don/Handbook_influenza_pandemic_dec05.pdf.

61. Margaret Chan, "Sharing of Influenza Viruses and Access to Vaccines and Other Benefits," Opening Remarks at the Intergovernmental Meeting on Pandemic Influenza Preparedness: Sharing of Influenza Viruses and Access to Vaccines and Other Benefits, 2008, http://www.who.int/dg/speeches/2008/20081208/en/; and Colin McInnes and Anne Roemer-Mahler, "From Security to Risk: Reframing Global Health Threats," *International Affairs* 93, no. 6 (January 2017): 1313–1337, esp. 1328, https://doi.org/10.1093/ia/iix187.

62. Lu Liang and Peng Gong, "Climate Change and Human Infectious Diseases," 100.

63. Gavin J. D. Smith, *et al.*, "Origins and Evolutionary Genomics of the 2009 Swine-Origin H1N1 Influenza A Epidemic," *Nature* 459, no. 7250 (2009): 1122–1125, https://doi.org/10.1038/nature08182.

64. GAO, *Avian Influenza: USDA Has Taken Actions to Reduce Risks but Needs a Plan to Evaluate Its Efforts* (April 2017), https://www.gao.gov/assets/690/684086.pdf.

65. *Ibid.*, 26–27.

66. The World Organisation for Animal Health (OIE), *Prevention and Control of Animal Diseases Worldwide: Economic Analysis—Prevention Versus Outbreak Costs* (Agra Ashford, U.K.: CEAS Consulting, September 2007), 12–14, https://www.oie.int/fileadmin/Home/eng/Support_to_OIE_Members/docs/ppt/OIE_-_Cost-Benefit_Analysis__Part_I_.pdf.

67. Mary Lea Killian, *et al.*, "Outbreak of H7N8 Low Pathogenic Avian Influenza in Commercial Turkeys with Spontaneous Mutation to Highly Pathogenic Avian Influenza," *Genome Announcements* 4, no. 3 (June 2016), 1, https://doi.org/10.1128/genomea.00457-16.

68. USDA Agricultural Research Service, *Epidemiologic and Other Analyses of Indiana HPAI/LPAI-Affected Poultry Flocks: February 10, 2016 Report* (Colorado, 2016), 2, https://www.aphis.usda.gov/animal_health/animal_dis_spec/poultry/downloads/indiana-epi-report.pdf.
69. GAO, *Avian Influenza*, 16.
70. Baleshwari Kurmi, *et al.*, "Survivability of Highly Pathogenic Avian Influenza H5N1 Virus in Poultry Faeces at Different Temperatures," *Indian Journal of Virology* 24, no. 2 (September 2013): 272–277, esp. 275, https://doi.org/10.1007/s13337-013-0135-2.
71. *Ibid.*
72. GAO, *Avian Influenza*, 21.
73. *Ibid.*
74. "Seizure, Quarantine, and Disposal," 7 U.S. Code § 8306(d)(2)-(3) (2002).
75. HSUS, "Comment on Environmental Assessment for High Pathogenicity Avian Influenza Control in Commercial Poultry Operations—A National Approach on Docket No. APHIS-2015-0058," October 5, 2015, 16–17, https://www.regulations.gov/document?D=APHIS-2015-0058-0006.
76. USDA APHIS, "Final Environmental Assessment," *High Pathogenicity Avian Influenza Control in Commercial Poultry Operations – A National Approach* (December 2015), https://www.regulations.gov/document?D=APHIS-2015-0058-0008.
77. Chan, "Sharing of Influenza Viruses."
78. Thanks to Travis at Jet Black Coffee for coming up with "Permacane Versus Sharknado."
79. Mike Rivington, *et al.*, *Extreme Weather and Resilience of the Global Food System: Synthesis Report* (August 2015), 5, https://www.researchgate.net/publication/281029049_Extreme_weather_and_resilience_of_the_global_food_system_-_Synthesis_Report.
80. Barry K. Goodwin and Daniel Hallstrom, "Modeling Catastrophic Weather Events and the Risks of animal Waste Spills in the Coastal Plain of North Carolina," Paper Prepared for 2004 AAEA Meetings August 2-4, 2004, 1, https://www.researchgate.net/publication/23505666_Modeling_Catastrophic_Weather_Events_And_The_Risks_Of_Animal_Waste_Spills_In_The_Coastal_Plain_Of_North_Carolina.
81. Robbin Marks, *Cesspools of Shame: How Factory Farm Lagoons and Sprayfields Threaten Environmental and Public Health* (Washington, D.C.: National Resource Defense Council and the Clean Water Network, July 2001), https://www.nrdc.org/sites/default/files/cesspools.pdf.
82. Environmental Working Group, "Landmark Report Maps Feces-Laden Hog and Chicken Operations in North Carolina" (last modified June 21, 2016), https://www.ewg.org/research/exposing-fields-filth.

83. GAO, "Concentrated Animal Feeding Operations, EPA Needs More Information," 30.
84. Wendee Nicole, "CAFOs and Environmental Justice: The Case of North Carolina," *Environmental Health Perspectives* 121, no. 6 (June 2013): 186, https://doi.org/10.1289/ehp.121-a182.
85. Marks, *Cesspools of Shame*, 13.
86. Federal Emergency Management Agency, *Animals in Disasters*. Module A, Unit 4, https://training.fema.gov/emiweb/downloads/is10_a-4.pdf.

Chapter 8: A Convoy 150 Years Long

1. International Humane Society, *Doings of the First Annual Meeting of the International Humane Society, International Humane Society Held at Cleveland, Ohio, October 9, 1877* (New York: Albert J. Wright: 1879), 18.
2. *Ibid.*, 16.
3. Joseph E. Rickenbacker, *Causes of Losses in Trucking Livestock* (Washington, D.C.: USDA, 1958), 1, https://babel.hathitrust.org/cgi/pt?id=uva.x030493299; Bernard Unti, *Protecting All Animals: A Fifty-Year History of the Humane Society of the United States* (Washington, D.C.: Humane Society Press, 2004), 59; and Joseph E. Rickenbacker, *Losses of Livestock in Transit in Midwestern and Western States* (Washington, D.C.: USDA, 1958), 3–4.
4. Rickenbacker, *Losses of Livestock*, 3–4; and U.S. Department of Transportation Bureau of Transportation Statistics, *Economic Census Transportation, 2012 Commodity Flow Survey*, February 2015, Table 5a, https://www.census.gov/content/dam/Census/library/publications/2015/econ/ec12tcf-us.pdf.
5. *Transportation of Animals Act*, U.S. Code 49 (1873), § 80502; U.S. Constitution, Amendment 19 (granting women the right to vote); and *Fair Labor Standards Act*, U.S. Code 29 (1938), § 206.
6. *Transportation of Animals Act*, § 80502.
7. *Ibid.*
8. Henry Bergh, "The Condition of Cattle on Their Arrival at the New York Stock Yards" *New York Times*, August 27, 1870; Bernard Unti, "The Quality of Mercy: Organized Animal Protection in the United States, 1866–1930" (Ph.D. diss., American University, 2002); and Diane L. Beers, *For the Prevention of Cruelty: The History and Legacy of Animal Rights Activism in the United States* (Athens, OH: Swallow Press/Ohio University Press, 2006), 69.
9. Bergh, "The Condition of Cattle."
10. *Ibid*; and Unti, "The Quality of Mercy."
11. Bergh, "The Condition of Cattle."

12. Hearings before the Committee on Interstate and Foreign Commerce, U.S. House of Representatives, January 23, 1906, esp. 3762–3800, esp. 3770–3773, https://www.govinfo.gov/content/pkg/GPO-CRECB-1906-pt4-v40/pdf/GPO-CRECB-1906-pt4-v40-13-1.pdf.

13. USDA, *Report to the Department of Justice, George P. McCabe* (1908) 766, https://goo.gl/MiGgUW.

14. *The Bill to Prevent Cruelty to Animals While in Transit*, HR 694, on June 4, 1872, 42nd Cong., 2d sess.: 4226.

15. *Ibid.*, 4228.

16. *Ibid.*, 4227–4228, 4236.

17. *Ibid.*

18. *Ibid.*, 4236.

19. "The Abuse of Live Stock on the Way to Market," *Scientific American* (1845–1908); Nov 15, 1879; Vol. XLI, No. 20.; and International Humane Society. *Doings*, 18, 19.

20. *The Bill to Prevent Cruelty to Animals While in Transit*, HR 694, 4226; and International Humane Society. *Doings*, 15.

21. U.S. Department of Labor/Bureau of Labor Statistics. CPI Inflation Calculator, n.d., https://data.bls.gov/cgi-bin/cpicalc.pl; USDA Bureau of Animal Industry. *The 28 Hour Law Regulating the Interstate Transportation of Live Stock: Its Purpose, Requirements, and Enforcement* by Harry Golding and A. Joseph Raub (Bulletin No. 589, 1918), 17; and USDA, *Report to the Department of Justice*, 763.

22. *N.C. & St. L.R.R. Co. v. Heggie*, 12 S.E. 363 (Ga. 1890).

23. *Ibid.*

24. USDA, *Report to the Department of Justice*, 763.

25. Penn University Archives & Records Center. Tuition and Mandated Fees, Room and Board, and Other Educational Costs at Penn 1900–1909, https://archives.upenn.edu/exhibits/penn-history/tuition.

26. Unti, "The Quality of Mercy," American Meat chapter at fn. 8; and "Comments and Reflections," *Journal of Zoophily* (April 1908): 129–130.

27. USDA Bureau of Animal Industry, *The 28 Hour Law*, 17; and USDA, *Report to the Department of Justice*, 763.

28. USDA, *Report to the Department of Justice*, 766; and International Humane Society, *Doings*, 17.

29. Unti, "The Quality of Mercy," American Meat chapter fn. 21.

30. Robert Fitzgerald and Ken Stalder, "Reducing Pig Transport Losses," *National Hog Farmer* (June 15, 2009), http://www.nationalhogfarmer.com/behavior-welfare/0615-reducing-transport-pig-losses.

31. National Pork Board, *Transport Quality Assurance Handbook: Version 5*, 37, https://d3fns0a45gcg1a.cloudfront.net/sites/all/files/documents/TQA/2014-Version5/TQAHandbookV5.PDF.

32. USDA National Agriculture Statistics Service, *Livestock Slaughter: 2018 Summary* (April 2019), 8, https://downloads.usda.library.cornell.edu/usda-esmis/files/r207tp32d/8336h934w/hq37vx004/lsslan19.pdf.

33. USDA National Agriculture Statistics Service, "Daily Hog and Pork Summary" (constantly updated), https://www.ams.usda.gov/mnreports/lsddhps.pdf.

34. USDA Office of the Solicitor, Farmer Cooperative Service, *The Twenty-Eight Hour Law Annotated*, by George P. McCabe (Washington, D.C.: USDA, 1961), 24. USDA (October 2, 1909): 22–23.

35. Rickenbacker, *Losses of Livestock*, 3–4.

36. Rickenbacker, *Loss and Damage in Handling and Transporting Hogs* (Washington, D.C.: USDA, 1961), 19–20.

37. *Fraud by Wire, Radio, or Television, U.S. Code* 18 (1952), § 1343.

38. DOJ, *Prosecuting Computer Crimes*, 110, https://www.justice.gov/sites/default/files/criminal-ccips/legacy/2015/01/14/ccmanual.pdf.

39. Oncale v. Sundowner Offshore Services, Inc., 523 U.S. 75, 79 (1998).

40. Letter of W. Ron DeHaven, Administrator USDA APHIS to Peter Brandt, p. 2 (September 22, 2006); and APHIS, Final Rule, "Tuberculosis, Brucellosis, and Paratuberculosis in Cattle and Bison; Identification Requirements," *Federal Register* 60, no. 181 (October 19, 1995): 48361–48622, esp. 48365, https://www.govinfo.gov/content/pkg/FR-1995-09-19/pdf/FR-1995-09-19.pdf.

41. George Orwell, *Politics and the English Language* (London: Horizon, 1946).

42. Temple Grandin, "Perspectives on Transportation Issues: The Importance of Having Physically Fit Cattle and Pigs," *Journal of Animal Science* 79 (E. Suppl.), July 2000, http://www.grandin.com/behaviour/perspectives.transportation.issues.html.

43. Mhairi A. Sutherland, *et al.*, "Health of Non-Ambulatory, Non-Injured Pigs at Processing," *Livestock Science* 116, no. 1 (July 2008): 244, https://doi.org/10.1016/j.livsci.2007.10.009; and P. D. Warriss, "The Welfare of Slaughter Pigs During Transport," *Animal Welfare* 7, no. 4 (November 1998): 365–381; Rickenbacker, *Loss and Damage*, 17.

44. H. Marg, *et al.*, "Influence of Long-time Transportation Stress on Reactivation of Salmonella Typhimurium DT104 in Experimentally Infected Pigs," *Berliner und Münchener tierärztliche Wochenschrift* 114, nos. 9–10 (September–October 2001): 385–388, https://doi.org/10.1016/s0378-1135, 99)00175-3.

45. Robert W. Wills, *et al.*, "Synergism Between Porcine Reproductive and Respiratory Syndrome Virus (PRRSV) and *Salmonella Choleraesuis* in Swine," *Veterinary Microbiology* 71 (2000): 177–192; Marg. *et al.*, "Influence of Long-time Transportation Stress, 385.

46. FAO, *Improved Animal Health for Poverty Reduction and Sustainable Livelihoods* (2002), http://www.fao.org/3/a-y3542e.pdf.

47. *Ibid.*

48. Centers for Disease Control and Prevention, "Zoonotic Diseases," n.d., https://www.cdc.gov/onehealth/basics/zoonotic-diseases.html.

49. Margaret Chan, "Sharing of Influenza Viruses and Access to Vaccines and Other Benefits," Opening Remarks at the Intergovernmental Meeting on Pandemic Influenza Preparedness: Sharing of Influenza Viruses and Access to Vaccines and Other Benefits, 2008, http://www.who.int/dg/speeches/2008/20081208/en/.

50. WHO, *WHO Handbook for Journalists: Influenza Pandemic* (updated December 2005): 2, 4, 6 http://www.who.int/csr/don/Handbook_influenza_pandemic_dec05.pdf.

51. Nan Nan Zhou, *et al.*, "Genetic Reassortment of Avian, Swine, and Human Influenza of Viruses in American Pigs," *Journal of Virology* 73 (1999): 8851–8856, https://doi.org/10.1128/JVI.73.10.8851-8856.1999.

52. WHO, Influenza at the Human–Animal Interface (Summary and Assessment, 21 April to 16 May 2017), http://www.who.int/influenza/human_animal_interface/Influenza_Summary_IRA_HA_interface_05_16_2017.pdf.

53. WHO, *WHO Handbook for Journalists: Influenza Pandemic*, 6.

54. Sundar S. Shrestha, *et al.*, "Estimating the Burden of 2009 Pandemic Influenza of (H1N1) in the United States (April 2009–April 2010)," *Clinical Infectious Diseases* 52 (2011): S75–S82, https://doi.org/10.1093/cid/ciq012.

55. Wuethrich. "Chasing the Fickle Swine Flu."

56. USDA, "Agriculture Census, 2017," https://www.nass.usda.gov/Publications/AgCensus/2017/Online_Resources/Ag_Atlas_Maps/17-M211-RGBDot1-largetext.pdf.

57. Declaration of Michael Terrill in Support of Motion for Preliminary Injunction, filed in *National Meat Assn. v. California*, Case No. 1:08-cv-01963-LJO-DLB (E.D. Cal.).

58. Sutherland, *et al.*, "Health of Non-Ambulatory, Non-Injured Pigs at Processing," 237–245.

59. Kevin McCoy, "Peanut Exec in Salmonella Case Gets 28 Years," *USA Today*, September 21, 2015.

60. U. S. Patent and Trademark Office, "Improvement in Stock-Cars Patent," Zadok Street, August 30, 1870, https://www.google.com/patents/US106888.
61. *Ibid.*
62. International Humane Society, *Doings*, 11.

Chapter 9: Rendered Insensible in the End

1. Charlotte Perkins Gilman, *Herland* (Mineola, N.Y.: Dover Publications, 1998).
2. USDA National Agricultural Statistic Service, *Livestock Slaughter: 2018 Summary* (April 2019), 8, https://downloads.usda.library.cornell.edu/usda-esmis/files/r207tp32d/8336h934w/hq37vx004/lsslan19.pdf; and USDA National Agricultural Statistic Service, *Poultry Slaughter: 2018 Summary* (April 2019), 5, https://www.nass.usda.gov/Publications/Todays_Reports/reports/pslaan19.pdf.
3. USDA National Agricultural Statistic Service, *Livestock Slaughter*, 8.
4. *Ibid.*, 4.
5. *Code of Federal Regulations*, title 9 (2019): § 310.1, https://www.govinfo.gov/content/pkg/CFR-2012-title9-vol2/pdf/CFR-2012-title9-vol2-sec310-1.pdf.
6. Clifford Rothman, "Last Frontier of Animal Rights? The Farm: Activism: With Their Rescues of Cows, Donkeys and Other Livestock, Gene and Lorri Bauston Give the Term *Sanctuary* a New Meaning," *Los Angeles Times*, July 6, 1995.
7. *U.S. ex rel Humane Soc'y of the U.S. v. Hallmark*, No. EDCV 08–00221–VAP, 2013 WL 4713557, at *13 (C.D. Cal. Apr. 30, 2013) (internal citations omitted).
8. Press-Enterprise, "Chino Slaughterhouse Regularly Brought, Abused Sick Cattle, Ex-Worker Says," September 13, 2008, http://www.pe.com/2008/09/13/chino-slaughterhouse-regularly-bought-abused-sick-cattle-ex-worker-says/.
9. Curt A. Gooch, "Concrete Flooring for Dairy Cows," Progressive Dairyman, March 31, 2017, https://www.progressivedairy.com/topics/barns-equipment/concrete-flooring-for-dairy-cows.
10. A. J. Webster, "Effects of Housing and Two Forage Diets on the Development of Claw Horn Lesions in Dairy Cows at First Calving and in First Lactation," *The Veterinary Journal* 162, no. 1 (2001): 56–65, https://doi.org/10.1053/tvjl.2001.0569.
11. Frank A. M. Tuyttens, "The Importance of Straw for Pig and Cattle Welfare: A Review," *Applied Animal Behaviour Science* 92, no. 3 (August 2005): 261–282, https://doi.org/10.1016/j.applanim.2005.05.007.

12. Evgenij Telezhenko and Christer Bergsten, "Influence of Floor Type on the Locomotion of Dairy Cows," *Applied Animal Behaviour Science* 93, nos. 3–4 (2005): 183–197, https://doi.org/10.1016/j.applanim.2004.11.021; and J. Rushen, and A. M. de Passillé, "Effects of Roughness and Compressibility of Flooring on Cow Locomotion," *Journal of Dairy Science* 89, no. 8 (August 2006): 2965–2972, https://doi.org/10.3168/jds. S0022-0302(06)72568-1.

13. USDA National Agricultural Statistic Service, *Milk Production*, 1 (viewed December 2019), https://www.nass.usda.gov/Publications/Todays_ Reports/reports/mkpr0120.pdf.

14. USDA National Agricultural Statistic Service, *Milk Production*, 1 (January 18, 1989), https://downloads.usda.library.cornell.edu/usda-esmis/files/ h989r321c/jw827d05h/9p290b384/MilkProd-01-18-1990.pdf.

15. L. B. Hansen, "Consequences of Selection for Milk Yield from a Geneticist's Viewpoint," *Journal of Dairy Science* 83, no. 5 (2000): 1145–1150, https://pdfs.semanticscholar.org/31bf/3da739a3d95dc3eca567d 0786d7307728a71.pdf; and Kent A. Weigel, "Prospects for Improving Reproductive Performance through Genetic Selection," *Animal Reproduction Science* 96, nos. 3–4 (August 2006): 323–330, https://doi. org/10.1016/j.anireprosci.2006.08.010.

16. Michael Greger, "Transgenesis in Animal Agriculture: Addressing Animal Health and Welfare Concerns." *Journal of Agricultural and Environmental Ethics* 24, no. 5 (2011): 451–472, https://doi.org/10.1007/ s10806-010-9261-7.

17. Lorraine M. Sordillo, "Factors Affecting Mammary Gland Immunity and Mastitis Susceptibility," *Livestock Production Science* 98, nos. 1–2 (2005): 89–99, https://doi.org/10.1016/j.livprodsci.2005.10.017.

18. USDA Office of Inspector General, Great Plains Region, *Audit Report: Evaluation of FSIS Management Controls Over Pre-Slaughter Activities*, 6 (2008), https://www.usda.gov/oig/webdocs/24601-07-KC.pdf.

19. Dave Wilkins, "Are Dairymen Responsible When Meat Recalls Occur?" *Progressive Dairymen*, June 30, 2014, http://www.progressivedairy.com/ topics/herd-health/are-dairymen-responsible-when-meat-recalls-occur; and David Wilson, "Dairy Veterinary Newsletter," Utah State University, December 2010, https://extension.usu.edu/dairy/files/Utah-State-Dairy-Vet-Newsletter-Dec-2010.pdf.

20. U.S. Congress, House, Subcommittee on Energy and Commerce, *Safety of the Food Supply: Hearing Before the House Subcommittee on Commerce of the House Committee on Energy and Commerce*, 110th Cong. 2:05:22 (2008) (testimony of Steve Mendell, president of Hallmark Meat Packing), https://www.c-span.org/video/?204391-1/safety-food-supply.

21. Mendell, *Safety of the Food Supply*, 1:58:39.
22. International Humane Society, *Doings of the First Annual Meeting of the International Humane Society, International Humane Society Held at Cleveland, Ohio, October 9, 1877* (New York: Albert J. Wright: 1879), 18.
23. James Joyce, *Dubliners* (Oxford: Oxford University Press, 2008), 75.
24. Richard Brooks, "Abuse Charges Filed in Chino Slaughterhouse Case," *Press-Enterprise*, February 16, 2008, http://www.pe.com/2008/02/16/abuse-charges-filed-in-chino-slaughterhouse-case/.
25. *Ibid.*
26. Jonathan R. Lovvorn and Nancy V. Perry, "California Proposition 2: A Watershed Moment for Animal Law," *Animal Law* 15, no. 2, (2008): 149–169, esp. 158.
27. Press-Enterprise, "Key Players in the Meat Recall," August 17, 2008, http://www.pe.com/2008/08/17/key-players-in-the-meat-recall/.
28. *Ibid.*
29. Press-Enterprise, "Chino Meat Plant Worker Gets 270 Days in Jail," September 25, 2008, http://www.pe.com/2008/09/25/chino-meat-plant-worker-gets-270-days-in-jail/.
30. Francisco Vara-Orta, "Former California Slaughterhouse Worker Sentenced in Cow Abuse Case," *Los Angeles Times*, September 25, 2008.
31. *New York Times* Editorial. "The Biggest Beef Recall Ever," February 21, 2008.
32. Mendell, *Safety of the Food Supply*.
33. *Ibid.*, 32:54.
34. U.S. Congress, House, Subcommittee on Energy and Commerce, *Safety of the Food Supply*, 1:10:00; and Associated Press, "Sick Cows Hit Food Supply, Beef Chief Says," *CBS News*, March 12, 2008.
35. U.S. Congress, House, Subcommittee on Energy and Commerce, *Safety of the Food Supply*, 1:07:50.
36. *False Claims Act, U.S. Code* 31 (1982), § 3729(a)(1)(G).
37. HSUS, "Meat Supplier Faces $150 Million Lawsuit for Using Sick, Injured Animals in School Lunch Program," May 1, 2009.
38. Associated Press, "California: Deal Reached in Suit Over Animal Abuse," *New York Times*, November 27, 2013.
39. Glynn T. Tonsor and Nicole J. Olynk, "U.S. Meat Demand: The Influence of Animal Welfare Media Coverage," Kansas State University, September 2010, 2, http://www.mercyforanimals.org/files/Kansas_State_Media.pdf.
40. *Ibid.*
41. USDA Economic Research Service. Statistics & Information, "Table 1. U.S. Beef Industry" (viewed September 24, 2019), https://www.ers.usda.gov/topics/animal-products/cattle-beef/statistics-information/.

42. USDA, "Per Capita Red Meat and Poultry Disappearance: Insights Into Its Steady Growth" (June 4, 2018), https://www.ers.usda.gov/amber-waves/2018/june/per-capita-red-meat-and-poultry-disappearance-insights-into-its-steady-growth/.

43. HSUS, "Meat Supplier Faces $150 Million Lawsuit," press release, May 2009.

44. Press-Enterprise, "Six Months Later, Did the Chino Beef Recall Produce Benefits?" August 17, 2008, http://www.pe.com/2008/08/17/six-months-later-did-the-chino-beef-recall-produce-benefits/.

45. Victoria Kim and Mitchell Landsberg, "Huge Beef Recall Issued," *Los Angeles Times*, February 18, 2008.

INDEX

"accommodation," 14

Adams, Virginia, 24–25

Addams, Jane, 21–22, 25, 44

adults
  apathetic and passive, 23–25, 43, 61–62
  exploitation of children and farm animals, 23–26
  responsibilities of, 44–45

advertising, truth in, 30–31

Africa, sub-Saharan, 124

agriculture, as single biggest land use, 85
  . *See also* animal agriculture; cattle industry; dairy farming; pig farming; poultry industry

air pollution
  lead, 78–79, 81–83, 95–96
  poultry industry, 103–4

alfalfa, 90, 92, 175

American Cancer Society (ACS), 15, 16

American College of Cardiology, 13

American Farm Bureau, 62

American Humane Association, 148

American Journal of Public Health, 87

American Smelting and Refining Company (ASARCO), 78, 80–81, 93–95
  "taller-is-safer" theory, 94

American Society for the Protection of Animals (ASPCA), 22, 146

American Veterinary Medical Association (AVMA), 30

ammonia, 105–7

Amtrak, 95, 142

animal activism, late nineteenth and early twentieth centuries, 22–26

animal agriculture
  ammonia produced by, 105–7
  business model, 61, 73, 153, 165
  calories wasted by, 85–87
  global expansion of, 88, 120, 122
  grazing not used, 89–90
  greenhouse gas (GHG) emissions, 117
  inefficiency of, 84–85
  "intensified," 7–8
  as major air and water polluter, 97–113
  methane (CH_4) produced by, 120–22, 127
  outsourced to other countries, 84
  reconsideration of, 83–85
  "we feed the world" line, 49–50, 62, 86–87

Animal and Plant Health Inspection Service (APHIS), 56

animal behaviorists, 28–30

anthropogenic climate change, 119–20

anthropomorphism, 27–29

antibiotics, 3
  80% consumed by farm animals, 53

lentils, 90–92
lifespan, vs. having a life, 32
livestock, as term, 169
"Livestock Protection Collars," 72
Lompoc, California, 102
Los Angeles Times, 160, 176
Lovvorn, Jonathan, 124, 175
low-ball markets, 40–41

macrolides, 57–58
"mad cow disease" (BSE), xv–xvi, 170
Maine, DeCoster egg facilities, 39
"mangler" machinery, 24–25
manure, 26, 86
    animals forced to lie or stand in, 38–39, 42
    cesspools, 57, 69, 74, 91, 99–106, 108, 135
    children diseased by, 106–7
    disease and, 54, 100, 106–7, 135
    GHG emissions and, 122
    half a billion tons generated by United States, 105
    pollution of streams by, 44–45, 57–58, 100, 135–36
    public health and environmental liability, 91
    spills, 134–36
    . *See also* waste
marginalized populations, climate change and, 128–29
Marion, Ohio, human trafficking case, 32–34
"marketing," 61
Marx Brothers, 102, 105
Mary (animal activist), 158–59, 163, 176–77
Maslansky and Partners, 61–62
McCabe, George P., 146–47
media attention, 173, 176
Megacrush, 115
Mendell, Steve, 158, 169–71, 172, 177–78

Mercy for Animals, 39
methane (CH_4), 120–22, 127
Mexico, class action lawsuit against DeCoster, 38–39
Michael Clayton (movie), 173
Midwest dairy farms, 31–32
The Mighty Boosh (British TV show), 8
Mississippi River, 100
monkeys, xii, xv
Morrill, Lot Myrick, 147
mother animals
    coyotes, 75
    dairy cows, 26, 32
    gorillas, 5–6
    pigs, 29–31
MRSA (multi-drug-resistant *Staphylococcus aureus*), 53–54
multi-drug-resistant *Staphylococcus aureus* (MRSA), 53–54
My Name, 115

National Association of Local Boards of Health, 106
National Geographic, 126
National Pork Board, 61, 149
Navarro, Daniel, 162, 166–67
"Nebraska Pioneer Farm Award," 101
needlessness of animal agriculture, xvi
New York dairy farms, 32
New Yorker review, 9
New York Society for the Prevention of Cruelty to Children, 22
New York State, animal transport, 146
New York Times, 10, 22, 56, 146, 170–71
Ninth Circuit Court of Appeals, 9, 39–40
nitrates, 101
nitrous oxide (N_2O), 120
NoMeansNo, 115

About the Author

PETER BRANDT is the Managing Attorney for Farm Animals at the nation's largest animal protection organization, the HSUS. In 2017, he was a Farm Animal Law and Policy Fellow with Harvard Law School's Animal Law & Policy Program. As an adjunct professor, he has taught classes on farm animal law and policy at Lewis & Clark's Northwestern School of Law. His writings on animal protection have been published in the *Los Angeles Times*, the *San Francisco Examiner*, and *Salon*.

About the Publisher

LANTERN PUBLISHING & MEDIA was founded in 2020 to follow and expand on the legacy of Lantern Books—a publishing company started in 1999 on the principles of living with a greater depth and commitment to the preservation of the natural world. Like its predecessor, Lantern Publishing & Media produces books on animal advocacy, veganism, religion, social justice, psychology and family therapy. Lantern is dedicated to printing in the United States on recycled paper and saving resources in our day-to-day operations. Our titles are also available as e-books and audiobooks.

To catch up on Lantern's publishing program, visit us at www.lanternpm.org.

facebook.com/lanternpm
twitter.com/lanternpm
instagram.com/lanternpm